OCEAN SHIPS

OCEAN SHIPS

B. Moody

LONDON

IAN ALLAN

This edition, 1971

SBN 7110 0214 2

Published by Ian Allan Ltd, Shepperton, Surrey and printed in Great
Britain by Crampton & Sons Ltd, Sawston, Cambridge

Contents

Notes on details
given in fleet lists

The Companies listed in the book are in alphabetical order in each section, Companies operating under other than the British flag have their country indicated in the heading.

The date quoted in the lists relates to the year of completion of each ship, and is not necessarily the year of launching.

Merchant ship tonnage is given in gross tons, which is not weight but volume, as one gross ton equals 100 cubic feet of enclosed space. In the same way, net tonnage is the gross tonnage less the non-earning spaces, such as the engine room, bunkers, crews' quarters, etc. The deadweight is the weight of the cargo, fuel, etc which can be carried—in other words, the difference in weight of the ship when empty and fully loaded. A number of cargo ships are classified as open/closed shelter deck vessels, and the gross tonnage is less by usually about 2,000 tons when operating under the open conditions than as a closed shelter deck vessel. In such cases the gross tonnage quoted is normally in respect of the open shelter deck conditions.

The length given in the tables is overall, and the speed quoted is the average service speed and not the maximum. One knot equal 6,080 feet per hour.

Space does not permit a comprehensive index of ship names but many of the companies name their vessels systematically with the same beginning or ending, while others have a theme. A list of classified naming systems will be found at the end of each section.

For the different types of machinery the following abbreviations are used:—

SR   Steam reciprocating engines (usually triple expansion).

ST   Steam turbines.

RT   Combined steam reciprocating and turbines.

TE   Steam turbines with electric drive.

M   Diesel engine.

ME   Diesel engine with electric drive.

GT   Gas turbine.

(A)   Engines aft. (Not quoted for tankers all of which are built thus).

(2)   Twin screw.

(3)   Triple screw.

(4)   Quadruple screw.

Preface

THIS EDITION of *Ocean Ships* has been completely revised with details of a number of additional shipping companies included. The principal ocean going companies of the World are covered, the book being divided into two sections, one for British and Foreign passenger liners, container and cargo ships, and the other section for tankers. The majority of the ships included are over 3,000 tons gross, but some smaller vessels are listed. The former names of the ships listed are also given where applicable.

Since the publication of the last edition of *Ocean Ships* there have been many changes in the shipping world. Several very popular liners like the two " Queens " have disappeared from the scene, but much of interest can still be found. Larger and larger tankers continue to be built. There are already in service several tankers with a deadweight tonnage of over 300,000 tons and even larger ones are already being constructed. The size of various bulk carriers has also increased considerably. Many of the new ships are fitted with bulbous bows which help to increase the speed of the vessel. The container ship has arrived and in view of the heavy costs of containerisation various shipping companies have grouped together to form consortiums such as The Atlantic Container Line, Associated Container Transportation Ltd, Dart Containerline Ltd and Overseas Containers Ltd.

Acknowledgments are due to various shipping companies and to all those who have kindly assisted with information and photographs.

So far as is possible the lists have been corrected up to the time of going to press.

March, 1971.

BERT MOODY.

The American liner UNITED STATES leaving Southampton on one of her last voyages of 1969 prior to being laid up

[Bert Moody]

PART ONE

Passenger Liners
and
Cargo Ships

BoT (Sea Transport): SIR PERCIVALE   [*Malcolm Cranfield*

Adriatica: SAN MARCO   [*Malcolm Cranfield*

BRITISH GOVERNMENT

Board of Trade Sea Transport Section

FUNNEL: *Grey, black top.*
HULL: *Grey.*

Name		Date	Tons Gross	Length (feet)	Breadth (feet)	Speed (knots)	Engines	Former Names
Sir Bedivere	..	1967	4474	413	59	17	M(A)(2)	
Sir Galahad	..	1966	4473	412	59	17	M(A)(2)	
Sir Geraint	..	1967	4473	412	59	17	M(A)(2)	
Sir Lancelot	..	1963	6390	415	60	17	M(A)(2)	
Sir Percivale	..	1968	4473	413	59	17	M(A)(2)	
Sir Tristram	..	1967	4473	413	59	17	M(A)(2)	

Ministry of Defence (Navy Department)

FUNNEL: *Grey, black top.*
HULL: *Grey.*

Name		Date	Tons Gross	Length	Breadth	Speed	Engines	Former Names
Bacchus*	.. ..	1962	4823	379	55	15	M(A)	
Engadine	.. ..	1967	6384	424	58	18	M	
Fort Dunvegan	..	1944	7243	442	57	11	SR	
Fort Rosalie	..	1945	7332	442	57	11	SR	
Fort Sandusky	..	1945	7288	442	57	11	SR	
Hebe*	.. ..	1962	4823	379	55	15	M(A)	
Lyness	.. ..	1966	14113	523	72	17½	M	
Regent	.. ..	1967	18029	640	77	17½	ST(A)	
Reliant	.. ..	1954	8460	469	62	16	M	ex Somersby 58
Resource	.. ..	1967	18029	640	77	17½	ST(A)	
Resurgent	..	1951	9357	477	62	15	M	ex Changchow 53
Retainer	..	1950	9498	477	62	15	M	ex Chungking 52
Stromness	..	1967	12359	524	72	17½	M	
Tarbatness	..	1967	12359	523	72	17½	M	

* owned by British India S.N. Co. Ltd.

(ITALY)

" ADRIATICA " Soc. per Azioni di Nav.

FUNNEL: *Yellow with bronze Venetian lion and narrow black, red and white bands at the top.*
HULL: *White with yellow line and blue boot-topping.*
ROUTE: *Adriatic or Tyrrhenian ports to Greece, Cyprus, Israel, Egypt, Lebanon, Anatolia, Turkey and Black Sea, Trieste, Venice, Dalmatian coast, Greece.*

"ADRIATICA" *(continued)*

Name	*Date*	*Tons Gross*	*Length (feet)*	*Breadth (feet)*	*Speed (knots)*	*Engines*	*Former Names*
Appia	1961	8017	402	62	17	M(A)	
Ausonia	1957	11879	523	70	21	ST(2)	
Bernina	1959	4410	358	54	16	M(2)	
Brennero	1959	4406	358	54	16	M(2)	
Enotria	1951	5173	383	54	17	M(2)	
Esperia	1949	9314	488	63	19½	M(2)	ex Ausonia 49
Illiria	1962	3851	333	48	16	M(2)	
Messapia	1952	5207	383	54	17	M(2)	
Palladio	1963	3630	363	49	16	M(A)	
San Giorgio ..	1956	4755	367	51	17	M(2)	
San Marco	1956	4755	367	51	17	M(2)	
Stelvio	1959	4408	358	53	16	M(2)	
ex Victoria	1953	11695					

Also smaller ships

(U.S.A.)

AMERICAN EXPORT ISBRANDTSEN LINES INC.

FUNNEL: *Tan, broad white band bordered top and bottom with narrower red bands, and blue top.*

HULL: *Black, white letters "American Export-Isbrandtsen" on each side.* (CONSTITUTION *and* INDEPENDENCE *have white hulls with special designs.*)

Atlantic	1953	11840	564	76	20	ST	ex Badger Mariner 57
Constitution* .. (to Atlantic Far East Lines; ren. OCEANIC CONSTITUTION)	1951	20269	683	89	22½	ST(2)	
Container Despatcher ..	1946	15461	583	78	16½	ST(A)	ex Transindia 66, ex Oremar 61, ex Lebore 48
Container Forwarder ..	1946	15462	583	78	16½	ST(A)	ex Transorient 66, ex Feltore 61
C.V. Lightning ..	1968	17902	611	78	21	ST(A)	
C.V. Sea Witch .. (to USA)	1968	17902	610	78	21	ST(A)	
C.V. Staghound ..	1969	17902	610	78	21	ST(A)	
Exbrook	1946	6452	473	66	16½	ST	
Exchester	1945	6452	473	66	16½	ST	
Executor	1845	6452	473	66	16½	ST	
Exford	1946	6451	473	66	16½	ST	
Expeditor	1943	6454	473	66	16½	ST	ex Paul Revere 49, ex Windsor 47.
Export Adventurer	1960	7849	493	73	19	ST	
Export Agent ..	1960	7849	493	73	19	ST	
Export Aide ..	1961	7808	493	73	19	ST	
Export Ambassador	1960	7808	493	73	19	ST	
Export Banner ..	1961	7939	493	73	19	ST(A)	
Export Bay	1961	7939	493	73	19	ST(A)	
Export Builder ..	1962	7939	493	73	19	ST(A)	
Export Buyer ..	1962	7939	493	73	19	ST(A)	
Export Challenger	1963	8128	493	73	19	ST(A)	
Export Champion	1963	8128	493	73	19	ST(A)	
Export Commerce	1963	8128	493	73	19	ST(A)	
Export Courier ..	1962	8128	493	73	19	ST(A)	
Exporter	1945	6452	473	66	16½	ST	
Flying Clipper ..	1944	8141	459	63	15	ST	ex Southampton 47.
Export Democracy	1952	9151					ex President Arthur

American Export Lines: C.V. SEA WITCH

[*John G. Callis*

American Export Lines: INDEPENDENCE before being laid up   [*Malcolm Cranfield*

Name	Date	Tons Gross	Length (feet)	Breadth (feet)	Speed (knots)	Engines	Former Names
Flying Cloud ..	1944	6214	460	63	15	ST	
Flying Endeavor ..	1941	6478	480	67	15	ST	ex Robin Tuxford 57
Flying Enterprise II	1944	6052	459	63	15	ST	ex Noonday 52
Flying Fish ..	1941	6478	480	67	15	ST	ex Robin Wentley 57
Flying Foam ..	1940	7620	492	70	16	ST	ex Kings Point 65, ex Howell Lykes 65, ex Empire Pintail 43, ex Howell Lykes 42.
Flying Hawk ..	1941	6479	480	67	15	ST	ex Robin Kettering 57
Independence*	1950	20269	683	89	22½	ST(2)	

to Atlantic Far East Lines (Pan.) ren OCEANIC INDEPENDENCE

* Laid up.

Great Republic (cont.) 1969 11757   *Morwacsky*

Young America "

(U.S.A.)

AMERICAN PRESIDENT LINES LTD.

FUNNEL: *Dark blue with white eagle and stars on red band.*

HULL: *Grey with dark grey boot-topping or black with red boot-topping.*

ROUTE: *(Round the World.) New York, Panama, U.S. Pacific ports, Japan, China, Philippines, Malaya, Ceylon, India, Pakistan.*

Name	Date	Tons Gross	Length (feet)	Breadth (feet)	Speed (knots)	Engines	Former Names
President Adams	1953	9277	564	76	20	ST	ex Palmetto Mariner 56
President Arthur ..	1952	9171	564	76	20	ST	ex Lone Star Mariner 59
President Buchanan	1952	8995	564	76	20	ST	ex Hoosier Mariner 59.
President Cleveland	1947	15456	610	76	19	TE(2)	
President Coolidge	1954	9277	564	76	20	ST	ex Cracker State Mariner 56
President Fillmore	1968	14764	574	82	23	ST	
President Garfield	1953	9171	654	76	20	ST	ex Magnolia Mariner 59
President Grant	1967	14762	574	82	23	ST	
President Harding	1945	7962	492	70	16½	ST	ex President Taft 68 ex Sea Thrust 45
President Harrison	1965	10411	564	76	20	ST	
President Hayes ..	1952	9277	564	76	20	ST	ex Old Dominion Mariner 55
President Hoover	1945	7963	492	70	16½	ST	ex President Grant 67, ex Sea Beaver 45
President Jackson	1952	9277	564	76	20	ST	ex Volunteer Mariner 55
President Lincoln ..	1961	13265	564	76	23	ST	
President McKinley	1968	14764	574	82	23	ST	
President Madison	1946	7924	492	70	16½	ST	ex Sea Starling 46
President Monroe	1966	10411	564	76	20	ST	
President Pierce ..	1945	7953	492	70	16½	ST	ex Sea Jumper 45
President Polk	1965	10411	564	76	20	ST	
President Taft ..	1967	14764	574	82	23	ST	
President Taylor ..	1954	9171	564	76	20	ST	ex Hawkeye Mariner 57
President Tyler	1961	13265	564	76	23	ST	
President Van Buren	1967	14762	574	82	23	ST	
President Wilson ..	1948	15456	610	76	19	TE(2)	

To American Export Democracy, ren Export Democracy

To Wakeman

To Orient Overseas, ren ORIENTAL PRESIDENT

to USA, ren Harding

To Waterman ren JOSEPH HEWES

To Ferrell, ren Austral Pilgrim

To Orient Overseas ren ORIENTAL PRINCESS

Ⓧ President Jefferson
President Johnson
President Madison
President Pierce

American President Lines: PRESIDENT HARRISON

[*A. Duncan*

Amsterdam N.V.: AMSTELPARK

[*J. Mathieson*

" AMSTERDAM " N.V., REEDERIJ

FUNNEL: *Black with red 'X' on white panel.*

HULL: *Black or grey.*

Name		Date	Tons Gross	Length (feet)	Breadth (feet)	Speed (knots)	Engines	Former Names
Amsteldiep†	..	1960	13950	559	73	14	M(A)	ex Nieuwe Tonge 63
Amstelhoek	..	1960	9473	509	64	14	M	
Amstelhof†	..	1964	19985	603	84	14	M(A)	
Amstellaan	..	1970	20000	604	84	14	M(A)	
Amstelmolen	..	1959	8533	492	62	14	M	
Amstelpark	..	1967	19850	603	84	15	M(A)	
Amstelsluis	..	1957	8539	492	62	13½	M	
Amstelstad	..	1962	9455	509	64	14½	M	
Amstelveen	..	1963	12256	535	70	14	M(A)	
Amstelveld	..	1960	8558	492	62	14	M	

† Owned by N.V. Stoomv, Maats " Nederland ".

ANCHOR LINE LTD.
Runciman Shipping Ltd.

FUNNEL: *Black.*

HULL: *Black, red boot-topping with white line.*

Eucadia	..	1961	8155	463	61	15	M	ex Linkmoor 68
Glenmoor	..	1953	7792	449	58	13	M	
Hazelmoor	..	1954	7792	449	58	13	M	
Kirriemoor	..	1965	22198	646	85	15	M(A)	
Star Acadia*	..	1969	19580	564	86	15½	M(A)	
CAMERONIA (bulk)		1974	30400				M	

* On charter to Star Bulk Co. (Norway).

CARL M. ANDERSEN
D/S Torm A/S.

FUNNEL: *Black with black 'T' on white band between two red bands.*

HULL: *Grey with red boot-topping.*

Alice Torm	..	1958	4890	452	59	16	M
Estrid	..	1967	15810	590	75	15½	M(A)
Gunhild Torm	..	1958	6694	481	62	15½	M
Gyda	..	1967	15810	590	75	15½	M(A)
Helvig	..	1965	21002	628	87	16	M(A)
Herdis	..	1965	21004	628	87	16	M(A)
Ragnhild	..	1967	15810	590	75	15½	M(A)
Thyra Torm	..	1963	5441	461	62	16	M

ASIATIC STEAM NAVIGATION CO. LTD.

FUNNEL: *Yellow.*

HULL: *Black with white line, red boot-topping.*

Name			Date	Tons Gross	Length (feet)	Breadth (feet)	Speed (knots)	Engines	Former Names
Kohinur†	..	..	1963	9874	508	65	14½	M	*To P&O ren. Strathudirn*
Nurjehant	..		1963	8380	482	63	14½	M	*To P&O ren. Strath nevis*
Nurmahal*	..	..	1959	8388	482	63	14	M	*" " " Strathnewton*
Rajah	..	..	1949	5791	443	57	14	RT	
Ranee	..	..	1950	5791	443	57	14	RT	

† Owned by Hain-Nourse Ltd.   * Owned by British India S.N. Co., Ltd.

ASSOCIATED CONTAINER TRANSPORTATION LTD.

(A container consortium formed by Ben Line Steamers Ltd, Blue Star Line, Cunard Steam Ship Company Ltd, Ellerman Lines, T. & J. Harrison and Port Line.)

FUNNEL: *White, narrow black top and ACT insignia in blue.*

HULL: *Grey.*

ACT 1	..	..	1969	24821	713	95	22	ST(A)
ACT 2	..	..	1969	24821	713	95	22	ST(A)

ATLANTIC CONTAINER LINE

(A container consortium formed by Cie. Generale Transatlantique (French Line), Cunard Steam Ship Company Ltd, Holland America Line, Swedish America Line, Rederi A/B Transatlantic, Wallenius Lines.)

FUNNEL: *Yellow, light grey or white, black top with ACL insignia on blue disc.*

HULL: *Black with ACL insignia in black and white.*

Cunard Steam Ship Co. Ltd.

Atlantic Causeway	1969	14946	696	92	23	ST(2)(A)
Atlantic Conveyor	1970	14950	696	92	23	ST(2)(A)

(FRANCE)
Cie. General Transatlantique (French Line)

Atlantic Champagne	1969	15351	696	92	23	ST(2)(A)
Atlantic Cognac	..	1970	15351	696	92	23	ST(2)(A)

Associated Container Transportation: ACT I passing the famous Opera House at Sydney, New South Wales
[J. Y. Freeman

Associated Container Transportation: ACT 2
[F. R. Sherlock

Atlantic Container Line: ATLANTIC CAUSEWAY alongside the container berth at Southhampton
[Bert Moody

Atlantic Container Line: ATLANTIC SAGA   [F. R. Sherlock

(NETHERLANDS)
Holland America Line

Name		Date	Tons Gross	Length (feet)	Breadth (feet)	Speed (knots)	Engines	Former Names
Atlantic Crown	..	1969	15469	696	92	23	ST(2)(A)	
Atlantic Star	..	1967	11839	647	87	21	M(A)	

(SWEDEN)
Swedish America Line

Atlantic Saga	..	1967	12232	647	87	21	M(A)	

(SWEDEN)
Rederi A/B Transatlantic

Atlantic Span	..	1967	11955	647	87	21	M(A)	

(SWEDEN)
O. Wallenius

Atlantic Song	..	1967	11771	647	87	21	M(A)	

(WEST GERMANY)
Wallenius Bremen G.m.b.H.

Atlantic Cinderella	1970	15470	696	92	23	ST(2)(A)	

AUSTASIA LINE LTD.

FUNNEL: *White with black top and black 'A' in black ring.*

HULL: *Grey with red boot-topping.*

Name		Date	Tons Gross	Length (feet)	Breadth (feet)	Speed (knots)	Engines	Former Names
~~Australasia~~†	..	1950	10854	505	65	16	M	ex Iberia Star 65, ex Anselm 63, ex Thysville 61, ex Baudouinville 57.
Malaysia† ..	..	1955	8062	439	60	15	ST	ex Hubert 64.
Mahsuri		1952	8230					ex Colorado Star

† Owned by Blue Star Line Ltd.

Austasia Line: AUSTRALASIA

AUSTRALIAN NATIONAL LINE
(Australian Coastal Shipping Commission)

FUNNEL: *Blue, black top, two wide white bands and a narrow red band.*
(Some ships have letters 'ANL' on funnel.)

HULL: *Cream with red boot-topping (passenger vessels), or black.*

Name	Date	Tons Gross	Length (feet)	Breadth (feet)	Speed (knots)	Engines	Former Names
Australian Emblem 1974 21,000 (cont'd)						M	
Australian Endeavour ..	1969	25144	713	95	22	ST(A)	ex ACT 3 69.
Australian Enterprise ..	1969	16580	596	82	21	M(A)	
Australian Trader	1969	7005	445	71	18	M(2)	
Baralga	1956	3895	405	53	14	M	
Bass Trader ..	1961	4129	323	57	14½	M(2)	
Boonaroo	1953	3904	405	53	12	M	
Brisbane Trader ..	1969	6326	448	71	18	M(2)	
Bulwarra	1954	4010	405	53	13	M	
Darling River ..	1966	33774	742	105	16	ST	
Darwin Trader ..	1970	8300	458	70	15½	M(A)	
Empress of Australia	1965	12035	445	71	17	M(2)	
Inyula	1954	4893	356	52	12	M	
Iranda	1957	4893	387	53	12	M(A)	
Jeparit	1964	6341	437	57	14	M(A)	
Lake Barrine ..	1956	7215	468	57	12	M(A)	
Lake Boga ..	1957	7327	468	58	12	M(A)	
Lake Colac ..	1958	7317	468	57	12	M(A)	
Lake Eyre ..	1956	7584	458	59	12	ST(A)	
Lake Illawarra ..	1958	7274	459	59	12	ST(A)	
Lake Macquarie ..	1958	7358	468	58	12	M(A)	
Lake Sorell ..	1959	7317	468	57	12	M(A)	
Lake Torrens ..	1957	7329	459	59	12	ST(A)	
Mount Keira ..	1960	10229	513	65	12½	M(A)	
Mount Kembla ..	1960	10112	513	65	12½	M(A)	
Musgrave Range ..	1964	14467	582	75	15	M(A)	To Panama, ren. SIMANGGANG
Nilpena	1954	1468	243	37	10½	M(A)	
North Esk ..	1957	1603	264	37	10½	M(A)	
Princess of Tasmania	1959	3981	372	58	18	M(2)	
South Esk	1959	1616	264	37	10½	M(A)	
Sydney Trader ..	1969	6326	448	71	18	M(2)	
Townsville Trader	1970	6326	448	71	18	M(2)	
Windarra	1953	2355	288	46	10	M(2)	ex Warringa 53.
Yanderra	1954	3446	330	47	11	SR(A)	
Yarra River ..	1970	32400	742	104	16	ST(A)	
Yarrunga	1955	3473	330	49	10	SR(A)	

AUSTRALIND STEAM SHIPPING CO. LTD.
Trinder, Anderson & Co. Ltd.

FUNNEL: *Yellow with black top and house flag on panel.*
HULL: *Black, red boot-topping with white line.*

Name	Date	Tons	Length	Breadth	Speed	Engines	
Araluen	1958	6545	525	61	14½	M	To Somalia, ren. TAI SHAN
Armadale	1971	10300	525	70	16	M(A)	
Australind	1961	6134	477	62	14½	M	

Australian National Line: AUSTRALIAN TRADER   [*J. Y. Freeman*

Australian National Line: LAKE ILLAWARRA   [*J. Y. Freeman*

AVENUE SHIPPING CO. LTD.
Trinder, Anderson & Co. Ltd.

FUNNEL: *Dark red with black top and blue 'A' on white diamond over blue cross on white panel.*

HULL: *Grey, with red boot-topping with white line.*

Name			Date	Tons Gross	Length (feet)	Breadth (feet)	Speed (knots)	Engines	Former Names
Antrim	..	..	1962	6305	460	59	14½	M	
Donegal	..	..	1957	6270	460	59	14	M	
Galway	..	..	1959	7167	525	61	14	M	

(SPAIN)

NAVIERA AZNAR S.A.

FUNNEL: *Yellow with red 'A'.*

HULL: *White with green boot-topping or black with red boot-topping.*

ROUTES: **A.** *Spanish ports to Canary Is., and South America.*
B. *London or Liverpool to Las Palmas, Tenerife.*

Name		Date	Tons Gross	Length	Breadth	Speed	Engines	Former Names
Monte Anaga	..	1959	6813	429	59	14	M to Mexico	
Monte Arucas	..	1956	4691	388	53	19	M	
Monte Naranco	..	1970	4600	384	53	17	M(A)	
Monte Pagasarri	..	1959	6305	474	61	14	M(A)	
Monte Penalara	..	1960	6305	474	61	14	M(A)	
Monte Saja	..	1965	6041	479	62	14	M	to BanglaDesh, ren. BANGLAR UPAHAR
Monte Sollube	..	1965	6044	479	62	14	M	
Monte Udala	..	1948	10170	487	62	16½	M	
Monte Ulia	..	1952	10123	487	62	16½	M	ex Monasterio de El Escorial 52.
Monte Umbe	..	1959	9971	508	62	16½	M	
Monte Urquiola	..	1949	8392	487	62	16½	M	ex Guadalupe 49. To Spore, ren Climax Garm
Monte Zalama	..	1968	15650	599	74	15	M(A)	
Monte Zamburu	..	1969	15650	599	74	15	M(A)	
Monte Zapola	..	1969	15490	601	74	15	M(A)	
Monte Zaraya	..	1968	15490	599	74	15	M(A)	
RoRo Monte Toledo		1973	13500					
RoRo Monte Granada		1974	13800					

Also many smaller ships.

| Monte Banderas | 1975 | 2800 | | | | | M | ferry |
| Monte Contes | 1974 | 3800 | | | | | M | ferry |

BANK LINE LIMITED
Andrew Weir & Co., Ltd.

FUNNEL: *Buff with black top.*

HULL: *Black with red boot-topping.*

ROUTES: *Numerous services mainly covering India, Far East, East and South Africa, North and South America, Australia and New Zealand.*

Australind Steam Shipping Co: ARALUEN *To Scualia* *ren TAI SHAN* [Malcolm Cranfield

Avenue Shipping Co: GALWAY [J. Y. Freeman

Bank Line: LOSSIEBANK [*F. R. Sherlock*

Bank Line: TWEEDBANK [*V. H. Young*

[handwritten: Clydebank 1974 11200]

[handwritten: Beaverbank 1974 11,500]

Name		Date	Tons Gross	Length (feet)	Breadth (feet)	Speed (knots)	Engines	Former Names
Ashbank	..	1959	6307	483	63	14½	M	
Avonbank	..	1961	6303	483	63	15	M	
Beechbank	..	1965	7355	508	67	15	M	
Carronbank	..	1957	6326	483	63	14½	M	
Cedarbank	..	1955	5671	455	59	14	M	*to Cyprus, ren - POLA MONIKA*
Crestbank	..	1957	6326	483	63	14½	M	
Dartbank	..	1958	6326	483	63	14½	M	
Elmbank	..	1960	6311	483	63	15	M	
Ernebank	..	1965	7355	508	67	15	M	
Firbank	..	1957	6168	487	62	14½	M	
Forresbank	..	1962	6154	488	62	15	M	
Foylebank	..	1955	5671	455	59	14	M	
Garrybank	..	1958	6307	483	63	15	M	
Gowanbank	..	1958	10365	513	68	14½	M	
Hazelbank	..	1954	10335	513	68	15	M	
Hollybank	..	1964	6163	437	62	15	M	
Inverbank	..	1962	6154	487	62	15	M	
Irisbank	..	1964	10349	513	68	15	M	*Somalia*
Laganbank	..	1955	5671	455	59	14	M	*To PIRAEUS, ren. POLA ANNA*
Larchbank	..	1961	6234	488	62	15	M	*GOLDEN SEA*
Laurelbank	..	1963	6167	487	62	15	M	
Levernbank	..	1961	6303	483	63	15	M	
Lindenbank	..	1961	6234	488	62	15	M	
Lossiebank	..	1963	6291	483	63	15	M	
Maplebank	..	1967	10365	513	68	15	M	
Marabank	..	1963	5969	486	63	15	M	
Minchbank	..	1958	6307	483	63	14½	M	
Nairnbank	..	1966	10363	513	68	15	M	
Nessbank	..	1953	5690	450	59	14	M	*to Cyprus, ren - PARIS*
Northbank	..	1957	6410	488	62	15	M	
Oakbank	..	1963	6167	487	62	15	M	
Olivebank	..	1962	6317	483	63	15	M	
Pinebank	..	1959	6311	483	63	14½	M	
Riverbank	..	1957	6168	487	62	14½	M	*To S'pore, ren 'GOLDEN SEASON*
Rosebank	..	1959	6307	483	63	14½	M	
Rowanbank	..	1963	6169	487	62	15	M	
Roybank	..	1963	6378	483	63	15	M	
Shirrabank	..	1966	10439	528	69	15	M	
Speybank	..	1962	5972	486	63	15	M	
Springbank	..	1962	6317	483	63	15	M	
Sprucebank	..	1964	6163	437	62	15	M	
Streambank	..	1958	6162	438	62	13½	M	
Taybank	..	1963	10141	508	67	15½	M	
Teakbank	..	1953	6160	438	62	13½	M	
Testbank	..	1961	6154	437	62	15	M	
Teviotbank	..	1967	10439	523	69	15	M	
Tweedbank	..	1964	10141	508	67	15	M	
Wavebank	..	1959	6160	437	62	13½	M	
Weirbank	..	1961	6234	438	62	15	M	
Weybank	..	1964	6378	433	63	15	M	
Willowbank	..	1960	6201	488	62	14½	M	
Yewbank	..	1959	6160	487	62	13½	M	

[handwritten: Moraybank 197]

BEN LINE STEAMERS LTD.

Wm. Thomson & Co.

FUNNEL: *Yellow.*

HULL: *Grey with green boot-topping.*

ROUTES: *U.K. and North Continent to Malaya, Singapore, Indonesia, Thailand, Borneo, Philippines, Hong Kong, China and Japan.*

Name		Date	Tons Gross	Length (feet)	Breadth (feet)	Speed (knots)	Engines	Former Names
Benalbanach		*1957*	*8800*					*ex Woodarra*
Benalbanach	..	1967	11466	563	75	21	M	
Benalligin ..	..	1945	9868	498	64	14½	M	ex City of Khartoum 68.
Benarkle ..	..	1946	9868	498	64	14½	M	ex City of Poona 68.
Benarmin ..	..	1963	10870	550	71	20	M	
Benarty ..	..	1963	10162	509	67	17½	M	
Benattow ..	..	1951	8038	501	64	15½	ST	ex Cuzco 65.
Bencairn ..	..	1951	10593	568	71	17	ST	ex City of Brisbane 70.
Bencleuch ..	..	1949	7769	475	60	15	ST	
Bencruachan	..	1968	12092	558	78	21½	ST	
Bendearg ..	..	1964	8199	533	70	19	M	
Bendoran ..	..	1956	9932	508	64	18	ST	
Bengloe ..	..	1961	10955	550	71	20	ST	
Benhope ..	..	1945	9846	497	64	15	M	ex Egidia 62.
Benkitlan ..	..	1946	9868	498	64	14½	M	ex City of Swansea 68.
Benlawers ..	..	1970	12900	600	82	21½	M	
Benledi ..	..	1965	11758	563	75	21	M	
Benlomond	..	1957	9927	508	64	18	ST	
Benloyal ..	..	1959	10929	550	71	20	ST	
Benmacdhui	..	1948	7755	475	60	15	ST	
Benmhor ..	..	1949	7755	501	64	16	ST	ex Penrith Castle 52.
Bennachie ..	..	1949	8494	474	62	16	ST	ex Eastern Glory 66.
Bennevis ..	..	1944	7841	492	70	16	ST	ex Bardic 59, ex Muncaster Castle 54, ex HMS Puncher.
Benreoch ..	..	1952	9707	504	64	17	ST	
Benrinnes ..	..	1944	8008	492	70	16	ST	ex Gallic 59, ex Greystoke Castle 54, ex HMS Trouncer.
Benstac ..	..	1968	12011	532	70	21	M	
Benvalla ..	..	1962	10926	550	71	20	M	
Benvannoch	..	1952	10594	568	71	15	ST	ex City of Winchester 70.
Benvenue ..	..	1948	7759	475	60	16	ST	
Benvrackie	..	1955	9757	508	64	18	ST	
Benwyvis ...	..	1966	11467	563	75	21	M	
Benwyvis		*1957*	*8800*					*ex Waroonga*
Tkr. Benvenue		*1975*	*1500*				*M*	

BERGEN LINE (Det Bergenske D/S)

FUNNEL: *Black with three narrow white bands.* JUPITER *and* VENUS *have yellow funnels with house flag.*

HULL: *Black with red boot-topping.* JUPITER *and* VENUS *have grey hulls with green boot-topping.*

ROUTES: *Various, West Norway to U.K. and N. European ports. Norwegian coastal services.*

Name			Date	Tons Gross	Length (feet)	Breadth (feet)	Speed (knots)	Engines	Former Names
Cruz	..	..	1958	2974	414	51	14	M	ex Cap Domingo 70.
Estrella	..	..	1961	5656	468	60	17	M	
Jupiter*	..	..	1966	9500	465	67	21	M(2)	
Leda	..	..	1953	6670	437	57	22	ST(2)	
Venus†			1966	9500	465	67	22	M(2)	*ex Sirius*
Nor News Express			*1970*	*499*					*ex Dowb*
Nor News service			*1969*	*498*					

Also many smaller ships.

* Jointly owned by Fred Olsen and operates as **Black Watch** by that company.

† Owned by Fred Olsen and operates as **Black Prince** by that company.

Ben Line: BENALBANACH [*John G. Callis*

Ben Line: BENHOPE [*A. P. Oakden*

BIBBY BROTHERS & COMPANY
Bibby Bros. & Co.

FUNNEL: *Pink with black top.*
HULL: *Black with yellow line, red boot-topping.*

Name		Date	Tons Gross	Length (feet)	Breadth (feet)	Speed (knots)	Engines	Former Names
Berkshire	..	1970	19100	600	87	15	M(A)	
Cheshire	..	1970	19100	600	87	15	M(A)	
Coventry City*	..	1966	7643	465	64	17	M	
Derbyshire	..	1966	9931	507	67	16	M	
Gloucestershire	..	1950	8640	471	63	15	M	ex Cingalese Prince 64, ex Gallic 62, ex Cingalese Prince 60.
Oxfordshire	..	1970	19100	600	87	15	M(A)	
Shropshire	..	1959	8775	491	64	15	M	
Staffordshire	..	1950	8685	471	63	15	M	ex Bardic 64, ex Eastern Prince 60.
Toronto City*	..	1966	7643	465	64	17	M	
Warwickshire	..	1967	10682	528	69	16	M	
Worcestershire	..	1965	9931	507	67	16	M	
Yorkshire	..	1960	8777	491	64	16	M	ex Eastern Princess 64, ex Yorkshire 63.

ren· Arya Bod *Warwickshire*
ex Tenbury 1965 8252

* On charter to Bristol City Line Ltd.

Britain Steamship Co. Ltd.

Atlantic Bridge	..	1968	44842	810	106	15½	M(A)
Ocean Bridge	..	1970	66150	850	134	15½	M(A)
Pacific Bridge	..	1967	44795	810	106	15½	M(A)
Westminster Bridge		1968	42202	805	106	15½	M(A)

(GHANA)
BLACK STAR LINE LTD.

FUNNEL: *Yellow, black top with red and green bands above and below black star.*

HULL: *Grey.*

Afram River	..	1962	7356	461	60	14½	M
Benya River	..	1965	7337	455	63	16	M
Bia River	..	1965	7479	455	63	15½	M
Birim River	..	1962	7354	461	60	14½	M
Klorte Lagoon	..	1969	7155	455	63	16	M
Korle Lagoon	..	1964	7337	455	63	16	M
Kulpawn River	..	1962	7356	461	60	14½	M
Lake Bosomtwe	..	1963	7356	461	60	14½	M
Nakwa River	..	1965	7446	455	63	15½	M
Nasia River	..	1962	7390	461	60	14½	M
Offin River	..	1961	7354	461	60	14½	M
Otchi River	..	1961	7378	461	60	14½	M
Oti River	..	1964	7478	455	63	15½	M
Pra River	..	1961	7351	461	60	15	M
Sakumo Lagoon	..	1964	7337	454	63	15½	M
Subin River	..	1968	7582	455	63	15	M

Bibby Line: WARWICKSHIRE [J. Mathieson

Black Star Line: BENYA RIVER [Malcolm Cranfield

BLUE FUNNEL LINE

(includes Ocean S.S. Co. Ltd., and China Mutual S.N. Co. Ltd.)

FUNNEL: *Blue with black top.*

HULL: *Black, pink boot-topping.* CENTAUR *has white hull.*

ROUTES: **A.** *U.K. and Rotterdam to Malaya, Singapore, Philippines, Hong Kong, China and Japan.*

       B. *U.K. and Continental ports to Indonesia.*

       C. *U.K. and Continental ports to Malaya, Singapore, Thailand, North Borneo and Sarawak.*

       D. *Gulf of Mexico and Atlantic ports of U.S.A. to Singapore, Malaya and Indonesia.*

       E. *Philippines, Hong Kong and Japan via Panama to Kingston (*Jamaica*) and Atlantic Coast ports of America.*

       F. *Singapore to Australia and Indonesia.*

Name			Date	Tons Gross	Length (feet)	Breadth (feet)	Speed (knots)	Engines	Former Names
Achilles	..	..	1957	7675	491	62	16	M	
Adrastus*	..	..	1953	7572	487	62	16	M	
Aeneas	..	..	1947	7436	487	62	15	M	
Ajax ..	..	..	1958	7667	481	62	16½	M	
Anchises	..	..	1947	7697	487	62	15	M	
Antilochus ..		..	1949	7378	487	62	15	M	
Ascanius	..	..	1950	7431	487	62	16	M	
Astyanax	..	..	1948	7436	487	62	15	M	ex Glenfriun 62, ex Astyanax 57.
Atreus	..	..	1951	7548	487	62	16	M	
Autolycus	..	..	1949	7420	487	62	15	M	
Automedon		..	1949	7392	487	62	15	M	
Calchas	..	..	1947	7436	487	62	15	M	ex Glenfinlas 62, ex Calchas 57.
Centaur	..	..	1964	8262	481	66	20	M(2)	
Clytoneus	..	..	1948	7401	487	62	15	M	
Cyclops	..	..	1948	7416	487	62	15	M	
Dardanus	..	..	1940	9371	507	66	17	M(2)	ex Glengarry 70, ex Empire Humber 46, ex Hansa 46, ex Meersburg, ex Glengarry.
Elpenor	..	..	1954	7425	487	62	16	M	
Eumaeus*	..	..	1953	7562	487	62	16	M	
Hector	..	..	1950	9718	523	69	18	ST	
Helenus	..	..	1949	9717	523	69	18	ST	
Ixion	..	..	1951	9724	523	69	18	ST	
Jason	..	..	1950	9715	523	69	18	ST	
Laertes*	..	..	1949	7467	487	62	16	M	
Laomedon	..	..	1953	7599	487	62	16	M	
Lycaon*	..	..	1954	7572	487	62	16	M	
Machaon	..	..	1959	8208	495	65	16½	M	
Maron	..	..	1960	8242	495	65	16½	M	
Memnon	..	..	1959	8242	494	65	16½	M	
Menelaus	..	..	1957	8242	495	65	16½	M	
Menestheus		..	1958	8220	495	65	16½	M	
Myrmidon	..	..	1945	7732	455	62	15½	ST	ex Ripon Victory 47.
Neleus	...	..	1953	7544	489	64	16	ST	
Orestes	..	..	1952	7552	489	64	16	ST	ex Glenaffric 70, ex Nestor 69.
Patroclus	..	..	1950	9754	516	68	18	ST	
Peisander	..	..	1967	12094	564	78	21	M	

to China Mutual Steam Nav.
PHILOCTETES
Patroclus

Blue Funnel Line: MEMNON

Blue Funnel Line: PEISANDER

Blue Star Line: ADELAIDE STAR [*V. H. Young*

Blue Star Line: QUEENSLAND STAR [*F. W. Hawks*

Name	Date	Tons Gross	Length (feet)	Breadth (feet)	Speed (knots)	Engines	Former Names
Phrantis	*1967*	*12299*					*ex Pembrokeshire*
Phemius	*1966*	*12824*				*M*	*ex Glenfinlas*
Peleus	1949	9747	516	68	18	ST	
Perseus	1950	9753	516	68	18	ST	
Phemius ..	1941	8953	513	66	17	M(2)	ex Glenorchy 70, ex Priam 48.
Polydorus	1952	7535	487	62	16	M	ex Alcinous 60.
Polyphemus*	1948	7401	487	62	15	M	ex Asphalion 66, ex Radnorshire 63, ex Achilles 49.
Priam ..	1966	12094	564	78	21	M	
Prometheus ..	1967	12094	564	78	21	M	
Protesilaus ..	1967	12094	564	78	21	M	
Pyrrhus ..	1949	9626	515	68	18	ST	
Radnorshire ..	1967	12089	164	78	21	M	
Rhexenor ..	1945	10195	497	64	15	M	
Stentor ..	1946	9833	497	64	15	M	ex Glenshiel 63, ex Stentor 58.
Talthybius	1944	7313	455	62	16	ST	ex Polydurus 60, ex Salina Victory 06.
Telamon ..	1950	8463	474	62	17	ST	ex Teucer 6, 4ex Silverlaurel 50.
Telemachus ..	1950	8469	474	62	17	ST	ex Teiresias 60, ex Silverelm 50.
Theseus ..	1955	7561	489	64	16	ST	
Ulysses	1949	8469	474	62	15½	ST	ex Silverholly 49.
Tantalus	*1972*	*120787 bulk*					

* These ships operate under the associated Dutch Company of Nederlandsche Stoomv. Maats. ' Ocean ' N.V. and fly the Netherlands flag.
See also Overseas Containers Ltd.

Agapenor and **Melampus** are detained in Suez Canal and abandoned to Insurers.

BLUE STAR LINE LTD.

FUNNEL: *Blue star on white disc on red funnels with black top divided by white over black bands.*

HULL: *Black, red boot-topping or lilac grey with blue boot-topping.*

ROUTES: **A.** *London to S. America calling at Lisbon, Canary Is., Rio, Santos, Montevideo and Buenos Aires.*

        B. *U.K. Ports to Australia calling at Teneriffe, Capetown, and other S. African Ports.*

        C. *U.K. Ports to New Zealand via Panama calling at Curacao.*

        D. *Glasgow and Liverpool to Pacific Coast of U.S.A. and Canada via Panama.*

(*A number of the ships shown hereunder are actually owned by associate companies such as Lamport and Holt Line and Union International Co. Ltd. but are operated by Blue Star Line Ltd.*)

Name	Date	Tons Gross	Length (feet)	Breadth (feet)	Speed (knots)	Engines	Former Names
Afric Star	*1974*	*9800*				*M*	
Adelaide Star ..	1950	12964	574	73	18	M(2)	
America Star ..	1964	7357	463	63	18	M	
Argentina Star ..	1947	10716	503	68	16	ST	
Australia Star ..	1965	10025	526	70	20	M	SOLD
Brasil Star ..	1947	10716	503	68	16	ST	
Canadian Star ..	1957	6274	473	63	15½	M	
Canterbury Star ..	1960	7437	463	63	17	M	
Colorado Star ..	1952	8292	466	63	12	M	ex Raeburn 58.
California Star	*1971*	*19095*					
Columbia Star	*1971*	*19095*	*35*				
Avila Star	*1975*	*9600*				*M*	
Andalucia Star	*1975*	*9700*				*M*	

Name	Date	Tons Gross	Length (feet)	Breadth (feet)	Speed (knots)	Engines	Former Names
Empire Star	1946	11085	541	71	16	M(2)	ex Empire Mercia 46.
~~English Star~~	1950	9864	506	70	16	M(2)	
Fremantle Star	1960	8403	519	70	18	M	
Halifax Star	1964	7327	463 540	63	18	M	
~~Imperial Star~~	1948	12885	572	70	17	M(2)	
~~Melbourne Star~~	1948	12895	572	70	17	M(2)	
Montreal Star	1963	7365	463	63	18	M	
~~Newcastle Star~~†	1956	8398	520	70	17	M	Montevideo
New York Star	1965	7372	463 540	63	18	M	
New Zealand Star	1967	11300	552	73	21	M	Brasilia
~~Queensland Star~~	1957	9911	512	68	17	M(2)	
Rockhampton Star	1958	10619	507	68	17	M	
Southland Star	1967	11300	552	73	21	M	
Tasmania Star	1950	12605	572	73	17	ST	
Timaru Star	1967	8366	497	65	18	M	
Ulster Star	1959	9708	519	70	17	M	
~~Uruguay Star~~	1948	10506	503	68	16	ST	
Wellington Star	1952	12539	574	73	18	M(2)	

Scottish Star is detained in Suez Canal and abandoned to Insurers.

† Operated by Compass Line between Australia and S. Africa.

Salient Shipping Co. (Bermuda) Ltd.

Name	Date	Tons Gross	Length	Breadth	Speed	Engines	
Auckland Star	1958	11799	572	73	17	ST	
~~Canberra Star~~	1956	8398	520	70	17½	M	Buenos Aires
Gladstone Star	1957	10635	516	70	17½	M	
Hobart Star†	1956	8398	520	70	17½	M	
Townsville Star	1957	10725	516	70	17½	M	

† Operated by Compass Line between Australia and S. Africa.

BOLTON STEAM SHIPPING CO. LTD.
North Yorkshire Shipping Co. Ltd.

FUNNEL: *Black.*
HULL: *Black with red boot-topping.*

Name			Date	Tons	Length	Breadth	Speed	Engines
Redcar			1956	10746	505	69	11½	M(A)
Ribblehead			1957	10741	505	69	11½	M(A)
Ribera			1965	18088	600	79	15	M(A)
Rievaulx			1958	10974	505	69	11½	M(A)
Ripon			1956	10731	505	69	11½	M(A)

BOOKER LINE Ltd.

FUNNEL: *Black with white band and red "B".*
HULL: *Grey with green boot-topping.*

Name	Date	Tons	Length	Breadth	Speed	Engines	
Booker Valiance†	1962	2811	375	51	14	M(A)	ex Johan Wessel 63.
Booker Vanguard	1963	5417	403	57	15	M(A)	
Booker Venture	1961	9516	530	63	14	M(A)	
Booker Viking	1967	5383 1041	403	57	15½	M(A)	ex Elrethorn

Also smaller ships.   † On charter.

Blue Star Line: NEW ZEALAND STAR

[John G. Callis

Booth Steamship Co: CLEMENT

[Malcolm Cranfield

BOOTH STEAMSHIP COMPANY LTD.

FUNNEL: *Black with blue 'B' over red St. Andrew's cross on white panel.*

HULL: *Black, red boot-topping. (Vessels on New York service have grey hulls.)*

ROUTES: *Liverpool and Portugal to Barbados, Trinidad and North Brazil (including River Amazon).*
New York to West Indies, North Brazil and Iquitos, Peru.
Canada to West Indies, Georgetown, North and Mid-Brazil.
(Note :- Several of these ships are owned by associated companies but are operated by Booth S.S. Co. Ltd.)

Name			Date	Tons Gross	Length (feet)	Breadth (feet)	Speed (knots)	Engines	Former Names
Clement	..	..	1959	1902	354	44	14	M(A)	
Crispin	..	..	1956	1816	358	44	13	M(A)	*To Salvador, ren ANNA*
Dominic	..	..	1953	3324	303	46	12	M	ex Makati 67, ex Jonna Dan 64.
Renoir	..	..	1953	4300	411	55	12½	M	ex Benedict 67, ex Mahsuri 66, ex Malay 64, ex Malay Star 53.
Rubens	..	..	1951	4472	411	55	12½	SR	ex Dunstan 67, *ex To Greec* Mandowi 66, *ex ren IRI* Crispin 53.
Veloz†	..	..	1959	1609	331	42	13	M(A)	ex Valiente 69, ex Spencer 61.
Venimos	..	..	1956	1607	330	42	13	M(A)	
Veras	..	..	1959	1616	330	42	13	M(A)	ex Siddons 62.
Viajero†	..	..	1957	1476	330	42	13	M(A)	

† Owned by Panama Shipping Co.

BERWELL ADVENTURE 1952 4459   *ex Rubens, ex Siddons -65 -55*

BOWATER S.S. Co. Ltd.
Cayzer, Irvine & Co. Ltd.

FUNNEL: *Yellow with Bowater housemark of black bow and arrow device over a series of narrow wavy white lines on blue.*

HULL: *Dark green with light green boot-topping.*

Name		Date	Tons	Length	Breadth	Speed	Engines	Former Names
Constance Bowater		1958	3914	325	50	12	M	
Elizabeth Bowater		1958	3914	325	50	12	M	
Gladys Bowater	..	1959	3917	325	50	12	M	
Nicolas Bowater	..	1958	6875	419	60	13	ST	*To Lb., ren VALL COMET*
Nina Bowater	..	1961	3866	325	50	12	M	
Phyllis Bowater	..	1960	3899	325	50	12	M	

BOWRING S.S. Co. Ltd.

FUNNEL: *Black with diagonal red cross on broad white band.*

HULL: *Grey with red boot-topping.*

Name		Date	Tons	Length	Breadth	Speed	Engines
Forth Bridge	..	1967	28467	674	98	16	M(A)
London Bridge	..	1967	28467	674	98	16	M(A)
Stephano	..	1965	16166	600	75	15	M(A)
Sydney Bridge	..	1970	34000	735	106	15½	M(A)
Trinculo	..	1957	11206	505	69	13	M(A)

Bowring S.S. Co: STEPHANO

[B. Reeves

Bowring S.S. Co: FORTH BRIDGE

[J. Mathieson

British India Steam Navigation: BANKURA [*F. W. Hawks*]

British India Steam Navigation: UGANDA [*Bert Moody*]

BRITISH INDIA STEAM NAVIGATION CO. LTD.

FUNNEL: *Black with two white bands close together.* BACCHUS *and* HEBE *have grey funnel with black top.*

HULL: *Black with white line, red boot-topping, except ships marked* which have white hulls with black line.* BACCHUS *and* HEBE *have grey hulls.*

ROUTES: *These are very numerous and form a network covering the whole of the Indian Ocean which is the main sphere of operations. Some of the services extend to the U.K., Japan and to New Zealand.*

The NEVASA *and* UGANDA *operate educational cruises throughout the year.*

Name			Date	Tons Gross	Length (feet)	Breadth (feet)	Speed (knots)	Engines	Former Names
Amra	..	..	1969	10031	504	70	17	M(A)	
Aska	..	..	1970	10030	504	70	17	M(A)	
Bacchus†	..	..	1962	4823	379	55	15	M(A)	
Bamora	..	..	1961	6745	426	59	16	M(A)	
Bankura	..	..	1959	6793	426	59	16	M(A)	
Barpeta	..	..	1960	6736	426	59	16	M(A)	
Bombala	..	..	1961	6745	426	59	16	M(A)	
Bulimba	..	..	1959	6791	427	59	16	M(A)	
Carpentaria	..	..	1949	7268	485	63	14½	M	
Chakdara	..	..	1951	7132	485	63	14½	M	
Chakdina	..	..	1951	7267	485	63	14½	M	
Chakla	..	..	1954	6565	485	64	15	M	
Chakrata	..	..	1952	7265	485	63	14½	M	ex Swiftpool 64. *To S'pore, ren. Golden Bear*
Chandpara	..	..	1949	7274	485	63	14½	M	
Chantala	..	..	1950	7349	485	63	14½	M	
Chilka	..	..	1950	7087	485	63	14½	M	
Chindwara	..	..	1950	7340	485	63	14½	M	
Chinkoa	..	..	1952	7102	485	63	14½	M	
Chupra	..	..	1944	6957	485	63	14½	M	
Dumra*	..	..	1946	4867	399	55	14	M	
Dwarka	..	..	1947	4851	399	55	14	M	
Hebe†	..	..	1962	4823	379	55	15	M(A)	
Howra	..	..	1952	6194	460	59	14	M	ex Limerick 69, ex Enton 55.
Jelunga	..	..	1953	7432	499	65	16	M	ex Middlesex 68.
Juna	..	..	1952	6796	489	63	16	M	ex Cornwall 67.
Juwara	..	..	1952	8227	499	65	16	M	ex Surrey 69.
Kampala*	..	..	1947	10304	507	66	16	ST(2)	
Karanja*	..	..	1948	10294	507	66	16	ST(2)	
Manora	..	..	1970	10000	515	76	19	M(A)	
Merkara	..	..	1970	10000	515	76	19	M(A)	
Nardana	..	..	1956	8511	515	68	16	ST	ex Baradine 68, ex *To Iran, ren.* Nardana 63. *Arya Fand*
Nevasa*	..	..	1956	20646	609	78	17	ST(2)	
Nowshera	..	..	1955	8516	514	68	16½	ST	*To Iran, ren. ARYA CHEHR*
Nuddea	..	..	1954	8598	514	67	16½	ST	
Nyanza	..	..	1956	8513	514	68	16	ST	*To Fran, ren. ARYA GOL*
Ozarda	..	..	1940	6895	442	57	12	M	
Purnea	..	..	1947	5340	432	55	11½	M	
Rajula	..	..	1926	8704	477	62	13	SR(2)	
Sirdhana*	..	..	1947	8608	479	63	14	M(2)	
Sirsa	..	..	1950	6722	432	55	11½	M	ex Betwa 66.
Tairea	..	..	1956	8199	500	65	15½	M	ex Aradina 70, ex Salsette 66.
Uganda*	..	..	1952	16907	540	71	16	ST(2)	
Waipara	..	..	1956	8569	472	63	16	M	ex Wharanui 69. *To S'pore, ren.*
Warina	..	..	1955	8573	472	63	16	M	ex Wainui 70, ex *Golden Lion* Whangaroa 65.

† On charter to Ministry of Defence as Store ships.

Bugsier-Reederei: NEUHARLINGERSIEL on charter to Dal Deutsche Africa-Linen

BUGSIER-REEDEREI UND BERGUNGS A.G.

FUNNEL: *Black with broad white band.*
HULL: *Black.*

Name		Date	Tons Gross	Length (feet)	Breadth (feet)	Speed (knots)	Engines	Former Names
Cuxhaven	..	1957	6507	535	63	17	M	
Geestemunde	..	1956	6507	535	63	17	M	
Hannoverland	..	1966	6991	534	69	18½	M	
Neuharlingersiel	..	1960	6971	533	65	18½	M	
Ostfriesland	..	1962	7016	533	65	18½	M	
Weserland	..	1970	6991	534	69	18½	M	
Vulkan		1974	1600					

BURIES MARKES LTD.

FUNNEL: *Black with blue " BM " on broad white band between two narrow red bands.*
HULL: *Black with white line and white boot-topping.*

Name		Date	Tons Gross	Length (feet)	Breadth (feet)	Speed (knots)	Engines	Former Names
La Chacra	..	1963	16599	617	75	14	M(A)	
La Colina	..	1958	7216	427	57	12	M(A)	
La Estancia	..	1965	28007	720	92	15	M(A)	
La Pampa	..	1970	17180	550	80	15	M(A)	
La Sierra	..	1966	28004	720	92	15	M(A)	
La Ensenada		1974	25200	bulk				

Montship Lines Ltd.

FUNNEL: *Black with blue " M " on broad white band between two narrow red bands.*

Name		Date	Tons Gross	Length (feet)	Breadth (feet)	Speed (knots)	Engines	Former Names
Montcalm	..	1960	4999	440	59	15	M	

BURNETT S.S. CO. LTD.

FUNNEL: *Black with broad yellow band.*
HULL: *Black with red boot-topping.*

Name		Date	Tons Gross	Length (feet)	Breadth (feet)	Speed (knots)	Engines	Former Names
Federal Tyne	..	1962	11563	507	69	14	M(A)	ex Scottish Trader 68.
Gosforth	..	1962	5675	410	56	14	M(A)	

CANADIAN PACIFIC STEAMSHIPS LTD.

FUNNEL: *Green incorporating a modern design with a triangle, a segment of a circle and part of a square.*

HULL: *White with green boot-topping.* (EMPRESS OF CANADA *has a wide green band on hull.*)

Name	Date	Tons Gross	Length (feet)	Breadth (feet)	Speed (knots)	Engines	Former Names
Beaverelm ..	1960	3959	355	49	14½	M	ex Roga 62.
Beaverfir ..	1961	4539	374	51	14½	M(A)	To Lib., ren MOIRA
Beaverpine ..	1962	4390	371	53	15	M	
CP Ambassador ..	1965	7105	466	57	15¾	M(A)	ex Beaveroak 70. To Lib., ren ATALAN
CP Discoverer ..	1970	16000	548	84	20	M(A)	
CP Trader ..	1970	16000	548	84	20	M(A)	
CP Voyageur ..	1970	16000	548	84	20	M(A)	
Empress of Canada	1961	25615	650	87	21	ST(2)	

Canadian Pacific (Bermuda) Ltd.

HULL: *Black.*

H. R. MacMillan ..	1968	21461	594	96	14½	M(A)	
J. V. Clyne ..	1968	21446	594	96	14½	M(A)	
N. R. Crump ..	1969	21445	594	96	14½	M(A)	
Pacific Logger ..	1969	10324	487	70	15	M(A)	
T. Akasaka ..	1969	33328	744	102	15	M(A)	
W. C. Van Horne..	1970	33300	744	102	15	M(A)	
W. M. Neal	1974	69,900				M	

(GREECE)

CHANDRIS GROUP

Various Companies

FUNNEL: *Blue with black top and white cross.* (QUEEN FREDERICA *has gold maltese cross.*)

HULL: *White, red boot-topping.* (AUSTRALIS *has light grey hull.*)

ROUTES:
A. *Southampton or Piraeus to Fremantle, Melbourne, Sydney and Auckland.*

B. *Piraeus, Messina, Palermo, Naples, Gibraltar, Halifax, New York.*

C. *Cruising.*

Amerikanis ..	1952	16485	577	74	19½	ST(2)	ex Kenya Castle 67.
Atlantis ..	1944	18920	623	76	20	ST(2)	ex President Roosevelt 70, ex Leilani 61, ex Laguardia 56, ex General W. P. Richardson 49.

ren EMERALD SEAS

Canadian Pacific Steamships Ltd: EMPRESS OF CANADA [*Fotoship*

Canadian Pacific Steamships Ltd: N. R. CRUMP [*R. J. Weeks*

Name			Date	Tons Gross	Length (feet)	Breadth (feet)	Speed (knots)	Engines	Former Names
Aurelia	..	..	1939	10480	488	60	15½	ME	ex Beaverbrae 54, ex Huascaran 47.
Australis	..	..	1940	26315	723	94	22	ST(2)	ex America 64, ex West Point 46, ex America 42.
Britanis	..	..	1932	18655	632	79	18	ST(2)	ex Lurline 70, ex Matsonia 63, ex Monterey 56.
Carina	..	..	1930	3891	341	51	19	ST(2)	ex Carina II 67, ex Helene 65, ex Princess Helene 63.
Ellinis	..	..	1932	18564	632	79	18	ST(2)	ex Lurline 63.
Fantasia	..	..	1935	4576	359	52	17	ST(2)	ex York 63, ex Duke of York 63.
Fiorita	..	..	1950	3524	377	54	17	ST(2)	ex Amsterdam 69.
Fiesta	..	..	1946	3158	345	47	16	ST(2)	ex Carina 64, ex Barrow Queen 63, ex Mona's Queen 62.
Patris	..	..	1950	16259	595	76	18½	M(2)	ex Bloemfontein Castle 59.
Queen Frederica	..		1927	16435	582	83	20	ST(2)	ex Atlantic 55, ex Matsonia 48, ex Malolo 37.
Regina *Prima*		..	1939	10153	494	64	17½	ST(2)	ex President Hoover 65, ex Panama 57 ex James Parker, ex Panama.
Romantica	..	..	1936	3743	326	45	13	SR	ex Mansour 60, ex Al Amir Saud 56, ex Fort Townshend 52.

Bon Vivant   6644

Romanza 12000   ex Aurelia

Victoria 16000

Australis and **Regina** fly Panamanian flag.

CHAPMAN & WILLAN LTD.

Carlton S.S. Co. Ltd., Cambay

S.S. Co. Ltd., and Somerston Shg. Co. Ltd.

FUNNEL: *Black with red and white flag between (and separate from) two narrow white bands.*

HULL: *Grey with red boot-topping.*

Name			Date						Former Names
Brighton	..	..	1960	5935	476	60	12	M	
Carlton	..	..	1964	16303	642	74	14	M(A)	
Demeterton		..	1967	16969	647	75	14½	M(A)	
Frumenton		..	1968	16702	594	75	14	M(A)	ex East Breeze 68.
Ingleton	..	..	1960	7809	452	60	14	M	ex Thistleroy 66.
Lynton	..	..	1957	5936	474	60	12	M	

CIE. MAR. DES CHARGEURS RÉUNIS

FUNNEL: *Yellow with red stars on white band.*

HULL: *Black with red boot-topping, except passenger ships and banana-carriers which have white hulls.*

ROUTES: *Hamburg, Bremen, Rotterdam, Amsterdam, Antwerp, Dunkirk, Le Havre, Rouen, Nantes, Bordeaux, Casablanca to West and South African ports.*
Hamburg, Bremen, Rotterdam, Antwerp, Dunkirk, Le Havre, Bordeaux, Algiers, Marseilles to Far East.
North America (East Coast) to West African ports and Far East.

Name			Date	Tons Gross	Length (feet)	Breadth (feet)	Speed (knots)	Engines	Former Names
Ango	..	..	1966	10427	517	72	18	M	
Bougainville		..	1967	10618	516	72	19	M(A)	
Capraia	..	..	1963	7225	507	69	15	M	
Circea	..	..	1964	7224	507	69	15	M	
Cypria	..	..	1964	7224	507	69	15	M	
Daloa	..	..	1949	6739	460	65	14	M	
Djiba	..	..	1960	10256	500	65	14	M(A)	ex Bonita 66.
Douka	..	..	1960	10246	500	65	14	M(A)	ex Aleppo 65.
Dracula	..	..	1961	10666	496	66	15	M(A)	ex Ringulv 69.
Dupleix	..	..	1967	10427	518	72	18	M(A)	
Forbin	..	..	1967	10427	517	72	18	M	
Joinville	..	..	1969	10618	515	72	19	M(A)	
Kanga	..	..	1960	4475	366	52	16	M	
Kerguelen	..	..	1968	10618	515	72	19	M(A)	
Loudima	..	..	1954	6801	460	56	14	M	
Louga	..	..	1954	6801	460	56	14	M	
Loulea	..	..	1950	6714	460	56	14	M	
Nara	..	..	1957	8896	495	63	15	M	ex Calliope 61.
Narval	..	..	1968	7900	472	66	17	M	
Nausicaa	..	..	1957	8924	495	63	15	M	ex Mary Sophia 61.
Norbella	..	..	1970	11500	510	75	19	M(A)	
Surcouf	..	..	1967	10618	515	72	19	M(A)	
Taboa	..	..	1958	7271	461	61	15	M	
Talassa	..	..	1957	6996	461	62	15	M	ToGabon, ren. Owendo
Tamba	..	..	1955	7278	461	61	15	M	ToGabon, ren. NYANGA
Tanagra	..	..	1958	7276	461	62	15	M	
Tatiana	..	..	1959	7271	461	62	15	M	
Tchibanga	..	..	1959	7271	461	62	16	M	
Tessa	..	..	1955	7275	461	61	15	M	To Gabon, ren. MANDJI
Tidra	..	..	1959	7271	461	62	16	M	ex Timla 58. To Ivory Coast, ren. AKROU
Tobago	..	..	1957	8773	475	62	15	M	
Tocansa	..	..	1958	8529	475	62	15	M	
Tourville	..	..	1970	11600	515	72	19	M(A)	
Frontenac			1974	13000					M
Atlantica Marseille			1972	13,100					M cont.

CHINA NAVIGATION CO. LTD.
John Swire & Sons Ltd.

FUNNEL: *Black with house flag.*

HULL: *Black with white line, red boot-topping.*

Chargeurs Reunis TOCANSA
[*T. Rayner*

China Navigation Co: KUALA LUMPUR, formerly the British troopship DILWARA
[*J. Y. Freeman*

Name			Date	Tons Gross	Length (feet)	Breadth (feet)	Speed (knots)	Engines	Former Names
Anshun	..	..	1951	5578	418	57	15	M	
Chengtu	..	..	1955	5832	422	56	14½	M	
Coral Chief		..	1957	5700	422	56	14½	M	ex Chekiang 69.
Hupeh	..	..	1961	7564	473	61	17	M(A)	ex Sidonoa 67.
Island Chief		..	1954	5709	422	56	14½	M	ex Chefoo 70.
Kuala Lumpur		..	1936	12598	517	65	14	M(2)	ex Dilwara 60.
Kwangsi	..	..	1960	5957	422	56	14½	M	
Kwangtung		..	1959	5810	422	56	14½	M	ex Norman 66, ex Kwangtung 65.
Kweichow	..	..	1959	5735	422	56	14½	M	ex Norman 68, ex ~~To Somalia,~~ Kweichow 66. ~~ten Orient Victory~~
Kweilin	..	..	1961	5902	422	56	14½	M	
Nanchang	..	..	1957	9820	518	64	14½	M(A)	ex Hervang 70, ex Amacita 65.
Ninghai	..	..	1945	9879	497	64	15	M	ex Athenian 65, ex Elysia 63.
Princess Leopoldina	1962	9696	478	61	18		M(2)	(Renamed Coral Princess)
Shansi	..	..	1950	8089	485	61	16	M	ex Berganger 69.
Six Stars	..	..	1955	5588	449	60	14½	M	ex Tientsin 69, ex Maroua 61, ex Frontenac 56.
Taiwan	..	..	1961	5150	397	53	17	M(2)	ex Olav 69, ex Kong Olav V 68.
Taiyuan	..	..	1949	6160	440	57	15	M	
Tsingtao	..	..	1954	5156	449	60	14½	M	ex Island Chief 70, ~~To Somalia,~~ ex Tsingtao 68, ex ~~ten Soochow~~ Manga 62, ex Duquesne 56.
Wanliu	..	..	1949	5393	476	64	15	M	ex Wanstead 64, ex Raeburn 64, ex Wanstead 63, ex Port Wanstead 60, ex Wanstead 57.
Wenchow	..	..	1950	5393	476	64	15	M	ex Wendover 65.
Woosung	..	..	1950	5393	476	64	15	M	ex Woodford 64, ex Rossetti 64, ex Woodford 63.
Yochow	..	..	1948	6861	472	60	14½	M	ex St. Thomas 65.
Yunnan	..	..	1948	6844	472	60	14½	M	ex St. Essylt 65.

CLAN LINE STEAMERS LTD.

Cayzer, Irvine & Co. Ltd.

FUNNEL: *Black with two red bands close together.*

HULL: *Black, pink boot-topping.*

ROUTES:
    A. *United Kingdom to South Africa and Mauritius.*
    B. *United Kingdom to East Africa, India, Pakistan and Ceylon.*
    C. *South and East Africa to Australia.*
    D. *Australia, Tasmania to United Kingdom.*

Name		Date	Tons	Length	Breadth	Speed	Engines
Clan Alpine	..	1967	8713	508	63	16½	M
Clan Macilwraith	..	1960	6894	494	62	14	M(A)
Clan Macinnes	..	1952	6517	471	61	15	M
Clan Macintosh	..	1951	6454	471	61	15	M

China Navigation Co: CORAL CHIEF

[J. Y. Freeman

Clan Line: CLAN RAMSAY

[Fotoship

Name		Date	Tons Gross	Length (feet)	Breadth (feet)	Speed (knots)	Engines	Former Names
Clan Macintyre	..	1952	6488	471	61	15	M	
Clan Maciver	..	1958	7413	494	62	14	M	
Clan Maclachlan	..	1947	6365	466	61	14½	ST	
Clan Maclaren	..	1946	6389	466	61	14½	M	
Clan Maclay	..	1949	6388	466	61	14½	M	
Clan Maclean	..	1947	6017	466	61	14½	M	
Clan Maclennan	..	1947	6357	466	61	14½	ST	
Clan Macleod	..	1948	6073	466	61	14½	M	
Clan Macnab	..	1961	9169	507	62	16	M	
Clan Mactaggart	..	1949	7994	506	66	15	ST	
Clan Mactavish	..	1949	7971	506	66	15	ST	
Clan Malcolm	..	1957	7326	503	66	16	M	
Clan Matheson	..	1957	7553	503	66	16	M	
Clan Menzies	..	1958	7315	503	66	16	M	
Clan Ramsay*	..	1965	7955	529	69	17½	M	
Clan Ranald*	..	1965	7955	529	69	17½	M	
Clan Robertson*	..	1965	7955	529	69	17½	M	
Clan Sutherland	..	1951	8338	513	66	15½	ST	

* Owned by Union Castle Mail S.S. Co. Ltd.

King Line Ltd.

King Alfred	..	1968	29119	714	97	16	M(A)	ex Hemsefjell 68, ex Angelus 68.
King Arthur	..	1953	5883	467	59	13	M	
King James	..	1970	29758	678	95	16	M(A)	
Kinnaird Castle	..	1956	7737	503	66	16	ST	ex South African Scientist 62, ex Clan Ross 61.
Clan Graham	..	1961	9022	497	63	16	M	
Clan Grant	..	1962	9022	497	63	16	M	
Clan Macgillivray		1962	8811	508	63	16	M	
Clan Macgregor	..	1962	8811	508	63	16	M	

Houston Line Ltd.

Ships as Clan Line but with Houston house flag.

ROUTE: *U.K. and Continent to S. and E. African Ports.*

Clan Macdougall	..	1944	9587	506	65	16	M	
Clan Ross	..	1966	7955	529	69	17½	M	
King Charles	..	1957	5980	467	59	13	M	
King George	..	1957	5976	467	59	13	M	
King Henry	..	1958	6119	467	59	13	M	

Hector Whaling Ltd.

King Alexander	..	1952	5883	467	59	13	M	
King Malcolm	..	1952	5883	467	59	13	M	

Clan Line: KING ALFRED　　　　　　　　　　　　　　　　　　[*F. R. Sherlock*

Common Bros-Hopemount Shipping Co: HOPECRAG　　　[*Malcolm Cranfield*

Neptune Shipping Co. Ltd. (Bermuda)

Name		Date	Tons Gross	Length (feet)	Breadth (feet)	Speed (knots)	Engines	Former Names
Clan Macindoe	..	1959	8991	494	62	14	M(A)	
Clan Macnair	..	1962	9137	506	62	15¾	M(A)	

Scottish Shire Line Ltd.

Argyllshire	..	1956	9141	535	69	16	ST	

See also Overseas Containers Ltd.

Scottish Tanker Co. Ltd.

Elbe Ore	..	..	1967	42425	818	106	15	M(A)	

CIA. COLONIAL DE NAVEGACAO
PORTUGUESA DE TRANSPORTES MARITIMOS **(PORTUGAL)**

FUNNEL: *Yellow with white band between two green bands.*

HULL: *Grey with green boot-topping.*

ROUTES: **A.** *Lisbon to Vigo, Funchal, Teneriffe, La Guaira, Curacao, San Juan, Miami.*

B. *Lisbon to Portugal West and East Africa.*

Name			Date	Tons				Engines	
Amboim	..	..	1949	5895	443	59	13	M	
Benguela	..	..	1946	5094	432	57	13	M	
Ganda	..	..	1948	5895	443	59	13	M	
Imperio	..	..	1948	13186	531	68	17	ST(2)	
Infante Dom Henrique	..	..	1961	23306	642	85	21	ST(2)	
Lobito	..	..	1959	5981	475	60	14	M	
Luanda	..	..	1948	5941	445	60	13	M	
Lugela	..	..	1926	5277	423	56	12½	ST	ex Dortmund 43.
Patria	..	..	1947	13196	531	68	17	ST(2)	
Porto	..	..	1968	9220	563	72	17	M	
Santa Maria	..	..	1953	20906	610	76	20	ST(2)	
Uige	..	..	1954	10001	477	63	16	M	
Vera Cruz	..	..	1952	21765	610	76	20	ST(2)	

Also smaller ships.

COMMON BROS. (MANAGEMENT) LTD.
Hindustan Steam Shg. Co. Ltd.

FUNNEL: *Black with white " C " on broad red band between two narrow white bands.*

HULL: *Black with white line, red boot-topping.*

Name		Date	Tons Gross	Length (feet)	Breadth (feet)	Speed (knots)	Engines	Former Names
Afghanistan	..	1957	11188	526	69	11½	M(A)	
Daghestan ..	..	1960	11204	526	69	14	M(A)	

Burnside Shipping Co. Ltd.

Simonburn	..	1965	21379	630	85	15	M(A)	

Hopemount Shipping Co. Ltd.

Hopecrag ..	..	1963	7308	501	64	15½	M	

Northumbrian Shipping Co. Ltd.

Caribbean Enterprise	..	1969	1547	312	57	16	M(2)(A)	
Caribbean Venture		1968	1547	312	57	16	M(2)(A)	

Home Line Ltd.

Nimos	..	..	1969	2634	372	56	15½	M(A) ex Berkel 69.

CONSTANTS LTD.

FUNNEL: *Black with broad red band between two narrow white bands.*
HULL: *Black with white line, red boot-topping.*

~~Lottinge~~	..	..	1956	4094	382	51	11½	M(A) *To England, now SAMANTHA M*
Lyminge	..	..	1967	4980	406	54	14	M(A)
Susan Constant	..	1958	3385	352	47	11	M(A)

CORY MARITIME LTD.

St. Denis Shg. Co. Ltd.

FUNNEL: *Black with black diamond on broad white band.*
HULL: *Black with red boot-topping.*

Name			Date	Tons Gross	Length (feet)	Breadth (feet)	Speed (knots)	Engines	Former Names
Dukesgarth	..	..	1961	10606	511	70	12½	M(A)	
Knightsgarth	..	..	1961	10591	511	70	12½	M(A)	
Monksgarth	..	..	1960	10611	511	70	12½	M(A)	
Queensgarth	..	..	1959	10609	511	70	12½	M(A)	

Also tankers, Coastal ships and tugs.

(ITALY)

COSTA, ARMATORI S.p.A.—" LINEA C "

FUNNEL: *Yellow with narrow blue top and blue ' C '.*
HULL: *White with blue line and blue boot-topping.*
ROUTES: **A.** *Genoa to Cannes, Barcelona, Lisbon, Funchal, Las Palmas Rio de Janeiro, Santos, Montevideo and Buenos Aires.*
         B. *Genoa to Cannes, Barcelona, Vigo, Teneriffe, the West Indies and Central America.*

Name			Date	Tons	Length	Breadth	Speed	Engines	Former Names
Alpe ..	..	..	1942	6893	485	64	15	M	ex Mario Rosselli.
Andrea C	..	..	1942	8604	467	57	13½	M	ex Ocean Virtue 48.
Anna C	..	..	1929	12030	524	65	18	M(2)	ex Southern Prince 47.
Bice Costa ..		..	1946	9628	498	64	16	TE	ex Beaverlake 62.
Carla C	..	..	1952	19975	600	80	23	M ST(2)	ex Flandre 68.
Cervinia	..	..	1959	8612	477	62	15	M	ex Lorenzo Marcello 64.
Cesana	..	..	1956	8520	477	63	15½	M	ex Enrico Dandolo 64.
Enrico C	..	..	1950	13607	579	73	18½	ST(2)	ex Provence 65.
Eugenio C ..		..	1966	30567	713	96	27	ST(2)	
Federico C		..	1958	20416	606	79	22	ST(2)	
Flavia	..	..	1947	15465	556	70	17	ST(2)	ex Media 61.
Franca C.	..	..	1914	6822	428	55	14	M	ex Roma 52, ex Medina 49.
Giovanna Costa		..	1947	9622	498	64	16	TE	ex Beavercove 63, ex Maplecove 56, ex Beavercove 52.
Luisa Costa		..	1946	9622	498	64	16	TE	ex Beaverdell 63, ex Mapledell 63, ex Beaverdell 52.
Maria Costa		..	1958	10714	551	71	16	ST(A)	
Paola Costa		..	1949	6594	479	61	16	M	ex Peter Maersk 63.
Pia Costa	..	..	1958	10729	551	71	16	ST(A)	
Sises	..	..	1948	6422	474	61	17	M	
Giovanna C.			1956	8986				M	ex Ommenkerk
Luisa C.			1954	7008				M	ex Oostkerk

Costa: ANDREA C at Las Palmas

Cunard Line: CARMANIA

CUNARD LINE LTD.

FUNNEL: *Red with black top and thin black rings except* QUEEN ELIZABETH 2.

HULL: *White, red boot-topping, except* QUEEN ELIZABETH 2 *which has charcoal grey hull and orange boot-topping.*

ROUTES: **A.** *Southampton, Le Havre to New York.*
B. *New York to Bermuda* (FRANCONIA).
C. *Cruises.*

Name	Date	Tons Gross	Length (feet)	Breadth (feet)	Speed (knots)	Engines	Former Names
Carmania	1954	21370	608	80	20	ST(2)	ex Saxonia 62.
Franconia	1955	21406	608	80	20	ST(2)	ex Ivernia 62.
Queen Elizabeth 2	1968	65863	963	105	28½	ST(2)	

⊗ *Cunard Countess 1976*   *MV*
Cunard Adventurer 1971 14151   *MV*
Cunard Conquest 1975 16700   *M*

Cunard Steam Ship Co. Ltd.

(Managers Cunard Brocklebank Ltd.)

Media	..	..	1963	5149	437	60	17	M(A)
Parthia	..	..	1963	5149	437	60	17	M(A)

See also Atlantic Container Line.

T. & J. Brocklebank Ltd.

(Managers Cunard Brocklebank Ltd.)

FUNNEL: *Black with blue band over white band.*

HULL: *Black with broad white line or white, red boot-topping.*

ROUTES: *U.K. and Continent to Colombo, Madras, Calcutta and E. Pakistan.*
Calcutta, E. Pakistan and Colombo to U.S.A. East Coast and Gulf ports.

Macharda	..	..	1960	6658	490	63	17½	ST	ex Andania 69.
Mahout	..	..	1963	6867	481	63	16	M	
Mahronda	..	..	1964	8783	515	60	17	M(A)	ex Saxonia 70.
Mahseer	..	..	1948	8774	508	67	15	ST	
Mahsud	..	..	1968	9416	505	63	18	M	
Maihar	..	..	1968	9416	505	63	18	M	
Maipura	..	..	1952	9625	509	67	15	ST	
Makrana	..	..	1957	8764	497	63	16½	ST	
Malancha	..	..	1960	6658	490	63	17½	ST	ex Alaunia 69.
Manaar	..	..	1950	8970	508	67	15	ST	
Mangla	..	..	1959	8643	497	63	16½	ST	
Manipur	..	..	1964	8780	515	60	17	M(A)	ex Ivernia 70.
Markhor	..	..	1963	6867	481	63	16½	ST	
Masirah	..	..	1957	8596	497	63	15½	ST	
Mathura	..	..	1960	8624	497	63	16½	ST	
Matra	..	..	1949	8858	508	67	15	ST	
Mawana	..	..	1958	8925	497	63	16½	ST	

The majority of the above vessels are owned by Cunard Steam Ship Co. Ltd.

Cunard Line: QUEEN ELIZABETH 2

[F. R. Sherlock

Cunard-Brocklebank-Line: MANGLA [*F. R. Sherlock*

Cunard-Brocklebank-Line: MAIHAR [*J. Y. Freeman*

CURRIE LINE LTD.

FUNNEL: *Black with broad white band.*
HULL: *Black with red boot-topping.*

Name	Date	Tons Gross	Length (feet)	Breadth (feet)	Speed (knots)	Engines	Former Names
Gothland	1961	16664	595	74	14½	M(A)	

Also smaller ships.

(NORWAY)

A/S THOR DAHL

FUNNEL: *Grey with blue fish (resembling a " C ") on broad white band between two narrow red bands.*
HULL: *Grey with red boot-topping.*

Name	Date	Tons Gross	Length	Breadth	Speed	Engines	Former Names
Thor I	1955	5135	442	58	15	M	
Thorscape	1954	4981	442	58	14	M	
Thorsdrake ..	1967	29249	700	96	15	M(A)	ex Amasone 67.
Thorsdrott ..	1964	4172	420	56	18	M	
Thorsgaard ..	1951	5077	442	58	15	M	
Thorshavn	1965	19816	630	84	15	M(A)	
Thorshope	1958	5756	479	61	17	M	
Thorsorient ..	1951	5684	462	62	15	M	ex Vigan 64.
Thorsoy	1964	4172	420	56	18	M	
Thorsriver ..	1959	5757	479	61	17	M	
Thorstind	1968	4211	420	56	18	M	
Thorstream ..	1960	5754	479	61	17	M	
Thorswave ..	1967	10133	524	71	16	M	

R. S. DALGLIESH LTD.
Watergate S.S. Co. Ltd.

FUNNEL: *Red " D " on blue with black top.*
HULL: *Black with white line, grey boot-topping.*

Name	Date	Tons Gross	Length	Breadth	Speed	Engines	Former Names
Pennyworth ..	1958	10978	505	69	11½	M(A)	
Ravensworth ..	1960	6805	426	57	11¼	M(A)	
Silksworth ..	1964	16553	599	75	15	M(A)	
Starworth	1970	19580	564	85	15	M(A)	
Tamworth	1968	11126	507	69	14	M(A)	
Warkworth ..	1962	9648	495	63	13	M	

(DENMARK)

A/S DET DANSK-FRANSKE D/S
E. Hahn—Petersen

FUNNEL: *White with black top and black " D-F ".*
HULL: *Grey.*

Name			Date	Tons Gross	Length (feet)	Breadth (feet)	Speed (knots)	Engines	Former Names
Afrika	..	..	1958	3897	411	56	15½	M	*To Cyprus*
Banana	..	..	1967	5388	456	64	16½	M(A)	
Belgien	..	..	1954	3654	412	54	14½	M	*To Greece, ren. PHILIPPAS*
Congo	..	..	1954	3654	412	54	14½	M	*To Ukwama*
Frankrig	..	..	1956	3405	422	52	14½	M	
Grønland	..	..	1961	2018	336	48	14	M(A)	*To Greece, ren. LORD NELSON*
Himmerland	..	..	1967	15374	580	75	15	M(A)	
Holland	..	..	1961	4877	478	57	16	M	
Kinshasa	..	..	1967	5388	456	64	16½	M(A)	
Mayumbe	..	..	1955	3899	412	56	15½	M	
Normandiet	..	..	1967	15572	584	75	15	M(A)	
Slesvig	..	..	1959	13393	580	66	14	M(A)	*To Finland, ren. ARKADIA*
Vinland	..	..	1960	13392	580	66	14	M(A)	*cont.*
Skotland	..	..	19__	9700					

DART CONTAINERLINE LTD.

A Container Consortium by Cie. Maritime Belge (Lloyd Royal) S.A., Bristol City Line Ltd., and Clarke Traffic Services Ltd.

FUNNEL: *Yellow with three white/red darts.*
HULL: *Orange brown, black boot-topping.*

(BELGIUM)
Cie. Maritime Belge (Lloyd Royal) S.A.

Breughel	..	..	1963	10375	517	66	16½	M
Dart Europe	..	1970	33400	760	100	22		M(A)
Jordaens	..	..	1963	10375	517	66	16½	M
Rubens	..	..	1963	10375	517	66	16½	M
Teniers	..	..	1964	10375	517	66	16½	M

Tynedale Shipping Company

Dart America	..	1970	33400	759	100	22	M(A)

Bristol City Line Ltd.

Dart Atlantic	..	1971	33400	759	100	22	M(A)

(WEST GERMANY)
Hans Kruger G.m.b.H.
(ON CHARTER)

Britta Kruger	..	1969	5383	386	59	17	M(A)
Jorg Kruger	..	1969	5383	386	59	17	M(A)

Flensburger Schiffs. Vereinigung A.G.
(ON CHARTER)

Juno	..	..	1969	5530	410	56	17	M(A)

Dansk-Franske: BANANA

Dart Container Line: RUBENS

J. & J. DENHOLM (MANAGEMENT) LTD.
Denholm Line Steamers Ltd.

FUNNEL: *Red with black top and white " D " on blue diamond on white square.*

HULL: *Black with red boot-topping.*

Name		Date	Tons Gross	Length (feet)	Breadth (feet)	Speed (knots)	Engines	Former Names
Clunepark ..	..	1957	9800	516	64	14½	M	ex Glafki 57. *TOG REECQ new JANE IOTA*
Mountpark	..	1965	21833	630	85	15	M	
Wellpark ..	..	1958	6859	426	57	11½	M(A)	ex Needles 60.
Mouach		*1972*	*1594*				*M*	*ex Mornes*

Scottish Ore Carriers Ltd.

FUNNEL: *Black with white " O " on white bordered red shield over St. Andrew's cross on broad red band between two narrow white bands.*

HULL: *Black with red boot-topping.*

Name		Date	Tons Gross	Length	Breadth	Speed	Engines
Arisaig ..	..	1957	6872	427	57	11	M(A)
Craigallian	..	1959	7088	427	57	11	M(A)
Crinan ..	..	1960	7086	427	57	11	M(A)

H. Clarkson & Co. Ltd.

FUNNEL: *Same as Scottish Ore Carriers Ltd., but white " C " on shield.*

HULL: *Black with red boot-topping.*

Name		Date	Tons Gross	Length	Breadth	Speed	Engines
Baknes ..	..	1969	13400	520	75	15	M(A)
Bellnes ..	..	1969	12404	522	71	15	M(A)
Binsnes ..	..	1966	10961	501	67	15	M(A)
Clarkavon ..	..	1958	6860	426	57	11	M(A)
Clarkeden ..	..	1958	6861	426	57	11	M(A)
Gallic Bridge	..	1967	42774	805	106	15	M(A)
Jersey Bridge	..	1966	22490	657	85	16	M(A)
Spey Bridge†	..	1969	66126	850	134	15	M(A)

† Bulk/oil carrier.

St. Andrews Shipping Co. Ltd.

FUNNEL: *Same as Scottish Ore Carriers Ltd., but white "SA" on shield.*

HULL: *Black with red boot-topping.*

Name		Date	Tons Gross	Length	Breadth	Speed	Engines
Dunadd ..	..	1955	10682	505	69	13	M(A)
Dunkyle ..	..	1957	10687	505	69	12	M(A)

British Steam Shipping Co. Ltd.

Name	Date	Tons Gross	Length (feet)	Breadth (feet)	Speed (knots)	Engines	Former Names
Duncraig	1957	10687	505	69	12	M(A)	
Sir Andrew Duncan	1958	10687	505	69	12	M(A)	

Scotspark Shipping Co. Ltd.

Name	Date	Tons Gross	Length (feet)	Breadth (feet)	Speed (knots)	Engines	Former Names
Scotspark	1969	16793	580	75	15	M(A)	

Scotscraig Shipping Co. Ltd.

Name	Date	Tons Gross	Length (feet)	Breadth (feet)	Speed (knots)	Engines	Former Names
Vancouver Forest	1969	17659	575	87	15	M(A)	

Scotstoun Shipping Co. Ltd.

Name	Date	Tons Gross	Length (feet)	Breadth (feet)	Speed (knots)	Engines	Former Names
Kyoto Forest	1970	17670	575	87	15	M(A)	

J. Macdonald-Buchanan & Others

Name	Date	Tons Gross	Length (feet)	Breadth (feet)	Speed (knots)	Engines	Former Names
Conon Forest	1969	17659	575	87	15	M(A)	

Haverton Shipping Ltd.

Name	Date	Tons Gross	Length (feet)	Breadth (feet)	Speed (knots)	Engines	Former Names
Haverton	1968	32409	760	96	15	M(A)	

Trader Navigation Co. Ltd.

Name	Date	Tons Gross	Length (feet)	Breadth (feet)	Speed (knots)	Engines	Former Names
Essex Trader	1968	13953	583	75	14½	M(A)	

Random Ltd.

Name	Date	Tons Gross	Length (feet)	Breadth (feet)	Speed (knots)	Engines	Former Names
Federal Hudson	1956	7240	445	59	14	M	ex Tuscany 70.

Falkland Shipowners Ltd.

Name	Date	Tons Gross	Length (feet)	Breadth (feet)	Speed (knots)	Engines	Former Names
Scotstoun	1964	11183	514	68	15	M	

Louis Drefus: PIERRE L. D. [R. J. Weeks

East Asiatic Co: ARANYA [F. R. Sherlock

LOUIS DREYFUS & CIE.

FUNNEL: *Black with blue ' LD&C ' on white band between two red bands.*
HULL: *Black with white line and red boot-topping.*

Name		Date	Tons Gross	Length (feet)	Breadth (feet)	Speed (knots)	Engines	Former Names
Alain L.D.	..	1969	12705	499	74	16	M(A)	*To Italy*
Charles L.D.	..	1962	21560	653	87	14	M(A)	
Francois L.D.	..	1962	16516	617	75	14	M(A)	
Gerard L.D.	..	1963	21536	653	87	14	M(A)	*To Greece, ren. SKAMANDROS*
Philippe L.D.	..	1958	6733	427	57	12	M(A)	
Pierre L.D.	..	1962	21536	653	87	14	M(A)	
Robert L.D.	..	1969	12705	499	74	16	M(A)	
Jean L.D.		*1974*	*24,000*				*M*	*bulk*
Alain L.D.		*1974*	*25200*					*bulk*
Gerard L.D.		*1974*	*24,000*					*bulk*

THE EAST ASIATIC CO. LTD.
Det Ostasiatiske Kompagni A/S

FUNNEL: *Yellow, with " EAC " in blue.*
HULL: *Black with white line and red boot-topping.*
ROUTES: *Scandinavia, Continent and United Kindom to*
    A. *Malaya, Singapore, Bangkok and Far East.*
    B. *India, Pakistan, Ceylon and Burma.*
    C. *Indonesia.*
    D. *Australia and New Zealand.*
    E. *From Denmark and United Kingdom to St. Thomas (Virgin Is.) and West Coast of North America and Canada.*

Name			Date					Engines
Alameda	..	..	1967	7569	545	74	20	M
Ancona	..	..	1965	7981	540	74	20	M
Andorra	..	..	1964	7610	523	68	19	M(A)
Aranya	..	..	1966	7745	540	76	20	M
Arosia	..	..	1966	7812	540	76	20	M
Asmara	..	..	1961	7638	524	68	17	M(A)
Atrevida	..	..	1968	8930	548	82	21	M(A)
Ayuthia	..	..	1960	7822	524	68	17	M(A)
Azuma	..	..	1966	8440	539	77	20	M
Basra	..	..	1959	8802	498	64	$17\frac{1}{2}$	M(A)
Beira	..	..	1958	6611	498	64	$17\frac{1}{2}$	M(A)
Bogota	..	..	1956	6586	498	64	$17\frac{1}{2}$	M(A)
Boma	..	..	1957	6584	497	64	$17\frac{1}{2}$	M(A)
Boribana	..	..	1961	8807	498	64	$17\frac{1}{2}$	M(A)
Busuanga	..	..	1957	6493	497	64	$17\frac{1}{2}$	M(A)
Magdala	..	..	1951	6241	475	61	15	M
Mombasa	..	..	1950	6010	475	61	15	M
Panama	..	..	1950	6525	481	62	16	M
Pasadena	..	..	1953	6292	480	61	16	M
Patagonia	..	..	1951	6266	475	61	16	M
Poona	..	..	1952	6292	480	61	16	M
Pretoria	..	..	1952	6256	475	61	16	M
Samoa	..	..	1953	6239	489	63	16	M
Sargodha	..	..	1956	6211	489	63	16	M
Sibonga	..	..	1953	6335	491	63	16	M
Siena	..	..	1954	6429	491	64	16	M
Simba	..	..	1955	6194	488	63	16	M
Sinaloa	..	..	1956	6415	491	64	16	M
Songkhla	..	..	1953	6235	489	63	16	M
Sumbawa	..	..	1954	6429	491	64	16	M

Meonia
Falstria

East Asiatic Co: BEIRA

[*Malcolm Cranfield*

Eastern & Australian S.S.: ARAKAWA

[*J. Mathieson*

EASTERN & AUSTRALIAN S.S. CO. LTD.

FUNNEL: *Black.*

HULL: *Black with white line and red boot-topping.*

Name			Date	Tons Gross	Length (feet)	Breadth (feet)	Speed (knots)	Engines	Former Names
Arakawa	..	..	1956	8199	500	65	15½	M	ex Salmara 66.
Arawatta	..	..	1958	5510	459	58	17	M	ex Charlotte 63, ex Anne-Marie Thorden 59.
Cathay	..	..	1957	13531	558	70	16	ST	ex Baudouinville 61.
Chitral	..	..	1956	13821	558	70	16	ST	ex Jadotville 61.
Tanda	..	..	1954	8774	482	63	14	ST	ex Arafura 70.

ELDER DEMPSTER LINES LTD.

FUNNEL: *Yellow.*

HULL: *Black with red boot-topping except* AUREOL *which has white hull with yellow line and green boot-topping.*

ROUTES:
    A. *Liverpool to Las Palmas, Bathurst, Freetown, Monrovia, Tema and Lagos.*
    B. *United Kingdom, Continental ports to West and South West Africa.*
    C. *New York and Montreal to West Africa.*
    D. *Mediterranean ports to West Africa.*

Name			Date	Tons	Length	Breadth	Speed	Engines	
Aureol	..	..	1951	14083	537	70	16	(M2)	To Greece, ren. MARIANNA
Dalla	..		1961	6385	465	63	14	M	
Degema	..	..	1959	5636	460	62	14	M	
Deido	..	..	1961	5909	460	63	14	M	
Dixcove	..	..	1959	5649	460	62	14	M	
Donga	..	..	1960	8986	465	63	14	M	
Dumbaia	..	..	1960	8876	465	63	14	M	
Dumurra	..	..	1961	5932	460	63	14	M	
Dunkwa	..	..	1960	5909	460	63	14	M	
Ebani	..	..	1952	9376	508	64	15½	M	
Eboe	..	..	1952	9380	508	64	15½	M	
Egori	..	..	1957	8331	509	64	15½	M	
Falaba	..	..	1962	7703	465	62	16	M	
Fian	..	..	1964	7689	465	62	16	M	
Forcados	..	..	1963	7689	465	62	16	M	
Fourah Bay	..	..	1961	7704	465	62	16	M	
Fulani	..	..	1964	7689	465	62	16	M	
Kabala	..	..	1958	5445	455	58	12½	M	To Cyprus, ren. PAPA MAURICE
Kaduna	..	..	1959	5599	455	58	12½	M	
Kohima	..	..	1959	5445	455	58	12½	M	ex Kalaw 66, ex Prahsu 64. ren. 'PAPAGEORGI To Cyprus
Kumba	..	..	1958	5439	455	58	12½	M	To S'pore, ren. REGENT LIBERT
Obuasi	..	..	1952	5895	450	60	12½	M	
Onitsha	..	..	1952	5386	449	62	12½	M	To Greece, ren. AMVOURGAN
Oti	..	..	1956	5485	450	62	12¾	M	
Owerri	..	..	1955	5798	450	62	12½	M	
Patani	..	..	1954	6183	450	60	11	M	
Perang	..	..	1954	6177	450	60	11	M	
Sherbro			1974	9200				M	Cont.
			1974	131,000				ST	To Abu Dhabi

Also smaller ships on West African local services.

Elder Dempster Lines: ONITSHA, photographed in the Bristol Channel 23.7.68
[*Malcolm Cranfield*

Ellerman Lines: CITY OF DUNDEE
[*J. Mathieson*

Ellerman Lines: CASTILIAN

Ellerman Lines: CITY OF EXETER

Guinea Gulf Line Ltd.

FUNNEL: *Red with black top.*

Name			Date	Tons Gross	Length (feet)	Breadth (feet)	Speed (knots)	Engines	Former Names
Bhamo	..	..	1957	5932	470	60	14½	M	
Daru	..	..	1958	6301	460	62	14	M	ex Yoma 67, ex Daru 65.
Freetown	..	..	1964	7689	465	62	16	M	
Pegu	..	..	1961	5764	466	60	14	M	

ELLERMAN LINES

This large group consists of the City Line, Hall Line, Ellerman and Papayanni Lines, Ellerman and Bucknall S.S. Co., and the Westcott and Laurance Line, all of which have the same funnel and hull colours. The managing company of a ship can only be distinguished by the different house flags. The routes are world-wide and too numerous to give in detail.

FUNNEL: *Buff with black top and white dividing band.*

HULL: *Grey, bright red boot-topping.*

Name		Date	Tons Gross	Length (feet)	Breadth (feet)	Speed (knots)	Engines	Former Names
Arcadian		1960	3402	367	54	13½	M	
Athenian		1966	2702	308	46	14	M(A)	
Castilian	.. ..	1955	3803	377	53	12	RT	ex Arabia 66, ex Castilian 66, ex City of Peterborough 64, ex Castilian 63.
Catanian	.. ..	1958	1408	270	43	12	M(A)	
City of Adelaide	..	1964	10316	511	67	17¾	M	
City of Auckland	..	1958	8181	507	67	15¼	M	
City of Bedford	..	1950	7341	485	62	14	ST	
City of Birkenhead		1950	7492	485	62	14	ST	
City of Birmingham		1949	7599	480	62	15	ST	
City of Canberra	..	1961	10543	511	67	17½	M	
City of Capetown		1959	9914	545	71	17	M	ex City of Melbourne 68.
City of Chester	..	1944	8380	493	64	16	M(2)	
City of Colombo	..	1956	7739	507	66	15	M	
City of Deltic	..	1956	7716	507	66	15	M	ex Benedin 70, ex City of Winnipeg 68.
City of Dundee	..	1961	4978	434	59	15	M	
City of Durban	..	1954	13345	541	71	16½	M(2)	
City of Eastbourne		1962	9704	508	67	17½	M(A)	
City of Exeter	..	1953	13253	541	71	16½	M(2)	
City of Glasgow	..	1963	9710	508	67	17½	M(A)	
City of Gloucester		1963	4803	434	59	15	M	
City of Guildford		1957	4945	434	59	14½	M	
City of Hereford	..	1958	4954	434	59	14½	M	
City of Hull	..	1970	10900	502	73	18	M	
City of Karachi	..	1951	7320	485	62	14	ST	
City of Lancaster	..	1958	4949	434	59	14½	M	
City of Lichfield	..	1961	4976	434	59	15	M	
City of Liverpool		1970	10900	502	73	18	M	
City of London	..	1971	11500	500	72	18	M	
City of Manchester		1950	7585	485	62	15	ST	
City of Newcastle		1956	7727	507	66	15	M	ex Benratha 70, ex City of Newcastle 68.
City of Ottawa	..	1950	7622	485	62	15	ST	
City of Oxford	..	1948	7593	480	62	15	ST	

Handwritten annotations: "ex-CITY OF FAMAGUSTA" (Arcadian), "ex-CITY OF VALLETTA" (Athenian), "TO CYPRUS, ren. MEDITERRANEAN SEA" (City of Exeter), "City of Exeter 1974 9213 M ex Strathdene"

City of Canterbury 1976
City of Winchester 1976
City of York 1976

ELLERMAN LINES (continued)

Name	Date	Tons Gross	Length (feet)	Breadth (feet)	Speed (knots)	Engines	Former Names
City of							
Port Elizabeth ..	1952	13278	541	71	16½	M(2)	
City of Ripon ..	1956	7713	507	66	15	M	
City of St. Albans	1960	4809	434	59	14½	M	
City of Singapore..	1951	7338	485	62	14	ST	
City of Sydney ..	1960	10242	512	67	17½	M	
City of Wellington	1956	7702	507	66	15	M	
City of Worcester	1960	4790	434	59	15	M	
City of York	1953	13250	541	72	16½	M(2)	
Flaminian	1956	3100	351	52	13½	M	
Florian	1955	3134	351	52	13½	M	
Malatian ..	1958	1407	270	43	12	M(A)	
Mediterranian ..	1968	1460	309	48	13	M(A)	

(handwritten) ren: City of Istanbul
(handwritten) 12 Mlk

Sea Containers Ltd.

(ON CHARTER)

Name	Date	Tons	Length	Breadth	Speed	Engines
Minho *(hw) ren. City of Milan*	1969	930	279	45	16	M(A)
Tagus *(hw) " " Lisbon*	1970	930	279	45	16	M(A)
Tormes *(hw) " " Oporto*	1970	930	279	45	16	M(A)

(handwritten) Tamega ren: City of Genoa

ELLERMAN'S WILSON LINE LTD.

FUNNEL: *Red with black top.*

HULL: *Dark green with red boot-topping, but several of the smaller ships have grey hulls. (SPERO has light grey hull.)*

ROUTES: *Hull, London and Leith to Mediterranean and Black Sea. (Smaller ships) Hull, London and U.K. ports to Scandinavia and Poland.*

Name	Date	Tons	Length	Breadth	Speed	Engines
Rapallo *(hw) City of Limassol* ..	1960	3402	366	54	13½	M
Spero *(hw) City of Sparta*	1966	6916	454	68	18	M(2)

Also many smaller ships.
(handwritten) Silvio ren. City of Patras
(handwritten) Salmo ren. City of Ankara
(handwritten) Salerno ren. City of Corinth

(ARGENTINE)

EMPRESA LINEAS MARITIMAS ARGENTINAS

FUNNEL: *Black with wide white band and two narrow blue bands, and blue flag incorporating an anchor and St. Andrew's cross.*

HULL: *Black or white, red boot-topping.*

ROUTES: *Buenos Aires, Montevideo, Rio de Janeiro to Lisbon, Havre, London also Mediterranean.*

Name	Date	Tons	Length	Breadth	Speed	Engines	Former Names
Argentina	1949	12459	530	71	18½	ST(2)	ex President Peron 55.
Libertad	1950	12653	530	71	18½	ST(2)	ex 17 de Octubre 55.
Rio Tunuyan ..	1951	11433	550	66	17	M(2)	
Uruguay	1950	12627	530	71	18½	ST(2)	ex Eva Peron 55.
(hw) Rio Esquel		6500				M	

Also a large fleet of cargo ships.

Fearnley & Eger: FERNRIVER

Fearnley & Eger: FERNGROVE

FEARNLEY & EGER
VARIOUS COMPANY TITLES

FUNNEL: *Black or grey with blue Maltese cross on white panel on broad red band.*

HULL: *Black or grey with red boot-topping.*

Name	Date	Tons Gross	Length (feet)	Breadth (feet)	Speed (knots)	Engines	Former Names
Fernbank	1955	6174	488	64	17	M	
Fernbrook	1960	6609	455	59	16½	M	
Ferncliff	1955	6174	488	64	17	M	
Ferndale	1970	14095	555	70	16	M(A)	
Fernfield	1970	14095	555	70	16	M(A)	
Ferngate	1961	6608	455	59	17	M	
Fernglen	1964	21205	628	87	15	M(A)	
Ferngrove	1965	13458	541	71	15	M(A)	
Ferngulf	1968	13731	520	70	15½	M(A)	
Fernlake	1961	6732	510	68	19	M	
Fernland	1964	6274	430	60	16	M(A)	
Fernleaf	1964	13458	541	71	15½	M(A)	to Holland, ren. Aalsum
Fernmoor	1955	7082	512	64	17	M	
Fernriver	1967	29506	708	96	16	M(A)	
Fernside	1970	14095	555	70	16	M(A)	
Fernspring	1967	29506	708	96	16	M(A)	
Fernstate	1958	6759	511	64	17	M	
Fernview	1961	6732	510	68	18	M	
Fernwind	1963	20322	631	85	15	M(A)	ex Cypress Liquid gas carr
~~Fernvalley~~	1969	16568					ex Gas Master " " "
Fernwood	1969	16573					

Norwegian Cruiseships A/S

Name		Date	Tons	Length	Breadth	Speed	Engines
Sea Venture	..	1970	19000	553	96	20	M

FEDERAL STEAM NAVIGATION CO. LTD.

FUNNEL: *Dark red with black top and replica of house flag.*

HULL: *Black, red boot-topping, with white line, or emerald green with dark green boot-topping.*

ROUTES: *U.K. to Australia and New Zealand.*
East Coast of North America and Canada to Australia and New Zealand via Panama.

Name		Date	Tons	Length	Breadth	Speed	Engines	
Cumberland	..	1948	11281	561	70	16	M(2)	
Devon†	..	1946	7237	495	65	16	ST	
Dorset	..	1949	7806	496	65	16	ST	
Essex	..	1954	10936	526	70	16	M	
Hertford	..	1948	11276	561	70	16	M(2)	
Huntingdon	..	1948	11281	561	70	16	M(2)	
Manapouri	..	1968	9505	540	75	20	M	
Northumberland	..	1955	10335	499	65	16	M	To S'pore, ren. GOLDEN CITY
Nottingham	..	1950	6689	480	62	15	M	
Somerset	..	1962	7602	488	66	16	M	
Sussex	..	1949	11276	561	70	16	M(2)	
Westmorland	..	1966	8230	528	71	20	M	
Wild Fulmar	1974	7000					M	

† Owned by Overseas Containers Ltd.

Federal Steam Navigation Co: MATAURA

Federal Steam Navigation Co: PIPIRIKI

New Zealand Shipping Company Ltd.

(MANAGERS)

Name			Date	Tons Gross	Length (feet)	Breadth (feet)	Speed (knots)	Engines	Former Names
Haparangi	..	..	1947	11281	561	70	16	M(2)	
Hauraki	..	..	1947	11272	561	70	16	M(2)	ex Norfolk 53.
Hinakura	..	..	1949	11272	561	70	16	M(2)	
Hurunui	..	..	1948	11276	561	70	16	M(2)	
Mataura*	..	..	1968	9504	540	75	20	M	
Otaio	..	..	1958	10792	526	73	16	M(2)	
Otaki	..	..	1953	10934	526	70	16	M	
Piako	..	..	1962	9986	488	66	16½	M	
Pipiriki	..	..	1944	7195	495	65	15½	ST	
Rakaia	..	..	1945	7934	474	63	12½	M	ex Empire Abercorn 46.
Taupo	..	..	1966	8219	528	71	20	M	
Tekoa	..	..	1966	8226	528	71	20	M	
Tongariro	..	..	1967	8233	528	71	20	M	
Turakina†	..	..	1960	7707	455	62	17	M	

† Operated by Crusader Shipping Co.
* Owned by P. & O. S.N. Co.

(FINLAND)

O/Y FINNLINES LTD.

VARIOUS SUB-TITLES

FUNNEL: *Black with black " F " in white oval interrupting blue band between two white bands.*

HULL: *Grey or black with green boot-topping.*

Name			Date	Tons Gross	Length	Breadth	Speed	Engines	Former Names
Finnalpino	..	..	1958	2883	375	51	13	M(A)	ex Besseggen 61.
Finnarrow	..	..	1965	6382	497	62	16	M	
Finnbirch	..	..	1953	2731	369	48	13	M	ex Martti Ragnar 59.
Finnboston	..	..	1964	6391	497	62	16	M	ex Finnenso 64.
Finncarrier	..	..	1969	5900	451	81	18	M(2)	
Finnclipper	..	..	1962	6450	493	62	15½	M	
Finneagle	..	..	1962	6450	493	62	15½	M	
Finn-Enso	..	..	1965	6384	497	62	16	M	
Finnfighter	..	..	1965	1682	300	46	14½	M(A)	
Finnforest	..	..	1963	6603	500	62	16	M	
Finnhansa	..	..	1966	7481	441	66	18	M(A)(2)	
Finnhawk	..	..	1965	6387	497	62	16	M	
Finnkraft	..	..	1956	1990	321	47	13	M	
Finnmaid	..	..	1965	6386	497	62	16	M	
Finnmill	..	..	1965	3205	387	54	15	M(A)	ex Concordia Finn 69, ex Finnmill 68, ex Finnbrod 67.
Finnseal	..	..	1964	2738	300	46	14	M(A)	
Finnstar	..	..	1955	2914	371	50	13	M	ex Raimo Ragnar 59.
Finntrader	..	..	1951	4022	410	55	15	M	To Pan, Nar SOVEREIGN SAPPH
Kotkumiemi	..	..	1968	12052	519	71	14½	M(A)	
Outokumpu	..	..	1958	3781	362	52	13	M(A)	
Finntimber			1974	16200				M	cont.

Finnlines Ltd: FINN-ENSO

[F. R. Sherlock

French Line: ANJOU

[Malcolm Cranfield

WM. FRANCE, FENWICK & CO. LTD.

FUNNEL: *Black with red " FF " on broad white band.*

HULL: *Black with red boot-topping.*

Name			Date	Tons Gross	Length (feet)	Breadth (feet)	Speed (knots)	Engines	Former Names
Chelwood	..	..	1964	5531	370	54	15	M(A)	*To England. ren. OSTWESTRA to Houlder*
Dalewood	..	..	1966	5513	370	54	15	M(A)	*" " " CYMBELINE GRA*
Granwood	..	..	1959	8025	487	61	14	M(A)	
Sherwood	..	..	1958	5279	414	55	12½	M(A)	*ex Thackeray 68. To PK... SPORE, NISYROS E*
Star Pinewood	..	..	1968	19577	564	86	15	M(A)	*To England. ren. STAR BULFORD*

Also smaller ships.

(FRANCE)

FRENCH LINE

C.G.T.—Compagnie Générale Maritime ~~Transatlantique~~

FUNNEL: *Dark red with black top.*

HULL: *Black, red boot-topping with white line, or white with red boot-topping.*

ROUTES:
A. *Havre, Southampton and New York.*
B. *Havre, Southampton, Vigo to W. Indies, Trinidad, Venezuela, Curacao and Colombia.*
C. *North European ports to U.S.A. including Gulf ports, Canada and Great Lakes.*
D. *North European ports to W. Indies, Central America and west coast of S. America.*
E. *Dieppe, Rouen to Guadeloupe, Martinique.*

Name			Date	Tons Gross	Length	Breadth	Speed	Engines	Former Names
Anjou	..	..	1968	8718	494	66	16½	M(A)	*Aubrac*
Auvergne	..	..	1968	8718	501	66	16½	M(A)	
Caraibe	..	..	1949	6079	459	60	15½	M	
Carbet	..	..	1949	6079	459	60	15½	M	
Carimare	..	..	1950	6079	459	60	15½	M	
Chicago	..	..	1959	8166	450	62	15	M(A)	
Cleveland	..	..	1960	8141	450	62	15	M(A)	
Comte de Nice	..	..	1966	7162	377	60	21	M(2)	
Corse	..	..	1966	7162	377	60	21	M(2)	
Desirade	..	..	1949	4321	421	55	13½	M	*ex Croisset 53 To Pan. ren. LUSON*
Fort Crevecoeur	..	..	1962	5020	374	52	17	M	
Fort d'Orleans	..	..	1962	5020	374	52	17	M	
Fort de France	..	..	1961	5014	374	52	17	M	*to Pan. ren. LORD DE FRAN*
Fort Fleur d'Epee	..	..	1961	5014	374	52	17	M	
Fort Frontenac	..	..	1958	4990	377	52	16½	M	
Fort Josephine	..	..	1964	5457	410	56	17	M	
Fort La Reine	..	..	1969	9873	487	67	20	M	
Fort Niagara	..	..	1958	4990	377	52	16½	M	

French Line: FRANCE

[F. R. Sher!ock

French Line: FORT CREVECOEUR

[John G. Callis

Name	Date	Tons Gross	Length (feet)	Breadth (feet)	Speed (knots)	Engines	Former Names
Fort Pontchartrain	1969	9873	487	67	20	M	
Fort Sainte Marie	1970	9870	473	66	20	M	
Fort Trinite	1964	5457	410	56	17	M	
France	1961	66348	1035	111	30	ST(4)	
Fred Scarmaroni ..	1966	6743	377	59	20	M(2)	
Guadeloupe	1949	4294	421	55	13½	M	ex Canteleu 53.
Guyane	1955	7062	458	60	17	M	ex Ville de Djibouti 65.
La Coubre	1948	4310	421	55	15	M	
La Hague ..	1947	4310	420	55	15	M	
Languedoc	1966	8688	441	66	20	M(2)(A)	ex Prinz Hamlet 70.
Magellan	1958	9186	490	62	16	M(A)	
Martinique ..	1949	4309	421	55	13½	M	ex Caumont 53.
Maryland	1958	9224	490	62	16	M(A)	
Mediterranee†	1948	5324	402	54	19	ST(2)	ex President de Cazalet 67.
Michigan	1959	9235	490	62	17	M(A)	
Mississipi	1960	9235	490	62	17	M(A)	
Napoleon	1959	5564	357	52	18	M(2)	
Pointe Alegre	1969	6800	449	69	19	M	
Pointe des Collbris	1969	6800	449	69	19	M	
Pointe Marin ..	1969	6800	449	69	19	M	
Rochambeau ..	1967	9848	491	69	19	M(A)	
Suffren	1967	9848	491	69	19	M(A)	
Ville de Marseille	1951	9576	466	64	21	ST(2)	ex Maroc 56, ex Ville de Marseille 51.
Winnipeg	1947	8697	538	64	16	M(2)	

† On charter.   Also smaller ships.   See also Atlantic Container Line.

FURNESS WITHY & CO. LTD.

FUNNEL: *Dark red with black top, black base and black band.*

HULL: *Grey with green boot-topping or black with red boot-topping.*

ROUTES: *Liverpool—St. Johns N.F., Halifax N.S. and Boston.*
U.K. ports to U.S., Gulf ports and Pacific coast ports via Panama.

Name	Date	Tons Gross	Length (feet)	Breadth (feet)	Speed (knots)	Engines	Former Names
Edenmore	1958	10792	505	67	12	M(A)	to Italy
Furness Bridge ..	1971	81000	965	145	15½	M(A)	
Newfoundland ..	1964	6660	429	62	16½	M	ex Cufic, ex Newfoundland
Nova Scotia ..	1964	6660	429	62	16½	M	ex Fedris, Nova Scotia
Pacific Envoy ..	1958	9305	501	63	15½	ST	ex Loch Ryan 70, ex Pacific Envoy 67.
Pacific Exporter†	1957	6311	475	64	17	M	ex Oropesa 70, ex Aramaic 68.
Pacific Northwest	1954	9337	501	63	15½	ST	
Pacific Ranger† ..	1956	6311	475	64	17	M	ex Oroya 70, ex Arabic 68.
Pacific Reliance ..	1951	9337	501	63	15½	ST	
Pacific Stronghold	1958	9337	501	63	15½	ST	
Sagamore	1957	10792	505	67	12	M(A)	to Houlder Bros.

rem: CUFIC (handwritten annotation)

† Owned by Pacific S.N. Co.

French Line: ROCHAMBEAU, registered at Dunkerque [Bert Moody

Geest Industries Ltd: GEESTPORT [Malcolm Cranfield

FYFFES GROUP LTD.

FUNNEL: *Yellow with black top, red band with white diamond.*

HULL: *Pale grey or white, red boot-topping.*

ROUTES: *Southampton and Continental ports to Jamaica direct or via Barbados and Trinidad or British Cameroons.*

Name			Date	Tons Gross	Length (feet)	Breadth (feet)	Speed (knots)	Engines	Former Names
Camito	..	..	1956	8502	448	62	17½	ST(2)	
Chuscal	..	..	1961	6095	411	57	18	ST	
Golfito	..	..	1949	8313	447	62	17½	ST(2)	
Matina	..	..	1969	6351	474	67	20	M	
Morant	..	..	1970	6348	474	67	20	M	
Motagua	..	..	1970	6348	474	67	20	M	
Pacuare	..	..	1948	5026	386	56	16	ST	ex Tivives 68.
Patia	..	..	1947	5026	386	56	16	ST	ex Yaque 69.
Patuca	..	..	1947	5026	386	56	16	ST	ex Sixaola 69.
Pecos	..	..	1948	5026	386	56	16	ST	ex Hibueras 69.
Rio Cobre	..		1945	6845	455	61	18	ST(2)	ex Junior 69.
Romano	..	..	1947	6573	455	61	18	ST(2)	ex Metapan 70.
Ronde	..	..	1945	6573	455	61	18	ST(2)	ex San Jose 70.
Roatan	..	..	1946	6845	455	61	18	ST(2)	ex Comayagua 69.
Dairen			1964	4970					ex Polarstern
Davao			1964	4851					ex Polarlicht

Surrey Shipping Co. Ltd.

HULL: *White.*

Telde	..	..	1961	6573	451	60	17½	ST
Tilapa	..	..	1961	6573	451	60	17½	ST
Tucurinca	..		1962	6738	451	60	17½	ST
Turrialba	..		1960	6573	451	60	17½	ST

(HONDURAS)
Empresa Hondurena de Vapores

Carrillo	..	..	1957	6687	451	59	17	ST	
Lempa	..	..	1952	3253	369	45	14	M(2)(A)	ex Leith Hill 66, ex Lempa 59.
Leon	..	..	1952	3245	369	45	14	M(2)(A)	ex Box Hill 66, ex Leon 59.
Olancho	..	..	1957	6095	411	57	18	ST	ex Chirripo 70.
Omoa	..	..	1957	6095	411	57	18	ST	ex Changuinola 70.
Orica	..	..	1958	6095	411	57	18	ST	ex Chicanoa 70.
Tenadores	..		1960	6738	451	60	17½	ST	
Tetela	..	..	1960	6712	451	60	17½	ST	

Soc. Geral De Comercio: BELAS

[*Fotoship*

German Atlantic Line: HAMBURG

[*F. R. Sherlock*

(NETHERLANDS)
Caraibische Scheepv. Maats. N.V.

Name			Date	Tons Gross	Length (feet)	Breadth (feet)	Speed (knots)	Engines	Former Names
Calamares	..	..	1956	6797	451	59	17	ST	
Cartago	..	..	1956	6797	451	59	17	ST	
Castilla	..	..	1947	5127	386	56	16	ST	ex Santo Cerro 69.
Chiriqui	..	..	1948	5127	386	56	16	ST	ex Ulua 70.
Choluteca	..	..	1947	5127	386	56	16	ST	ex Cibao 70.
Copan	..	..	1947	5127	386	56	16	ST	ex Quisqueya 69.
Coppename	..	..	1948	5127	386	56	16	ST	ex Morazan 69.
Talamanca	..	..	1945	6729	455	61	18	ST(2)	ex Limon 70.
Tanamo	..	..	1947	6573	455	61	18	ST(2)	ex Heredia 70.
Toloa	..	..	1945	6573	455	61	18	ST(2)	ex Esparta 70.
Toltec	..	..	1947	6726	455	61	18	ST(2)	ex Parismina 70.

GEEST INDUSTRIES LTD.

FUNNEL: *White with insignia of two narrow blue bands with yellow diamond outlined in red and red 'G' on diamond on either superstructure or funnel. (Chartered vessels have a buff funnel with white band and insignia.)*

HULL: *White with green boot-topping.*

Name			Date	Tons	Length	Breadth	Speed	Engines
Geestbay	..	..	1964	7891	488	62	21	M
Geestcape	..	..	1966	7679	490	63	21	M
Geesthaven	..	..	1966	8042	490	63	21	M
Geestport	..	..	1964	7891	488	62	21	M

(NETHERLANDS)
Waling van Geest & Zonen

Name			Date	Tons	Length	Breadth	Speed	Engines
Geestland	..	..	1960	1937	328	44	17	M(A)
Geeststar	..	..	1960	1927	326	45	17	M(A)

Also smaller ships.

(PORTUGAL)
SOC. GERAL DE COMERCIO INDUSTRIA E TRANSPORTES

FUNNEL: *Black with black 'SG' on white band between two red bands.*
HULL: *Black or grey.*

Name			Date	Tons	Length	Breadth	Speed	Engines	Former Names
Alcobaca	..	..	1948	5289	450	59	14	M	
Alcoutim	..	..	1943	7057	442	57	13	SR	ex Fort Fidler 46.
Alenquer	..	..	1949	5289	450	59	14	M	
Alfredo da Silva	..		1950	3374	338	46	13	M	
Almeirim	..	..	1948	5289	450	59	14	M	
Ambrizete	..	..	1948	5503	450	59	14	M	
Amelia de Mello	..		1956	10195	501	65	19	ST	ex Zion 66.
Ana Mafalda	..	..	1951	3318	338	46	13	M	
Belas	..	..	1949	4448	425	54	14	M	
Borba	..	..	1948	4457	425	54	14	M	
Braga	..	..	1948	4455	425	54	14	M	
Braganca	..	..	1948	4455	425	54	14	M	
Manuel Alfredo	..		1954	3468	338	45	13	M	

German Atlantic Line: HANSEATIC   [*John G. Callis*

Gibbs & Co: WELSH HERALD   [*Fotoship*

Glen Line: GLENALMOND   [R. J. Wecks

Glen Line: GLENLYON   [Fotoship

GERMAN ATLANTIC LINE

FUNNEL: *Red with white German cross.*
HULL: *White.*
ROUTES: *Mainly cruising.*

Name	Date	Tons Gross	Length (feet)	Breadth (feet)	Speed (knots)	Engines	Former Names
Hamburg	1969	25002	638	87	23	ST(2)	*ex Russia, ren MAXIM GORKY*
Hanseatic	1964	25320	628	82	20	ST(2)	ex Shalom 67.

GIBBS & CO. (SHIP MANAGEMENT) LTD.
Welsh Ore Carriers Ltd.

FUNNEL: *Narrow black top, red with red lion and black ladder on white diamond.*

Name	Date	Tons Gross	Length (feet)	Breadth (feet)	Speed (knots)	Engines	Former Names
Welsh Herald ..	1963	19543	615	84	14	M(A)	
Welsh Minstrel ..	1968	18776	645	75	15	M(A)	

GLEN LINE LTD.

FUNNEL: *Red with black top.*
HULL: *Black, pink boot-topping.*
ROUTE: *United Kingdom and North Continent to Malaya, Thailand, Hong Kong, China, Philippines, Japan.*

Name	Date	Tons Gross	Length (feet)	Breadth (feet)	Speed (knots)	Engines	Former Names
Cardiganshire ..	1950	7427	487	62	16	M	ex Bellerophon 57.
Flintshire ..	1962	11537	544	75	20	M	
Glenalmond ..	1966	12299	564	78	21	M	
Glenbeg ..	1956	7698	491	62	16	M	ex Diomed 70.
Glenfalloch ..	1963	11537	544	75	20	M	
Glenfinlas ..	1966	12094	564	78	21	M *to Blue Funnel, ren PHEMIUS*
Glenfruin ..	1956	7672	491	62	16	M	ex Dolius 70.
Glengyle ..	1940	8887	507	66	17	M(2)	
Glenlochy ..	1957	7672	492	62	16½	M	ex Antenor 70.
Glenlyon ..	1962	11537	544	75	20	M	
Glenogle ..	1962	11537	544	75	20	M	
Glenroy ..	1955	7690	491	62	16	M	ex Demodocus 70.
Pembrokeshire ..	1967	12299	564	78	21	M *to Blue Funnel, ren PHRONTIS*

PRUDENTIAL

GRACE LINE INC.

FUNNEL: *Green with white and black bands of equal width at top.*
HULL: *Grey or black with red boot-topping.*
ROUTES:
A. *New York and U.S. Atlantic ports to West and North Coast of South America.*
B. *San Francisco and Pacific ports to West Coast of Mexico, Central and South America.*

GRACE LINE INC. (continued)

Name			Date 1963	Tons Gross 12,700	Length (feet)	Breadth (feet)	Speed (knots)	Engines ex C.E.Dant	Former Names
Santa Alicia	..		1944	7840	492	70	17½	ST	ex Mormacrey 66.
Santa Ana	..	..	1943	8007	492	70	17	ST	ex Mormacmar 66, ex Custer 48.
Santa Anita	..		1944	7840	492	70	17½	ST	ex Mormacsurf 66, ex Grundy 48.
Santa Barbara	..		1967	9322	560	82	20	ST	
Santa Clara	..		1966	9322	560	82	20	ST	
Santa Cruz	..		1966	9313	560	82	20	ST	
Santa Elena	..		1967	9322	560	82	20	ST	
Santa Eliana	..		1944	8010	492	60	17	ST	ex Mormacwind 66, ex P. & T. Seafarer 57, ex Mendocino 47.
Santa Fe	..	..	1944	6643	418	60	14	ST	ex Mexico 54, ex Agwiprincess 50, ex Cape Spear 48.
Santa Flavia	..		1943	6507	459	63	15½	ST	ex Norseman 47, ex Santa Barbara 46.
Santa Isabel	..		1967	9323	560	81	20	ST	
Santa Juana	..		1942	6507	459	63	16	ST	ex Silver Star 47, ex Santa Cecilia 46.
Santa Lucia	..		1966	9313	560	81	20	ST	
Santa Magdalena			1963	11219	545	79	20	ST	
Santa Maria	..		1963	11219	545	79	20	ST	
Santa Mariana	..		1963	11219	545	79	20	ST	
Santa Mercedes	..		1964	11219	545	79	20	ST	
Santa Paula	..		1958	11353	584	84	20	ST(2)	
Santa Regina	..		1941	7954	492	70	17	ST	ex Mormactide 66, ex Lyon, 46 ex Mormactide 42.
Santa Rosa	..		1958	11353	584	84	20	ST(2)	
Santa Victoria	..		1944	6689	418	60	14	ST	ex Santa Anita 66, ex Cape Cumberland 55.

Prudential Oceanjet
Prudential Seajet

(SWEDEN)
GRANGESBERG-OXELOSUND TRAFIK A/B

FUNNEL: *Black with yellow ' G ' within yellow ring on broad blue band.*
HULL: *Grey with red boot-topping.*

Name			Date	Tons	Length	Breadth	Speed	Engines	Former Names
Adak	..		1959	10629	490	64	14¼	M(A)	
Anaris	..	..	1962	10349	490	64	14¼	M(A)	
Arvidsjaur	..		1958	10824	490	64	14¼	M(A)	
Aurivaara	..		1961	10861	490	64	14¼	M(A)	
Avafors	..		1959	10810	490	64	14¼	M(A)	
Laidure	..		1964	24810	656	89	15½	M(A)	
Laponia	..		1963	24810	656	89	15½	M(A)	
Luossa	..		1962	18152	584	78	14½	M(A)	
Nikkala	..		1966	44005	800	124	16	M(A)	
Nuolja	..		1966	44001	800	124	16	M(A)	
Pajala*	..		1969	58808	831	131	15	M(A)	
Raunala*	..		1964	42314	798	115	16	M(A)	
Rautas*	..		1965	42220	798	115	16	M(A)	
Vasara*	..		1954	16170	596	75	14½	M(A)	
Virihaure*	..		1958	16098	597	75	14½	M(A)	
Viris*	..		1959	15967	596	75	14½	M(A)	
Vistasvagge*			1955	16207	596	75	14½	M(A)	
Vittangi*	..		1953 1968	16479 58589	596	75	14½	M(A)	ex Flowergate

* Ore/oil carrier. Also smaller ships and tugs.

M (BULK)

torne 1974

Grace Line: SANTA ROSA   [*A. Duncan*

Grangesburg-Oxelosund: RAUNALA   [*Malcolm Cranfield*

Grangesberg-Oxelosund: NUOLJA
[F. W. Hawks

Great Eastern: JAG DEV
[Malcolm Cranfield

GREAT EASTERN SHIPPING CO. LTD.

FUNNEL: *Yellow with red and green house flag and letters ' AHB '.*
HULL: *Grey.*

Name		Date	Tons Gross	Length (feet)	Breadth (feet)	Speed (knots)	Engines	Former Names
Jag Anand	..	1963	11070	508	68	15	M(A)	ex Cedar 68.
Jag Anjli	..	1963	11066	508	68	15	M(A)	ex Cypress 68.
Jag Arti	..	1959	10132	518	64	15	M(A)	ex Belvera 67.
Jag Asha	..	1963	10947	506	68	15	M(A)	ex Dageld 67.
Jag Darshan		1969	13341	532	75	16½	M(A)	
Jag Dev	..	1968	13326	532	75	16½	M(A)	
Jag Jawan	..	1966	23942	635	92	16	M(A)	
Jag Kisan	..	1966	23706	635	92	16	M(A)	
Jag Laxmi	..	1957	8798	490	62	14	M	
Jag Manek	..	1957	8747	467	61	14	M	ex Fernleaf 63.
Jag Shanti	..	1962	9069	490	62	14	M	
Jag Vijay	..	1962	9069	490	62	14	M	
Mahajagmitra	..	1959	5468	387	53	14	M	ex Jag Matri 69, ex Raj Kumar 59.
Tkr. Jag Prakash		1974	15500				M	
Jag Doot		1974	13300				M	bulk
Jag Manek		1967	13765				M	ex
Jag Shanti		1972	15498				M	ex Cunard Campaigner bulk

(Handwritten: Andrea Brovig, Cunard Campaigner bulk, Caravel)

GREEK LINE

FUNNEL: *Trident device on broad blue band between black top and yellow base.*

HULL: *White with red boot-topping.*

ROUTES: *Mediterranean ports to New York, and cruising.*

Name	Date	Tons Gross	Length (feet)	Breadth (feet)	Speed (knots)	Engines	Former Names
Olympia	1953	17434	611	79	21	ST(2)	
Queen Anna Maria	1956	21716	640	85	21	ST(2)	ex Empress of Britain 64. To Carnival Cruise Line ren. Carnivale

CHRISTIAN HAALAND
VARIOUS COMPANY TITLES

FUNNEL: *White with black top and black " H " on white.*
HULL: *Black with white band.*

Name		Date	Tons Gross	Length (feet)	Breadth (feet)	Speed (knots)	Engines	Former Names
Concordia Capo	..	1943	5226	412	60	14	M	ex Nyhaug 55, ex Cape San Antonio 47.
Concordia Fjord	..	1955	5818	466	62	17	M	
Concordia Fonn	..	1945	5869	475	59	17	M	ex Knut Bakke 54.
Concordia Lago	..	1961	5005	440	59	15½	M	ex Montrose 63.
Concordia Sky	..	1955	4953	426	57	17	M	
Concordia Star	..	1952	4701	420	57	17	M	
Concordia Sun	..	1954	4710	420	57	17	M	
Concordia Tadj	..	1958	6480	492	68	17	M	
Concordia Taleb	..	1960	6480	492	68	17	M	
Concordia Tarek	..	1958	6480	492	68	17	M	
Concordia Viking	..	1960	6937	495	68	17	M	
North Isle	..	1963	4908	430	57	17	M	
North Star	..	1948	4001	416	53	17½	M	
Northern Lights	..	1950	4001	416	53	17½	M	
Northland	..	1962	4908	430	57	17	M	

Greek Line: QUEEN ANNA MARIA [*A. Duncan*

Christian Haaland: CONCORDIA TALEB [*Fotoship*

HAIN-NOURSE LTD.

FUNNEL: *Blue with HN motif in white.*
HULL: *Blue.*

Name	Date	Tons Gross	Length (feet)	Breadth (feet)	Speed (knots)	Engines	Former Names
Jumna	1962	9890	508	65	15	M	*To P&O, ren. STRATHNAVER*
Trebartha	1962	7277	508	65	15	M	*" " " STRATHTAY*
Trecarne	1959	6286	476	61	13½	M	*To Cyprus, ren. GOLDEN ARROW*
Trecarrell	1959	6280	476	61	13½	M	
Trefusis	1961	7277	508	65	15	M	*To P&O, ren. STRATHTEVIOT*
Tremeadow	1958	6304	476	61	13½	M	*To England, ren. RELIANCE EXPRESS*
Treneglos	1963	6975	505	65	15	M	*To P&O, ren. STRATHTRUIM*
Trevalgan	1961	6433	488	63	14	M	
Trevaylor	1959	6286	472	61	13½	M	
Trewidden	1960	6469	488	63	14	M	

British India Steam Navigation Co. Ltd.

Name		Date	Tons Gross	Length (feet)	Breadth (feet)	Speed (knots)	Engines
Buccleuch ..	..	1965	25293	675	90	15½	M(A)
Cotswold ..	..	1966	25291	675	90	15½	M(A)

Charter Shipping Co. Ltd.

Name		Date	Tons Gross	Length (feet)	Breadth (feet)	Speed (knots)	Engines
Duhallow ..	..	1966	25368	675	90	15½	M(A)

Peninsular & Oriental S.N. Co. Ltd.

Name		Date	Tons Gross	Length (feet)	Breadth (feet)	Speed (knots)	Engines
Atherstone..	..	1965	25991	676	90	16	M(A)
Fernie ..	..	1967	42446	825	106	16	M(A)

HALL BROS.

FUNNEL: *Red with black top and house flag on broad grey band between two narrow white bands.*
HULL: *Grey or black with white line, red boot-topping.*

Hall Bros. S.S. Co. Ltd.

Name		Date	Tons Gross	Length (feet)	Breadth (feet)	Speed (knots)	Engines
Cilurnum ..	..	1968	1428	253	39	12½	M(A)
Embassage ..	..	1968	1428	253	39	12½	M(A)

Duff, Herbert & Mitchell Ltd.

Name		Date	Tons Gross	Length (feet)	Breadth (feet)	Speed (knots)	Engines
Melbrook ..	..	1964	11075	523	66	14	M(A)

Hain-Nourse: TREWIDDEN [John G. Callis

Hamburg America Line: ALSTER EXPRESS [R. J. Weeks

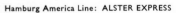

HAMBURG AMERICA LINE (HAPAG)

FUNNEL: *Yellow with black, white and red bands at top.*

HULL: *Black with red boot-topping.*

ROUTES: *Hamburg, Bremen, Rotterdam (or Amsterdam) and Antwerp to*
   A. *New York and U.S. Atlantic ports.*
   B. *Canada and the Great Lakes.*
   C. *Pacific ports of N. America.*
   D. *Cuba and Mexico and/or U.S. Gulf ports.*
   E. *West Indies.*
   F. *Pacific Coast of Central America.*
   G. *Pacific Coast of S. America.*
   H. *Australia and Far East.*

Services are run in conjunction with the Norddeutscher Lloyd.

Name		Date	Tons Gross	Length (feet)	Breadth (feet)	Speed (knots)	Engines	Former Names
Alemannia	..	1965	8094	540	73	20	M	
Alster Express	..	1969	14071	561	81	20	M(A)	
Bavaria	..	1966	8092	540	73	20	M	
Blumenthal	..	1961	6841	520	63	18	M	
Borussia	..	1965	8092	539	73	20	M	
Braunschweig	..	1953	6811	522	63	17	ST	
Darmstadt	..	1954	7044	530	63	17	ST	Cyprus
Dortmund	..	1954	7043	530	63	17	ST	To Pan., ren. MIGUEL TOSCA
Dresden	..	1957	9221	547	73	18	M	
Dusseldorf	..	1953	7047	530	63	17	ST	
Elbe Express	..	1968	14069	561	81	20	M(A)	
Erlangen	..	1970	13073	540	61	17	M	
Essen	..	1953	6821	522	63	17	ST	
Flensburg	..	1959	3011	399	54	14	M(A)	ex Amazonas 62.
Frankfurt	..	1967	5940	443	63	18	M	
Göttingen	..	1954	6782	522	63	17	ST	ex Hoechst 70. TO USA
Hagen	..	1967	5620	446	63	18	M	
Hamburg	..	1967	5866	446	63	18	M	
Hammonia	..	1965	8095	539	73	20	M	
Hanau	..	1967	5620	446	63	18	M	
Hannover	..	1967	5939	446	63	18	M	
Hattingen	..	1967	5665	446	63	18	M	
Havelland	..	1958	6646	499	62	17½	M	
Heidelberg	..	1967	5619	446	64	18	M	
Heilbronn	..	1967	5863	446	64	18	M	
Holsatia	..	1966	8092	539	73	20	M	
Iserlohn	..	1958	3312	397	54	14¾	M	
Kulmerland	..	1961	6957	516	63	18	M	
Lawanti	..	1956	6341	510	61	17	M	ex Erlangen 69.
Ludwigshafen	..	1969	14500	540	81	18	M(A)	
Munchen	..	1958	9186	547	73	18	M	
Munsterland*	..	1960	6965	516	63	18	M	
Nurnberg	..	1961	6842	520	63	18	M	
Pantjaran Sinar†	..	1951	5057	441	56	13	M	ex Odenwald 66.
Rendsburg	..	1959	4127	428	54	16	M(A)	ex Tove Lilian 65.
Rheinland	..	1959	6705	499	62	17½	M	
Saarland	..	1957	6646	499	62	17	M	
Speyer	..	1967	5617	446	64	18	M	
Stuttgart	..	1953	5635	498	59	16½	M	
Sydney Express	..	1970	27000	743	101	23	ST(A)	
Thuringia	..	1966	8136	539	72	20	M	
Trier	..	1967	5619	446	63	18	M	

Tokio Express   58088

Melbourne Express   25558

Mannheim   1971   25200   ex Roland Bremen

Main Express   197

Rhein Express   ex Oriental Exporter

Name			Date	Tons Gross	Length (feet)	Breadth (feet)	Speed (knots)	Engines	Former Names
Tubingen	..	..	1953	6828	525	63	17	ST	ex Leverkusen 70.
Twadika	..	..	1955	6341	510	61	17	M	ex Gottingen 69.
Vogtland	..	..	1959	6170	499	62	17½	M	
Weimar	..	..	1957	6388	510	61	17	M	
Westfalia	..	..	1964	8097	539	73	20	M	
Wien	..	..	1957	6380	510	61	17	M	
Wiesbaden	..	..	1957	6354	510	61	17	M	
Wolfsburg	..	..	1962	6850	520	63	18	M	
Worms	..	..	1959	6474	510	61	17½	M	

Hoechst

Also smaller ships.   † On charter to Indonesian operators.
* Detained since 1967 in Suez Canal.   Fleet to be merged with Norddeutscher Lloyd.

(WESTERN GERMANY)
HAMBURG SOUTH AMERICA LINE

FUNNEL: *White with red top.*

HULL: *White with red boot-topping.*

ROUTE: *Hamburg, Bremen, Rotterdam, Antwerp, Las Palmas, Recife, Salvador, Rio de Janeiro, Santos, S. Brazilian ports, Montevideo, Buenos Aires.*

Atlas Pioneer 1976   *livestock carrier*

Name		Date	Tons	Length	Breadth	Speed	Engines	
Cap Finisterre	..	1956	6433	502	61	17½	M	
Cap Norte		1955	6755	507	62	16	M	*To Somalia, ren. AIHUA*
Cap San Antonio	..	1962	7636	502	70	17	M	
Cap San Augustin		1961	7611	523	70	17	M	
Cap San Diego	..	1962	7626	522	70	17	M	
Cap San Lorenzo		1961	7625	522	70	17	M	
Cap San Marco	..	1961	7608	523	70	17	M	
Cap San Nicolas	..	1961	7620	502	70	17	M	
Cap Vilano	..	1955	6897	498	62	16	M	
Polarlicht	..	1964	3413	451	59	15	M	
Polar Argentina	..	1968	5623	485	64	22½	M	
Polar Colombia	..	1968	5623	485	64	22½	M	
Polar Ecudor	..	1967	5617	485	64	22½	M	
Polar Paraguay	..	1968	5639	485	64	22½	M	
Polar Uruguay	..	1968	5636	485	64	22½	M	
Santa Rita	..	1954	6535	479	61	13	M	
Santa Rosa	..	1954	6571	479	61	13	M	

Columbus Coromandel 1975
Columbus Capricorn
Columbus Caribic 1974 8413

Rudolf A. Oetker

Name			Date	Tons	Length	Breadth	Speed	Engines
Belgrano	..	..	1968	15119	613	75	17	M(A)
Cap Blanco	..	..	1955	6190	499	62	17	M
Cap Bonavista	..	..	1960	4118	348	53	15	M(A)
Cap Roca	..	..	1956	6834	498	63	17	M

Also smaller ships and ocean tankers.

Hamburg America Line: HATTINGEN

Hamburg America Line: FRANKFURT

Hamburg South America Line: CAP SAN NICOLAS

[*F. R. Sherlock*

Hansa: OCKENFELS

[*John G. Callis*

"HANSA"

Deutsche Dampfschiffahrts Ges.

FUNNEL: *Black with black iron cross on broad white band between two narrow red bands.*

HULL: *Grey with red boot-topping.*

Name		Date	Tons Gross	Length (feet)	Breadth (feet)	Speed (knots)	Engines	Former Names
Altenfels*	.. ..	1969	9393	485	69	16	M(A)	ex Marita Leonhardt 69.
Argenfels	.. ..	1950	8162	476	61	13	M	
Axenfels	.. ..	1958	5724	470	61	13½	M	ex Schelde 69.
Barenfels	.. ..	1951	6974	512	61	15	M(A)	
Birkenfels	.. ..	1967	9565	500	67	19	M(A)	
Braunfels	.. ..	1952	6977	512	61	13½	M(A)	
Crostafels	.. ..	1966	9600	499	67	19	M(A)	
Drachenfels	.. ..	1953	5781	470	60	13½	M	
Ehrenfels	.. ..	1953	5560	470	61	13½	M	
Falkenfels	.. ..	1967	9565	500	67	19	M(A)	
Frauenfels	.. ..	1953	5772	470	61	13½	M	
Freienfels	.. ..	1953	5755	470	61	13½	M	
Goldenfels	.. ..	1970	10743	503	75	20	M(A)	
Greiffenfels	.. ..	1945	6312	474	61	12	M	
Gutenfels	.. ..	1970	10750	503	75	20	M(A)	
Hohenfels	.. ..	1967	9433	500	67	19	M(A)	
Kandelfels	.. ..	1954	7311	512	61	16	M(A)	
Kybfels	.. ..	1967	9427	500	67	19	M(A)	
Lichtenfels	.. ..	1954	6800	461	59	15½	M(A)	
Liebenfels	.. ..	1955	6670	464	59	15½	M(A)	
Lindenfels	.. ..	1955	6612	464	59	15½	M(A)	
Marienfels	.. ..	1955	6736	464	59	15½	M(A)	
Neidenfels	.. ..	1955	6632	464	59	15½	M(A)	
Neuenfels	.. ..	1956	6612	464	59	15½	M(A)	
Ockenfels	.. ..	1956	6660	464	59	15½	M(A)	
Rabenfels	.. ..	1956	6740	461	59	15½	M(A)	
Rotenfels	.. ..	1947	8212	476	61	13	M	ex Mariposa 56, ex Empire Nene 54.
Schonfels	.. ..	1967	9442	500	67	19	M(A)	
Schwartzenfels	.. ..	1958	9336	482	63	14½	M(A)	
Spitzfels	.. ..	1958	9335	476	63	14½	M(A)	
Steinfels	.. ..	1970	10500	—	—	19	M(A)	
Sternenfels	.. ..	1970	10500	—	—	19	M(A)	
Tannenfels	.. ..	1959	9209	476	63	14½	M(A)	
Trautenfels	.. ..	1959	9212	476	63	14½	M(A)	
Treuenfels	.. ..	1959	9255	476	63	14½	M(A)	
Uhenfels	.. ..	1959	10363	514	73	14½	M(A)	
Wachtfels	.. ..	1962	9555	500	67	18½	(MA)	
Wallenfels	.. ..	1962	9717	500	67	18½	M(A)	
Wasserfels	.. ..	1963	9555	499	67	18½	M(A)	
Werdenfels	.. ..	1962	9718	500	67	18½	M(A)	To China, ren Dade
Wildenfels	.. ..	1962	9717	500	67	18½	M(A)	cont.
Atlantica Livorno		1971	10600				M	
Thomasturm		1974	800				M	
Lukasturm		1974	800					
Ochsenturm		1974	500				M	
Jonasturm		1974					M	
Medensturm		1974	950				M	

Also smaller ships.   * Owned by Leonhardt & Blumberg.

J. & C. HARRISON LTD.

FUNNEL: *Black with black " H " on broad white band.*

HULL: *Grey with white line, red boot-topping.*

Name		Date	Tons Gross	Length (feet)	Breadth (feet)	Speed (knots)	Engines	Former Names
Harmattan	..	1959	10411	546	63	13½	M	
Harpagus	..	1958	10152	541	62	13½	M *Too reece, ren-IRINIKOS*
Harpalyce	..	1958	10152	541	62	13½	M *Too reece, ren. EFCHARIS*
Harpalycus	..	1959	10248	546	62	13½	M	

HARRISON LINE

Thos. & James Harrison Ltd.

The Charente Steamship Co. Ltd.

FUNNEL: *Black with red band between two red bands.*

HULL: *Black with red boot-topping.*

ROUTES: **A.** *Glasgow, Liverpool, and South Wales to West Indies, Jamaica, Venezuela, Colombia, Panama, Canal Zone and Mexico.*

B. *Middlesbrough, London and Continental ports to South Africa.*

C. *London to West Indies and Demerara.*

D. *Glasgow, Liverpool, South Wales to South Africa, Mauritius, East Africa, and Red Sea ports.*

Name		Date	Tons	Length	Breadth	Speed	Engines	Former Names
Administrator	..	1958	8714	489	62	14¾	M	
Adventurer	..	1960	8971	490	65	14¾	M(A)	
Author	..	1958	8715	489	62	14¾	M	
Barrister	..	1954	8366	465	59	13	M *Tolib, ren. GEORGE*
Crofter	..	1951	8377	468	60	12	RT	
Custodian	..	1961	8847	488	62	16	M(A)	
Dalesman	..	1961	7200	440	60	15½	M	
Defender	..	1955	8165	465	59	13	M	
Diplomat	..	1953	8202	464	59	13	M	
Discoverer	..	1964	6162	407	57	16	M	
Explorer	..	1961	7200	440	60	15½	M	
Factor	..	1948	6533	464	57	14	M	
Forester	..	1952	8203	468	60	12	RT	
Governor	..	1952	8202	464	59	13	M	
Historian	..	1968	8454	494	63	18	M(A)	
Inventor	..	1964	9171	483	63	17	M	
Journalist	..	1954	8366	465	59	13	M	
Linguist	..	1966	6488	417	59	16	M(A)	
Magician	..	1968	8454	494	63	18	M	
Merchant	..	1964	5349	457	60	17½	M(A)	ex Scythia 69.
Naturalist	..	1965	6162	407	57	16	M	
Novelist	..	1965	6162	407	57	16	M	
Philosopher	..	1964	6162	407	57	16	M	
Plainsman	..	1959	8732	489	62	15	M	
Scholar	..	1965	5837	457	60	17½	M(A)	ex Samaria 69.
Statesman	..	1964	6162	407	57	16	M	
Tactician	..	1961	8844	488	62	16	M(A)	
Trader	..	1966	6448	418	59	16	M(A)	
Wayfarer	..	1951	8032	460	59	12	M	
Warrior (Bulk)		1974	16300				M	

Harrison Line: LINGUIST, pictured in March 1969

[John G. Callis

Harrison Line: NOVELIST

[Fotoship

HARRISONS (CLYDE) LTD.
Monarch S.S. Co. Ltd.

FUNNEL: *Red with black top.*
HULL: *Black with white line, red boot-topping.*

Name	Date	Tons Gross	Length (feet)	Breadth (feet)	Speed (knots)	Engines	Former Names
British Monarch*..	1965	18616	611	83	15½	M(A)	

* Owned by Scotts Shipbuilding & Engineering Co. Ltd.

Aiden Shipping Co. Ltd.

Vennacher ..	..	1965	18451	611	83	15	M(A)
Volnay ..	..	1968	22189	634	90	15½	M(A)

Orient Bulk Carriers Ltd.

Verdala ..	..	1968	14771	522	75	15	M(A)

HEADLAM & SON
Rowland & Marwood's S.S. Co. Ltd.

FUNNEL: *Black with blue cross on broad white band.*
HULL: *Black or grey with red boot-topping.*

Egton ..	..	1962	7175	508	66	14½	M
Runswick ..	..	1956	6101	476	62	14	M

(GREECE)

HELLENIC LINES LTD.
VARIOUS COMPANY TITLES

FUNNEL: *Black with blue ' E ' on white diamond on broad blue band between two narrow white bands.*
HULL: *Grey or black with red boot-topping and white line.*

Anghyra ..	..	1946	1892	301	44	10½	SR	ex Egypte 58.
Anglia ..	..	1944	1920	302	44	10½	SR	ex Kampar 57, ex Empire Gallery, 47, ex Weserburg 45.
Athinai ..	..	1956	2862	366	49	16	M	
Berolinon ..	..	1945	1892	301	44	10½	SR	ex Espagne 58, ex Breendonk 50.

Name	Date	Tons Gross	Length (feet)	Breadth (feet)	Speed (knots)	Engines	Former Names
Cypros	1945	3799	338	50	$12\frac{1}{2}$	M(A)	ex Ciudad de Caracas 60, ex Double Loop 47.
Egyptos	1945	3805	339	50	$12\frac{1}{2}$	M(A)	ex Krios 61, ex Coastal Monitor 47.
Germania	1946	2016	308	43	12	SR	ex Kittiwake 55.
Grigorios C III ..	1944	7227	442	57	$10\frac{1}{2}$	SR	ex Michael Anagnos 47.
Hellas	1956	2862	366	49	16	M	
Hellenic Beach ..	1944	7229	442	57	$10\frac{1}{2}$	SR	ex Oscar Underwood 47.
~~**Hellenic Charm**~~ ..	1944	7989	460	63	15	ST	ex Maipo 66, ex Oriental 47.
Hellenic Destiny ..	1960	7297	507	62	16	M(A)	
Hellenic Dolphin	1943	7989	460	63	15	ST	ex Imperial 65, ex Flying Mist 46.
Hellenic Glory ..	1956	7510	486	64	16	M	
Hellenic Halcyon	1943	7989	460	63	15	ST	ex Copiapo 66, ex Golden Gate 46.
Hellenic Hero ..	1957	7068	499	66	16	M	
Hellenic Laurel ..	1961	7293	507	62	16	M	
Hellenic Leader ..	1962	6666	473	63	16	M(A)	
Hellenic Pioneer ..	1962	6659	473	63	16	M(A)	
Hellenic Sailor ..	1939	6281	459	63	14	M	ex Mongala 54, ex Kamran 48, ex Mormacwren 47.
Hellenic Sky ..	1943	7200	442	57	$10\frac{1}{2}$	SR	ex Gilbert Stuart 47.
Hellenic Spirit ..	1957	7063	499	66	16	M(A)	
Hellenic Splendor	1959	9550	507	62	$15\frac{1}{2}$	M	
Hellenic Star ..	1943	7254	442	57	$10\frac{1}{2}$	SR	ex Keith Vawter 47.
Hellenic Sunbeam	1944	7989	460	63	15	ST	ex Aconcagua 65, ex Ocean Telegraph 46.
Hellenic Torch ..	1946	7510	486	64	$15\frac{1}{2}$	M	
Hollandia	1956	2863	366	49	16	M	
Italia	1946	6727	436	59	13	M	ex Ciudad de la Habana 67, ex Canadian Challenger 58.
Livorno	1952	4995	386	51	16	M	ex Adele 66, ex Sunadele 66, ex Adele 52.
Patrai	1945	2754	360	51	10	RT	ex Empire Patrai 53, ex Empire Towy 50.
Rodopi	1944	1923	300	44	10	SR	ex Empire Gavel 46, ex Setubal 45.
Roumania	1954	3654	360	53	15	M	ex Prinses Maria 70, ex Van Waerwyck 66.
Turkia	1956	2863	366	49	14	M	
Vorios Hellas ..	1944	1923	300	44	10	SR	ex Empire Gatwick 47, ex Sanga 45.
Hellenic Faith	*1972*	*10329*				M	

(NORWAY)
SIGURD HERLOFSON & CO. A/S
VARIOUS COMPANY TITLES

FUNNEL: *Yellow with black diamond between two black bands at top.*
HULL: *Grey.*

[Fotoship

Charles Hill & Sons: HALIFAX CITY

Name		Date	Tons Gross	Length (feet)	Breadth (feet)	Speed (knots)	Engines	Former Names
Black Eagle	..	1955	5700	484	61	17	M	
Black Osprey	..	1960	6027	484	61	17½	M	
Black Swan	..	1961	5827	484	61	17½	M	
Bulk Enterprise	..	1956	13825	536	71	14	M(A)	To Greece, ren. Silver City
Bulk Explorer	..	1968	11656	543	68	15	M(A)	
Bulk Pioneer	..	1967	11659	543	67	15	M(A)	
Bulk Prospector*	..	1970	21815	635	86	16	M(A)	
Bulk Trader	..	1959	10542	518	65	14	M(A)	
Bulk Venture	..	1965	23345	636	92	16	M(A)	
Hoegh Heron	..	1950	5406	459	58	15	M	ex Black Heron 69.
Pacific Express	..	1964	6310	455	61	17½	M	To E. Germany, ren. FRITZ REUTER

* Operates under W. German flag.

G. HEYN & SONS LTD.

Ulster S.S. Co. Ltd.

FUNNEL: *Black, white band and red hand on white shield.*
HULL: *Black with red-boot topping.*

Name		Date	Tons	Length	Breadth	Speed	Engines
Carrigan Head	..	1958	8116	459	62	15½	ST
Inishowen Head	..	1965	9101	485	64	15	M
Roonagh Head	..	1952	6058	455	60	15	ST
Torr Head	..	1961	7967	455	62	15	M

Also smaller ships.

Donaldson Line Ltd.

Name			Date	Tons	Length	Breadth	Speed	Engines
Santona	..	..	1959	3218	355	45	12½	M(A)

CHARLES HILL & SONS

Bristol City Line Ltd.

FUNNEL: *Black with blue star on white band.*
HULL: *Red or black with red boot-topping.*

Name		Date	Tons	Length	Breadth	Speed	Engines
Coventry City†	..	1966	7643	465	64	17	M
Halifax City	..	1964	6533	440	58	16	M
Montreal City	..	1963	6502	440	58	14	M
Toronto City†	..	1966	7643	465	64	17	M

† Owned by Bibby Line Ltd.

LEIF HOEGH & CO. A/S

FUNNEL: *White with blue top on which houseflag interrupts white band.*

HULL: *Grey with red boot-topping.*

Name	Date	Tons Gross	Length (feet)	Breadth (feet)	Speed (knots)	Engines	Former Names
Hoegh Ailette ..	1958	4766	381	53	15	M(A)	
Hoegh Aurore ..	1959	4777	381	53	15	M(A)	
Hoegh Banniere ..	1962	5759	425	58	15	M(A)	
Hoegh Belle ..	1962	5761	425	58	15	M(A)	
Hoegh Benin ..	1961	5290	406	56	15	M(A)	
Hoegh Biscay ..	1961	5296	406	56	15	M(A)	
Hoegh Breeze ..	1964	9377	494	66	15	M	ex Janecke Reed 70.
Hoegh Dene ..	1959	9796	516	64	16½	M	
Hoegh Dyke ..	1962	9848	515	64	17	M	
Hoegh Elan ..	1963	10719	515	65	17	M	
Hoegh Elite ..	1963	10732	515	65	17	M	
Hoegh Mallard ..	1966	16428	586	75	15	M(A)	
Hoegh Marlin ..	1966	16504	586	75	15	M(A)	
Hoegh Merchant	1966	16464	586	75	15	M(A)	
Hoegh Merit ..	1966	16464	586	75	15	M(A)	
Hoegh Minerva ..	1969	15743	591	75	15½	M(A)	
Hoegh Miranda ..	1969	15744	592	75	15½	M(A)	
Hoegh Mistral ..	1970	15743	592	75	15½	M(A)	
Hoegh Musketeer	1967	16464	586	75	15	M(A)	
Hoegh Opal ..	1967	9874	515	67	17	M(A)	
Hoegh Orchid ..	1968	9874	515	67	17	M(A)	
Hoegh Orris ..	1968	9874	515	67	17	M(A)	
Hoegh Pilot ..	1970	9843	515	68	17	M(A)	
Hoegh Pride ..	1970	9800	515	68	17	M(A)	
Hoegh Trader ..	1958	23581	690	90	16	ST(A)	ex Esso Genova 69, ex Esso Windsor 63.
Hoegh Transporter	1958	22245	696	90	16	ST(A)	ex Winchester 70, ex Esso Winchester 69.

H. HOGARTH & SONS LTD.

SCOTTISH SHIP MANAGEMENT LTD.

FUNNEL: *Yellow with black top.*

HULL: *Grey with red boot-topping.*

Baron Ardrossan	1970	14400	534	75	15	M(A)	
Baron Cawdor ..	1968	13580	528	75	15	M(A)	
Baron Dunmore ..	1968	12660	530	71	15	M(A)	
Baron Forbes ..	1967	12649	530	71	15	M(A)	
Baron Renfrew ..	1970	13600	528	75	15	M(A)	

Leif Hoegh: HOEGH MUSKETEER

[*John G. Callis*

Leif Hoegh: HOEGH MARLIN

[*Fotoship*

H. Hogarth & Sons: BARON CAWDOR   [*Malcolm Cranfield*

Holland America Line: ROTTERDAM   [*F. R. Sherlock*

INCOTRANS B.V. **(NETHERLANDS)**
HOLLAND-AMERICA LINE
Nederlandsche—Amerikaansche Stoomv. Maats.

FUNNELS: *Yellow with white band between two green bands.* NIEUW AMSTERDAM *has two funnels.* ROTTERDAM *has twin exhausts aft.*

HULLS: *Black with yellow line and red boot-topping.* NIEUW AMSTERDAM, STATENDAM, ROTTERDAM, *and* RYNDAM *have grey hulls.*

ROUTES: **A.** *Rotterdam, Havre, Southampton to New York some calling at Cobh, Galway and Halifax.*

   B. *Holland to U.S. and Canadian ports.*

   C. *Rotterdam, Antwerp to Gulf ports of U.S.A., Mexico and Havana.*

   D. *Rotterdam to Pacific Coast of U.S.A. and Vancouver.*

Name		Date	Tons Gross	Length (feet)	Breadth (feet)	Speed (knots)	Engines	Former Names
Gaasterdyk	..	1960	7222	534	68	17	M(A)	
Gorredyk	..	1963	7298	534	68	17	M(A)	To ren·Hellenic Grace
Grebbedyk	..	1962	7259	534	68	17	M(A)	Greece ren·Hellenic sky
Grotedyk	..	1962	7251	534	68	17	M(A)	
Kamperdyk	..	1959	5019	460	62	16	M To Ghana, ren. VOLTA PEACE	
Katsedyk	..	1961	5376	464	62	16	M	
Korendyk	..	1959	5019	460	62	16	M	
Moerdyk	..	1965	10931	546	69	17	M(A)	
Nieuw Amsterdam		1938	36982	759	88	21½	ST(2)	
Poeldyk	..	1964	3551	413	55	16½	M To Nigeria, ren·RIVER GONGOLA	
Rotterdam	..	1959	37783	749	94	22	ST(A)(2)	
Ryndam	..	1951	15051	503	69	16½	ST	ex Waterman 68, ex Ryndam 68.
Statendam	..	1957	24294	643	81	19	ST(2)	
Prinsendam		1973	8566				M	

See also Atlantic Container Line.

Volendam   1958   15257   ex Brasil

ren·Monarch Sun

(PANAMA)
HOME LINES INC.

FUNNEL: *Yellow with blue top and yellow castellated crown on blue disc.* HOMERIC *has two funnels.*

HULL: *White with green boot-topping.*

ROUTE: *Cruising mainly in the Bahamas and the Caribbean.*

Name			Date	Tons Gross	Length	Breadth	Speed	Engines	Former Names
Homeric	..	..	1931	18563	638	79	21	ST(2)	ex Mariposa 54.
Oceanic	..	..	1965	27645	782	97	26	ST(A)(2)	

Holland America Line: **NIEUW AMSTERDAM** [*R. J. Weeks*

Houlder—Alexander Shipping Co: WESTBURY [*J. Y. Freeman*

HOULDER BROS. & CO. LTD.

FUNNEL: *Black with white maltese cross on broad red band.*

HULL: *Black or grey with 'red boot-topping, some have white band on hull.*

ROUTES: **A.** *London, Liverpool, U.K. ports amd Antwerp to Montevideo, Buenos Aires and River Plate.*

B. *General world-wide trading including Australia/New Zealand.*

ex SAGAMORE 1957 10,792

Name	Date	Tons Gross	Length (feet)	Breadth (feet)	Speed (knots)	Engines	Former Names
Hardwicke Grange	1961	9234	489	66	16	ST	
Ocean Transport..	1962	8608	463	63	15	M(A)	
Oswestry Grange	1952	9406	475	62	12½	M	
Royston Grange ..	1959	9035	489	66	16	ST	*to Holland*
Swan River.. ..	1959	9637	487	64	13½	M	

Oswestry Grange 1964 5531

Also tankers.

ex Chelwood

Alexander Shipping Co. Ltd.

Queensbury	..	1953	5799	457	60	13½	M	
Shaftesbury	..	1958	8365	457	62	13½	M	
Tenbury	..	1965	8252	462	63	14	M	*TO Bibby*
Tewkesbury	..	1959	8532	457	62	13½	M	
Westbury	..	1960	8414	457	62	13½	M	

Ore Carriers Ltd.

Mabel Warwick	..	1960	11632	506	69	13	M(A)	
Oredian	.. ..	1955	6859	427	57	12½	M(A)	
Oregis	.. ..	1955	6858	427	57	12½	M(A)	
Orelia	.. ..	1954	6858	427	57	12½	M(A)	
Oremina	.. ..	1956	6858	427	57	12½	M(A)	
Oreosa	.. ..	1954	6856	427	57	12½	M(A)	
Orepton	.. ..	1955	6859	427	57	12½	M(A)	
Orotava Bridge	..	1968	28880	716	92	15½	M(A)	ex Orotava 69.

South American Saint Line Ltd.

St. Margaret	..	1960	11871	514	69	14	M(A)	ex Joya McCance 66.
St. Merriel*	..	1954	8695	477	62	13¼	M	ex Thorpe Grange 66. *To Sporea ren-Joo Hong*

* Owned by Houlder Line Ltd.

Warwick & Esplen Ltd.

(Vessel jointly owned by Houlder Line, Empire Transport Co., and Hadley Shipping Co.)

Clyde Bridge	..	1967	24024	662	92	15	M(A)	ex Clydesdale 68.

HUNTING & SON LTD.
Northern Petroleum & Bulk Freighters Ltd.

FUNNEL: *Black with seven-pointed blue star over narrow red and white bands.*

HULL: *Black with red boot-topping.*

Name		Date	Tons Gross	Length (feet)	Breadth (feet)	Speed (knots)	Engines	Former Names
Avonfield	..	1967	13195	571	74	14½	M(A)	ex Bjorn Stange 67.
Derwentfield	..	1959	11540	528	67	14	M(A)	ex Betty 67.
Gretafield	..	1952	10856	523	68	13	M(A)	
Wearfield	..	1964	17624	617	75	14	M(A)	

Also tankers.

William Baird Mining Ltd.

Dalhanna	..	..	1958	11452	504	69	12	M(A)

Argyll Shipping Company Ltd.

Argyll	..	..	1962	39665	737	106	14½	ST(A)
Coral Venture	..	1943	9121	466	68	12	TE(A)	

(INDIA)
INDIA STEAMSHIP CO. LTD.

FUNNEL: *Black with yellow star on broad red band.*

HULL: *Black, red boot-topping with white line.*

Indian Exporter	..	1945	7659	455	62	16	ST	ex Temple Victory 47.
Indian Industry	..	1959	5429	387	53	13	M	
Indian Merchant	..	1944	7659	455	62	16	ST	ex Lewiston Victory 47.
Indian Pioneer	..	1944	7657	455	62	16	ST	ex Dominican Victory 47.
Indian Reliance	..	1955	7422	531	63	17½	ST	
Indian Renown	..	1955	7422	531	63	17½	ST	
Indian Resolve	..	1956	7391	534	63	17½	ST	
Indian Resource	..	1956	7391	534	63	17½	ST	
Indian Security	..	1958	7156	508	66	17½	M	
Indian Shipper	..	1944	7660	455	62	16	ST	ex United States Victory 47.

Name	Date	Tons Gross	Length (feet)	Breadth (feet)	Speed (knots)	Engines	Former Names
Indian Splendour	1957	7275	508	66	17½	ST	
Indian Strength ..	1958	7185	508	66	17½	M	
Indian Success ..	1959	7185	508	66	17½	ST	
Indian Trader ..	1944	7657	455	62	16	ST	ex Norway Victory 47.
Indian Tradition ..	1960	7150	508	66	17½	ST	
Indian Tribune ..	1963	8611	508	63	16	M	ex Clan Macgowan 69.
Indian Triumph ..	1960	7185	508	66	17½	M	
Indian Trust ..	1960	7172	508	66	17½	M	

INDO-CHINA S.N. CO. LTD.

FUNNEL: *Red with black top.*

HULL: *Black with white line, red boot-topping.*

Name	Date	Tons Gross	Length	Breadth	Speed	Engines	Former Names
Eastern Argosy ..	1956	6907	467	63	17	ST	
Eastern Cape† ..	1956	8977	496	64	17	M	ex Hoegh Cape 67.
Eastern Cliff† ..	1956	8977	496	64	17	M	ex Hoegh Cliff 67.
Eastern Maid ..	1955	3606	385	53	12½	M	ex West Breeze 57.
Eastern Moon ..	1947	5338	441	56	15	M	ex Hoegh Silvermoon 60.
Eastern Muse ..	1955	3602	385	53	12½	M	ex East Breeze 55.
Eastern Ranger ..	1962	4408	404	57	15	M	*To Pan., ren GREEN ISLAND*
Eastern Rover ..	1961	4408	404	57	15	M	*" " " TSING YI ISLAND*
Eastern Trader ..	1959	6914	481	62	14	M	

† Owned by Dominion Far East Line.

IRISH SHIPPING LTD.

FUNNEL: *Yellow with green band between two narrow white bands.*

HULL: *Grey with white line, green boot-topping.*

Name	Date	Tons Gross	Length	Breadth	Speed	Engines	Former Names
Irish Alder ..	1957	6218	476	61	14½	M	
Irish Ash ..	1958	5971	476	61	14½	M	
Irish Cedar ..	1962	10477	504	68	15	M(A)	
Irish Elm ..	1968	22186	632	92	15	M(A)	
Irish Plane ..	1963	10449	504	68	15	M(A)	
Irish Poplar ..	1956	5908	449	62	15	ST	*to Pan., ren GoldenLion*
Irish Rowan ..	1962	10323	500	67	15	M(A)	*To Greece, ren AVRA*
Irish Spruce ..	1957	5918	449	62	15	ST	
Irish Star ..	1969	19580	564	86	15	M(A)	
Irish Stardust ..	1970	19500	564	85	15	M(A)	
Irish Sycamore ..	1961	10333	500	67	15	M(A)	*To Greece, ren MARIA*
Irish Larch	*1973*	*16700*				*M(A)*	
Irish Pine						*M(A)*	

Indo-China Steam Navigation Co: EASTERN CLIFF　　　　　　　　[J. Y. Freeman

Irish Shipping Ltd: IRISH SYCAMORE　　　　　　　　[D. C. McCormick

"ITALIA" Soc. per Azioni di Nav.

FUNNEL: *White with red top and separate narrow green band.*
HULL: *Black with white line or white with green line.*
ROUTES: **A.** *Italy to North America.*
B. *Italy to Brazil and River Plate.*
C. *Italy to Central America and Pacific Coast of S. America.*
D. *Italy (Adriatic and Tyrrhenian ports) to Central America and Pacific Coast of N. America.*

Name	Date	Tons Gross	Length (feet)	Breadth (feet)	Speed (knots)	Engines	Former Names
Alessandro Volta ..	1954	8086	535	64	16	M(2)	ex Clement Ader 56.
Antonio Pacinotti	1953	8086	535	64	16	M(2)	ex Edouard Branly 57.
Augustus	1952	27090	680	88	21	M(2)	
Cristoforo Colombo	1954	29429	701	90	23	ST(2)	
Donizetti	1951	13226	528	69	18	M(2)	ex Australia 63.
Galileo Ferraris ..	1953	8101	535	64	16	M(2)	ex Henri Poincare 57.
Giulio Cesare ..	1951	27078	681	88	21	M(2)	
Leonardo da Vinci	1960	33340	767	92	23	ST(2)	
Michelangelo ..	1965	45911	905	102	27	ST(2)	
Nereide	1943	7180	442	57	10	STR	ex Norman Hapgood 47.
Paolo Toscanelli ..	1948	7172	485	62	15½	M	
Raffaello	1965	45933	905	102	27	ST(2)	
Rossini	1951	13225	528	69	18	M(2)	ex Neptunia 63.
Stromboli ..	1944	7154	442	57	11	SR	ex Morgan Robertson 47.
Tritone	1944	7169	442	57	10	SR	ex Alexander Majors 47.
Verdi	1951	13226	529	69	18	M(2)	ex Oceania 63.
Vesuvio	1944	7170	442	58	10½	SR	ex William P. Duval 47.
CRISPI	1966	4500					
D'AZEGLIO	1966	4500					
MAZZINI	1966	4500					
Italica cont.	1975					ST	
Americana cont.	1975					ST	

JOHN I. JACOBS & CO. LTD.

FUNNEL: *Yellow with black top.*
HULL: *Black with red boot-topping.*

Name			Date	Tons	Length	Breadth	Speed	Engines	Former Names
Oakwood ..	..		1965	22211	645	85	15	M(A)	

Also tankers.

St. Helen's Shipping Co. Ltd.

Name			Date	Tons	Length	Breadth	Speed	Engines	Former Names
Beechwood ..	..		1960	12718	525	70	14	M(A)	ex Bishopsgate 69.
Cherrywood ..	..		1958	10885	503	70	12¾	M(A)	ex Silvercrag 69.

Italia: RAFFAELLO

[*Michael D. J. Lennon*

Anders Jahre: JANOVA

[*J. Mathieson*

ANDERS JAHRE

FUNNEL: *Black with white and blue houseflag on broad red band, or yellow with white and blue houseflag.*

HULL: *Grey with green boot-topping.*

Name			Date	Tons Gross	Length (feet)	Breadth (feet)	Speed (knots)	Engines	Former Names
Jacara	..	..	1965	13313	541	70	16	M(A)	
Jagona	..	..	1960	10648	496	66	15	M(A)	
Jalanta	..	..	1966	13313	541	71	16	M(A)	
Janita	..	..	1965	19750	605	86	16	M(A)	
Jannetta	..	..	1968	13388	542	71	16	M(A)	*To S'pore, ren. Ivory Neptune*
Janova	..	..	1968	19667	605	86	16	M(A)	
Japana	..	..	1965	19750	605	86	16	M(A)	
Jarabella	..	..	1963	13173	553	72	15	M(A)	
Jaraconda	..		1967	33586	743	102	16½	M(A)	
Jarilla	..	..	1959	15012	564	74	15	M(A)	
Jarosa	..	..	1963	16321	612	75	16	M(A)	
Jasaka	..	..	1967	33586	743	102	16½	M(A)	
Javara	..	..	1962	10434	496	66	16	M(A)	
Jawaga	..	..	1965	13313	541	71	16	M(A)	
Kronprins Harald			1961	7019	454	59	19	M(2)	
Prinsesse Ragnhild			1966	7715	463	66	19	M(2)	

Also tankers.

JOHNSON LINE
Red. A/B Nordstjernan

FUNNEL: *Black with blue ' J ' on yellow star on broad blue band between two narrow yellow bands.   Some now have yellow base.*

HULL: *Grey with red boot-topping.*

ROUTES: **A.**   *Swedish ports and Antwerp to Curacao, Panama, West Coast of Central and North America and Hawaii.*

   B.   *Swedish ports to Recife, Salvador, Rio de Janeiro, Santos, Paranagua, Rio Grande, Montevideo and Buenos Aires.*

   C.   *Scandinavian ports and Antwerp to N. and W. Coasts of S. America.*

Name			Date	Tons Gross	Length	Breadth	Speed	Engines	Former Names
Aconcagua Valley			1968	9611	506	69	21	M(A)	*Antonia Johnson*
Annie Johnson	..		1969	16288	572	85	21	M(2)	
Axel Johnson	..		1969	16284	572	85	21	M(2)	
Bahia Blanca	..		1964	10351	569	63	18½	M(2)	
Bolivia	..	..	1946	7042	455	57	17	M(2)	
Brasil	..	..	1944	6942	440	56	16	M(2)	*to Pan., ren. Char Ming*
Brasilia	..		1960	10287	569	63	18½	M(2)	
Buenos Aires	..		1957	10348	569	63	18½	M(2)	
California	..		1953	6629	500	64	19	M(2)	
Canada	..	..	1953	7211	500	64	19	M(2)	
Golden Gate	..		1948	6951	500	64	19	M(2)	
Guayana	..		1948	7065	455	57	17	M(2)	

Johnson Line: BAHIA BIANCA

Johnson Line: SAN JOAQUIN VALLEY

Name	Date	Tons Gross	Length (feet)	Breadth (feet)	Speed (knots)	Engines	Former Names
Hood River Valley	1965	6200	450	57	20	M	
Lions Gate	1950	7224	500	64	19½	M(2)	TO Lebanon
Los Angeles ..	1948	6600	500	64	19½	M(2)	
Margaret Johnson	1970	16111	572	85	21	M(2)	
Montevideo ..	1958	10402	569	63	18½	M(2)	
Okanagan Valley	1966	6235	450	57	20	M	
Panama	1945	7072	455	57	17	M(2)	
Paraguay	1947	7011	455	57	17	M(2)	
Portland	1952	9024	500	64	19	M(2)	
Rio de Janeiro ..	1957	10347	569	63	18½	M(2)	
Rosario	1960	10283	569	63	18½	M(2)	
San Francisco ..	1970	16290	572	85	21	M(2)	
San Joaquin Valley	1968	9638	506	62	21	M(A)	
Santos	1959	10364	569	63	18½	M(2)	
Seattle	1947	6581	500	64	19	M(2)	
Silver Gate ..	1952	6617	500	64	19	M(2)	
Star Altair ..	1959	6140	485	62	14½	M	ex Vimeira 66, ex Port Denison 65, ex Vimeira 60, ex Fair Lady 59.
Star Bellatix ..	1956	6492	479	63	15	M	ex Capetan Cardamilitis 59.

Also smaller ships.

(PANAMA)
Cia de la Paloma Soc. Anon
AND OTHER COMPANIES

Star Aldebaran ..	1962	6299	485	62	16	M	ex Kensington 63.
Star Antares ..	1956	6500	491	63	15	M	ex Solholt 63, ex Ivaran 62.
Star Arcturus ..	1939	6523	459	63	14	M	ex Mormachawk 47.
Star Betelgeuse ..	1939	6525	459	63	14	M	ex Betelgeuse 47, Mormaclark 47.
Star Procyon ..	1966	11543	—	—	15	M	

JOHNSTON WARREN LINES, LTD.

FUNNEL: *Dark red with black top, black base and black band.*
HULL: *Black.*

African Prince ..	1955	3596	372	53	13½	M	ex Pinemore 65.
Mystic† ..	1959	6656	480	64	17	M	
Rowanmore ..	1956	8274	467	63	14	M	ex Madulsima 60, TO Cyprus, ren ex Rowanmore 58. ANDRIANA I

† On charter to Shaw Savill & Albion.

Johnson Line: AXEL JOHNSON   [*F. R. Sherlock*

Jugoslav Line: ZADAR   [*Fotoship*

JUGOSLAVENSKA LINIJSKA PLOVIDBA
Yugoslav Line

FUNNEL: *Blue with black top and separate white band with red star.*
HULL: *Black or grey with white line and green boot-topping, or dark cream with blue line.*

Name			Date	Tons Gross	Length (feet)	Breadth (feet)	Speed (knots)	Engines	Former Names
August Cesarec		..	1967	6276	496	66	18	M	
Avala	..	..	1952	3172	384	50	17	M	
Bakar	..	..	1969	6270	499	66	17	M	
Baska	..	..	1960	4705	447	60	$16\frac{1}{2}$	M	
Bosna	..	..	1969	6963	509	67	16	M	ex Pleiades 69.
Crna Gora	..		1951	5824	462	59	17	M	
Dinara	..	..	1953	3073	384	50	17	M	
Dreznica	..	..	1962	4964	447	62	$16\frac{1}{2}$	M	
Frano Supilo		..	1961	2284	348	47	15	M	
Goran Kovacic		..	1967	8736	493	66	18	M	
Grobnik	..		1963	4964	447	61	$16\frac{1}{2}$	M	
Hrvatska	..		1969	6952	509	67	16	M	ex Cassiopeia 69.
Ivan Mazuronic		..	1961	2308	349	47	14	M	
Jesenice	..	..	1960	7378	509	68	18	M	
Kastav	..	..	1968	6269	499	66	17	M	
Klek ..	..	..	1965	7759	489	67	18	M	
Kosovo	..	..	1959	10562	519	65	15	M(A)	
Kostrena	..	..	1963	7378	509	68	18	M	
Kraljevica	..	..	1968	6276	499	66	17	M	
Kranjcevic	..	..	1966	8359	496	66	18	M	
Krk ..	..	..	1945	3789	398	53	14	M	ex Ada Gorthon 61 .
Kumrovec	..	..	1967	6276	493	66	17	M	
Kvarner	..	..	1946	3589	398	53	14	M	ex Alida Gorthon 61.
Lika ..	..	..	1957	6211	479	60	$13\frac{1}{2}$	M	
Lovcen	..	..	1954	3383	392	50	$15\frac{1}{2}$	M	
Makedonija	..	..	1939	6141	476	61	14	M	ex Viktoria.
Matko Laginja		..	1962	2308	349	47	14	M	
Nehaj	..	..	1967	7662	496	67	18	M	
Nikola Tesla		..	1957	6102	479	60	13	M	
Novi Vinodolski		..	1961	4714	447	60	$16\frac{1}{2}$	M	
Pag ..	..	..	1969	5521	487	67	18	M(A)	ex Lagatec 70.
Pazin	..	..	1969	6275	497	66	17	M	
Primorje	..	..	1961	7001	509	68	18	M	
Pula ..	..	..	1950	2400	353	46	14	M	
Rijeka	..	..	1950	2400	353	47	14	M	
Romanija	..	..	1953	3073	384	50	16	M	
Sarajevo	..	..	1949	3265	334	46	$13\frac{1}{2}$	M(A)	
Skopje	..	..	1949	3265	334	46	$13\frac{1}{2}$	M(A)	
Slovenija	..	..	1951	5523	462	59	17	M	
Srbija	..	..	1949	6634	475	61	15	M	ex Drvar 49.
Titograd	..	..	1950	3265	333	46	14	M(A)	
Treci Maj	..	..	1957	6211	479	60	13	M	
Trepca	..	..	1958	6211	479	60	13	M	
Triglav	..	..	1954	3383	392	50	17	M	
Trsat	..	..	1966	7662	508	68	18	M	
Tuhobic	..	..	1965	7759	489	67	18	M	
Ucka	..	..	1945	3133	365	50	14	M	ex Locchi 51.
Uljanik	..	..	1957	6212	480	60	13	M	
Velebit	..	..	1954	3383	392	50	$15\frac{1}{2}$	M	
Vis ..	..	..	1935	2086	322	44	11	RT	ex Malaga 47.
Visevica	..	..	1964	7759	489	67	17	M	
Vojvodina	..	..	1940	3555	397	51	12	M	ex Srem 51, ex Balcic.
Zadar	..	..	1950	2400	353	47	14	M	
Zagreb	..	..	1949	3265	339	46	$13\frac{1}{2}$	M(A)	
Zvir ..	..	..	1966	7760	490	67	18	M	

Also smaller ships.

KAYE, SON & CO. LTD.
Jamaica Banana Producers S.S. Co. Ltd.

FUNNEL: *Blue with black top and two white bands.*

HULL: *White with red boot-topping.*

Name	Date	Tons Gross	Length (feet)	Breadth (feet)	Speed (knots)	Engines	Former Names
Jamaica Planter ..	1959	6159	446	57	17	ST	
Jamaica Producer	1962	5781	397	56	17	M	

(NORWAY)

JACOB KJODE A/S
A. S. Inger

FUNNEL: *Black or yellow with white ' K ' on broad blue band.*

HULL: *Grey with red boot-topping or light green with dark green boot-topping.*

Name		Date	Tons	Length	Breadth	Speed	Engines
Baie Comeau	..	1960	8412	453	67	15½	M(A)
Elin Hope ..	..	1961	9139	508	62	16	M
Elin Horn ..	..	1968	30549	707	100	15	M(A)
Ingeren	..	1970	12638	520	74	15	M(A)
Ingerseks	..	1958	5000	386	53	13½	M(A)
Ingertre	..	1954	5078	389	54	11½	SR(A)

Also smaller ships.

(NORWAY)

A. F. KLAVENESS & CO. A/S
VARIOUS SUB-TITLES

FUNNEL: *Black with white ' K ' on broad red band.*

HULL: *White with blue line and red boot-topping.*

Name		Date	Tons	Length	Breadth	Speed	Engines
Bonneville ..	..	1950	5839	462	59	15½	M
Bougainville	..	1947	5792	462	59	15½	M
Bronxville ..	..	1950	5838	462	59	15½	M
Corneville ..	..	1955	3474	398	54	16	M
Kingsville ..	..	1956	6563	505	64	17½	ST
Libreville ..	..	1956	3477	398	54	16	M
Queensville	..	1957	7586	505	64	17	ST
Roseville ..	..	1961	5267	452	58	17	M
Sangstad ..	..	1966	21596	644	85	15½	M(A)
Sunnyville ..	..	1949	5806	462	59	15½	M

Also tankers.

122

A. F. Klaveness: SANGSTAD

[F. R. Sherlock

Lamport & Holt Line: ROSSETTI

[Fotoship

LAMBERT BROS. (SHIPPING) LTD.
Euxine Shipping Co. Ltd.
(Managers: Scottish Ship Management)

FUNNEL: *Black with red pyramid on broad white band.*
HULL: *Black, white line, red boot-topping.*

Name		Date	Tons Gross	Length (feet)	Breadth (feet)	Speed (knots)	Engines	Former Names
Temple Arch	..	1969	13543	528	75	16	M(A)	

LAMPORT & HOLT LINE LTD.

FUNNEL: *Light blue with broad white band and black top.*
HULL: *Black with white band at the Plimsoll mark.*
ROUTES: *U.K. ports to Brazil, Uruguay and Argentina.*
New York to N. Brazil and River Amazon via West Indies.

Name			Date	Tons Gross	Length (feet)	Breadth (feet)	Speed (knots)	Engines	Former Names
Cuthbert	..	..	1962	1869	358	44	14½	M	ex Spenser 67.
Cyril	..	..	1961	1849	358	44	14½	M	ex Sheridan 67.
Devis	..	..	1942	9141	488	63	14	M(2)	ex Caledonia Star 69, ex Royal Star 61, ex Empire Wisdom 46.
Raphael	..	..	1953	7852	473	62	13½	M	
Roland	..	..	1950	7344	497	65	16	ST	ex Dunedin Star 68.
Romney	..	..	1952	8138	470	63	15	ST	
Ronsard	..	..	1957	7840	473	62	15	M	
Rossetti	..	..	1956	4693	436	57	15	M	ex Boniface 67, ex Rossetti 63.
Rossini	..	..	1952	4459	436	57	15	M	ex Bernard 67, ex Rubens 65, ex Siddons 55.

VERGOCEAN
LARRINAGA S.S. CO. LTD.

FUNNEL: *Black with two red bands alternating with three yellow.*
HULL: *Black with white line and red boot-topping.*

Name	Date	Tons Gross	Length (feet)	Breadth (feet)	Speed (knots)	Engines	Former Names
Niceto de Larrinaga	1959	7292	559 ..	62	15	M ToGreece	
Rupert de Larrinaga	1969	9268	463	67	15	M	

J. LAURITZEN

FUNNEL: *Red with white band with white 'J' above and white 'L' below, some having black top and base.*
HULL: *Pale grey or cream some with red line, black with white line or all red.*

Name		Date	Tons Gross	Length (feet)	Breadth (feet)	Speed (knots)	Engines	Former Names
Arabian Reefer	..	1957	4714	435	59	18	M(2)	ToGreece, ren·APOLLONIAN CHAMPION
Belgian Reefer	..	1958	4686	435	59	18	M(2)	" " " " GRACE
Chilean Reefer	..	1959	4981	436	59	18	M(2)	
Ecuadorian Reefer		1962	4981	436	59	18	M(2)	
Erika Dan	..	1958	2648	299	46	14	M	
Frida Dan	..	1957	2676	301	46	14	M	
Helga Dan	..	1957	4040	350	52	14½	M	
Italian Reefer	..	1968	6004	477	69	22	M	
Nella Dan	..	1961	2206	247	47	15	M	
Nippon Reefer	..	1969	6004	478	69	22	M	
Perla Dan	..	1959	2353	275	43	12½	M(A)	
Persian Reefer	..	1970	6010	478	69	22	M	
Ritva Dan	..	1961	3065	318	46	13½	M	To Canada, ren· KAKAWI
Roman Reefer	..	1970	6010	478	69	22	M	
Sarma Dan	..	1962	3065	323	46	13½	M	
Thala Dan	..	1957	2000	247	45	12	M(A)	
Thora Dan	..	1956	4041	350	52	14½	M	To Cyprus, ren· ELIAS K.
Kyoto Reefer								

Also smaller ships.

Reena Dan 1972 4210   M   Montlaurier
To Bermuda, ren· Union Sydney

(ITALY)

ACHILLE LAURO

FUNNEL: *Blue with white star and black top.*

HULL: *White or black.* (ACHILLE LAURO *and* ANGELINA LAURO *have blue*).

ROUTES: **A.** *Southampton to Australia.*
   B. *Genoa to Australia.*
   C. *Mediterranean services.*

Name			Date	Tons	Length	Breadth	Speed	Engines	Former Names
Achille Lauro	..		1947	23629	631	82	22	M(2)	ex Willem Ruys 65.
Angelina Lauro	..		1939	24377	656	84	21	M(3)	ex Oranje 64.
Callao			1956	10567	504	67	15	ST(A)	ex Cornwall 66.
Capriolo	..	..	1970	12379	530	75	17	M	
Cervo	..	..	1971	12379	530	75	17	M	
Fede	..		1957	9975	521	63	15	ST(A)	ex Patmos 66, ex Andros Gale 60.
Gazella	..	..	1970	12379	530	75	17	M	
Lavoro	..	..	1938	7624	483	59	11	M	
Liana	..	..	1956	9938	525	63	15½	ST(A)	ex Piraeus 68, ex National Progress 61.
Lucrino	..	..	1942	7040	442	57	10½	SR	ex Saint Edward 62, ex Ocean Vista 48.
Napoli	..	..	1940	7460	451	57	12	M	ex Araybank 48.
Pegaso	..	..	1958	9093	502	61	14½	M	ex Continental Shipper 68, ex Woodburn 66, ex Continental Trader 62.
Pomona	..	..	1956	9975	521	63	15	ST(A)	ex Leros 66, ex Andros Glamour 60.
Ravello	..	..	1941	8452	473	63	12	M	
Tigre	..	..	1970	12379	530	75	17	M	
Valparaiso	..	..	1958	10727	504	67	15	ST(A)	ex Dorset 66.

Lauro: ACHILLE LAURO berthing at Malta; *dghajsas* in foreground   [*Malcolm Cranfield*

Lloyd Triestino: GALILEO GALILEI   [*Bert Moody*

LEONHARDT & BLUMBERG

FUNNEL: *Black with red ' × ' and black ' + ' combined on broad white band.*

HULL: *Black.*

Name	Date	Tons Gross	Length (feet)	Breadth (feet)	Speed (knots)	Engines	Former Names
Adolf Leonhardt ..	1964	22056	662	86	15	M(A)	
Altenfels	1969	9393	485	69	16	M(A)	ex Marita Leonhardt 69.
August Leonhardt	1958	10738	523	64	13½	M(A)	
Bernd Leonhardt	1955	6135	485	61	13	M	
Finn Leonhardt ..	1969	9406	458	69	16	M(A)	
Frank Leonhardt ..	1955	6145	485	61	13	M	
Heide Leonhardt..	1969	9400	458	69	16	M(A)	ex Finn Heide 70.
Ingrid Leonhardt	1954	5932	485	61	13	M	
Klaus Leonhardt ..	1969	9406	458	69	16	M(A)	
Marie Leonhardt	1958	10736	523	63	13½	M(A)	
Otto Leonhardt ..	1967	23414	664	94	16	M(A)	

LLOYD TRIESTINO
Soc. per Azioni di Nav.

FUNNEL: *Yellow with blue top and narrow blue band.*

HULL: *White with blue line and boot-topping or black.*

ROUTES: *Trieste, Venice or Genoa, Naples and/or Messina to:—*

    A. *Aden, Colombo, to Djakarta, Fremantle, Melbourne, Sydney.*

    B. *India, Pakistan and Far East.*

    C. *West and South Africa.*

Name	Date	Tons Gross	Length	Breadth	Speed	Engines	Former Names
Adige	1950	5449	435	63	15	M(A)(2)	ex St. Matthieu 56, ex Nord 50.
Africa	1952	11434	523	68	19½	M(2)	
Amerigo Vespucci	1949	7021	485	62	15½	M	ex Giuseppe Majorana 49.
Antoniotto Usodimare ..	1949	6895	485	62	15½	M	ex Vittorio Miccagotta 49.
Aquileia	1955	4908	428	60	14½	M	
Asia	1953	11693	522	68	19¾	M(2)	
Cellina	1951	5451	435	63	15	M(A)(2)	ex St. Jean 57.
Esquilino	1963	6956	505	66	18	M	
Europa	1952	11440	522	68	19½	M(2)	
Galileo Galilei ..	1963	27907	701	94	25	ST(2)	
Guglielmo Marconi	1963	27905	701	94	25	ST(2)	
Isarco	1950	5347	435	63	15	M(A)(2)	ex St. Marc 56.
Isonzo	1962	5522	456	61	18	M	
Livenza	1951	5385	435	63	15	M(A)(2)	ex Saint Luc 57.
Marco Polo ..	1948	7026	485	62	15½	M	ex Nicolo Giani 48.
Palatino	1963	6956	504	66	18	M	
Piave	1955	4907	428	60	14½	M	
Mediterraneo	1973	26,900					

London & Overseas Freighters: LONDON CITIZEN [*Fotoship*

Lykes Bros: NANCY LYKES [*Malcolm Cranfield*

Name	Date	Tons Gross	Length (feet)	Breadth (feet)	Speed (knots)	Engines	Former Names
Quirinale	1963	6957	504	66	18	M	
Rosandra	1956	5045	428	60	14½	M	
Sebastiano Caboto	1947	7179	485	62	15½	M	ex Mario Visentin 47.
Ugolini Vivaldi ..	1947	7130	485	62	15½	M	ex Ferruccio Buonapace 47.
Victoria	1953	11695	522	68	19¾	M(2)	to Adriatica
Viminale	1963	6956	504	66	18	M	

Also smaller ships.

LONDON & OVERSEAS FREIGHTERS LTD.

FUNNEL: *Yellow with red star on white over blue band.*
HULL: *Black, boot-topping black with white line.*

London Advocate	1964	7142	516	66	17	M	
London Banker ..	1963	7142	516	66	17	M	
London Citizen ..	1965	7862	531	67	17	M	
London Craftsman	1963	7862	531	68	17	M	
London Explorer	1959	15934	593	80	14	ST(A)	ex Overseas Explorer 67.
London Pioneer ..	1958	15934	593	80	14	ST(A)	ex Overseas Pioneer 67.
London Prestige ..	1954	16010	592	80	13½	M(A)	
London Resolution	1958	16025	593	80	14	ST(A)	
London Statesman	1963	8077	531	68	17	M	
London Tradition	1957	15947	593	80	14	ST(A)	

Also tankers.

Mayfair Tankers Ltd.

Mayfair Splendour	1953	16054	592	80	13½	M(A)	ex London Splendour 70.

LYKES BROS. STEAMSHIP CO. INC.

FUNNEL: *Black with white ' L ' on blue diamond on broad white band. Some ships without funnels have the ' L ' and diamond on the sides of the bridge.*

HULL: *Black with red boot-topping.*

Almeria Lykes	1973	21667	875		20	ST	
Adabelle Lykes ..	1963	9296	495	69	18	ST	
Aimee Lykes ..	1963	9398	491	69	18	ST	
Allison Lykes ..	1963	9397	495	69	18	ST	
Almeria Lykes ..	1945	7854	492	70	16½	ST	
Ashley Lykes ..	1963	9244	495	69	18	ST	
Brinton Lykes ..	1962	9244	495	69	18	ST	
Charlotte Lykes ..	1963	9296	495	69	18	ST	
Christopher Lykes	1963	9398	495	69	18	ST	

Name	Date	Tons Gross	Length (feet)	Breadth (feet)	Speed (knots)	Engines	Former Names
Doctor Lykes (hw)	*1972*	*29667*	*875*	*107*	*20*	*ST*	*Seabee* (hw)
Doctor Lykes ..	1945	7854	492	70	16½	ST	
Dolly Turman ..	1967	10723	540	76	20	ST	
Elizabeth Lykes ..	1965	10955	540	76	20	ST	
Elizabeth Lykes ..	1945	8067	459	63	15½	ST	
Frank Lykes ..	1944	8068	459	63	15½	ST	ex Fair Wind 47.
Frederick Lykes ..	1966	10723	540	76	20	ST	
Genevieve Lykes ..	1967	10723	540	76	20	ST	
Gibbes Lykes ..	1944	8068	459	63	15½	ST	ex Orpheus 47.
Harry Culbreath ..	1945	8067	459	63	15½	ST	
Howell Lykes ..	1967	10723	540	76	20	ST	
James Lykes ..	1960	9218	495	69	17	ST	
James McKay ..	1945	8067	459	63	15½	ST	ex Canvasback 47.
Jean Lykes ..	1961	9239	495	69	17	ST	
Jesse Lykes ..	1945	8067	459	63	15½	ST	ex Simoon 47.
John Lykes ..	1960	9218	495	69	17	ST	
Joseph Lykes ..	1960	9218	495	69	17	ST	
Kenneth McKay ..	1945	8067	459	63	15½	ST	
Leslie Lykes ..	1962	9239	495	69	18	ST	
Letitia Lykes ..	1968	10723	540	76	20	ST	
Lipscomb Lykes ..	1945	7854	492	70	16½	ST	
Louise Lykes ..	1965	10955	540	76	20	ST	
Louise Lykes ..	1945	8068	459	63	15½	ST	
Mallory Lykes ..	1966	10718	540	76	20	ST	
Margaret Lykes ..	1963	9397	495	69	18	ST	
Marjorie Lykes ..	1962	9244	495	69	18	ST	
Mason Lykes ..	1966	10723	540	76	20	ST	
Mayo Lykes ..	1963	9296	495	69	18	ST	
Nancy Lykes ..	1961	9239	495	69	17	ST	
Norman Lykes ..	1945	7854	492	70	16½	ST	
Reuben Tipton ..	1945	8067	459	63	15½	ST	
Ruth Lykes ..	1965	10723	540	76	20	ST	
Sheldon Lykes ..	1963	9296	495	69	18	ST	
Shirley Lykes ..	1962	9244	495	69	18	ST	
Solon Turman ..	1961	9239	495	69	17	ST	
Stella Lykes ..	1966	10723	540	76	20	ST	
Stella Lykes ..	1945	8067	459	63	15½	ST	
Sue Lykes ..	1945	8067	459	63	15½	ST	ex Tornado 45.
Thompson Lykes ..	1960	9218	495	69	17	ST	
Tillie Lykes ..	1945	7854	492	70	16½	ST	
Tyson Lykes ..	1945	8067	459	63	15½	ST	ex National Eagle 45.
Velma Lykes ..	1967	10723	540	76	20	ST	
Velma Lykes ..	1945	8067	459	63	15½	ST	
William Lykes ..	1945	8067	459	63	15½	ST	ex Red Gauntlet 47.
Zoella Lykes ..	1960	9218	495	69	17	ST	
Tillie Lykes (hw)	*1973*	*21668*	*875*	*107*	*20*	*ST*	*Seabee* (hw)

LYLE SHIPPING CO. LTD.

SCOTTISH SHIP MANAGEMENT LTD.

FUNNEL: *Yellow.*

HULL: *Grey with red boot topping.*

Name	Date	Tons	Length	Breadth	Speed	Engines	
Cape Clear ..	1967	12624	530	71	15½	M(A)	*To Greece, ren. KIKKI YEN* (hw)
Cape Franklin ..	1959	11674	525	70	12½	M(A)	
Cape Howe ..	1962	19032	608	80	13	M(A)	
Cape Nelson ..	1961	12351	525	70	12	M(A)	
Cape Rodney ..	1965	11950	527	68	14	M(A)	
Cape Sable ..	1969	13532	528	75	16	M(A)	
Cape St. Vincent* ..	1966	12835	528	72	15½	M(A)	
Cape Wrath ..	1968	13532	528	75	16	M(A)	
Cape York	1969	13543	528	75	16	M(A)	

* On charter from William Dennison Ltd.

Lyle Shipping Co: CAPE RODNEY

[F. R. Sherlock

Manchester Liners: MANCHESTER CONCORDE

[Fotoship

MacANDREWS & CO. LTD.

FUNNEL: *Yellow.*
HULL: *White with green boot-topping.*

Name		Date	Tons Gross	Length (feet)	Breadth (feet)	Speed (knots)	Engines	Former Names
Cervantes	..	1967	1470	301	44	16	M(A)	
Churruca	..	1968	1455	301	44	16	M(A)	
Pacheco	..	1961	1242	245	42	15½	M(A)	
Palacio	..	1961	1096	248	42	15½	M(A)	
Palomares	..	1963	1196	245	42	15½	M(A)	
Pelayo	..	1963	1196	245	42	15½	M(A)	
Sailor Prince		1957	2055	334	46	15½	M	ex Velarde 69.
Vargas	..	1959	2052	334	46	15½	M	
Verdaguer	..	1958	2049	334	46	15½	M	
Vives	..	1955	1216	285	38	15½	M(A)	

MANCHESTER LINERS LTD.

FUNNEL: *Dark red with black top and black band.   Several ships have no funnel, but have twin exhausts aft.*

HULL: *Black with red boot-topping, or red with white letters " MAN-CHESTER LINERS ".*

ROUTE: **A.** *Manchester to Saint John N.B. Halifax, Quebec, Montreal, Toronto, Hamilton, Detroit, Chicago and other Great Lake ports.*

Name		Date	Tons Gross	Length (feet)	Breadth (feet)	Speed (knots)	Engines	
Manchester Renown		1974	12500	529	63	19½	M(A)	conti
Manchester Challenge	..	1968	11899	530	64	19½	M(A)	
Manchester City	..	1964	8734	502	62	17	M(A)	
Manchester Commerce	..	1963	8724	502	62	17	M(A)	
Manchester Concorde†	..	1969	11899	530	64	19½	M(A)	
Manchester Courage		1968	11899	529	64	19½	M(A)	
Manchester Merit		1970	2850	327	50	14½	M(A)	
Manchester Miller		1959	8378	468	62	17	ST(A)	(Renamed Manchester Quest)
Manchester Port	..	1966	8168	502	62	17½	M(A)	
Manchester Progress		1967	8176	502	62	17½	M(A)	
Manchester Concept Renown*	..	1964	8742	502	62	17	M(A)	
Manchester Reward		1974	12000					M	

† Owned by Nile S.S. Co. Ltd.   * Owned by Beaver Industries Ltd.

(BELGIUM)

CIE. MARITIME BELGE (LLOYD ROYAL) S.A.

FUNNEL: *Yellow.*
HULL: *Grey with red boot-topping.*

Manchester Liners: MANCHESTER PROGRESS

Cie Maritime Belge: MONTFORT

CIE. MARITIME BELGE (LLOYD ROYAL) S.A. (continued)

ROUTES:
  A. *Antwerp, Teneriffe, Lobito, Matadi, Boma and Pointe Noire.*
  B. *Antwerp, Rotterdam, Bremen, Hamburg, Mombasa, Tanga, Zanzibar, Dar-es-Salaam, Beira.*
  C. *Antwerp, Zeebrugge to New York and other East Coast ports of U.S.A.*
  D. *Matadi, Boma, Lobito to New York and other East Coast ports of U.S.A.*
  E. *Antwerp to Brazil, Uruguay and Argentina.*

Name	Date	Tons Gross	Length (feet)	Breadth (feet)	Speed (knots)	Engines	Former Names
Albertville	1948	10575	504	65	16	M	
Lualaba	1950	8223	480	63	14	M	ex Sakura 52. *To Engl. re*
Lukuga	1956	8750	482	62	16	M	*MOUNT C*
Lulua	1956	8750	482	62	16	M	
Lusambo	1956	8750	482	62	16	M	
Mineral Gent	1967	40304	802	105	15	M(A)	
Mineral Seraing	1965	33023	754	106	15	M(A)	
Moanda	1957	8992	483	62	14	M	
Mobeka	1958	8992	483	62	14	M	
Moero	1958	8992	483	62	14	M	
Mohasi	1958	8992	483	62	14	M	
Mokambo	1959	9013	483	62	14	M	
Mokaria	1964	10978	523	66	16½	M	
Mokoto	1959	9013	483	62	14	M	
Mol	1962	9009	483	62	14½	M	
Moliro	1960	9013	483	62	14½	M	
Montaigle	1968	11519	528	76	20	M	
Montalto	1960	9309	483	62	14½	M	
Montenaken	1969	11519	528	76	20	M	
Montfort	1969	11519	528	76	20	M	
Monthouet	1961	9309	483	62	14½	M	

See also Dart Containerline Ltd.

(U.S.A.)

MATSON NAVIGATION COMPANY

FUNNEL: *Yellow, blue top with blue ' M ' on disc.*
HULL: *Black or white.*

Californian	1946	13636	633	72	15	ST(A)	ex Mount Greylock 51.
Hawaiian	1946	14113	633	72	15	ST(A)	ex Mount Rogers 51. *To US*
Hawaiian Builder	1945	7898	492	70	16	ST	ex Sea Blenny 47.
Hawaiian Citizen	1944	12589	492	70	16	ST	ex Sea Wren 47. *to USA*
Hawaiian Enterprise	1970	17000	721	95	23	ST(A)	
Hawaiian Farmer	1944	7865	492	70	16	ST	ex Sea Sturgeon 47.
Hawaiian Legislator	1946	11178	523	72	16	ST	ex Coast Progress 63, ex Nevadan 57, ex Willis Vickery 51.
Hawaiian Merchant	1945	7882	492	70	16	ST	ex Sea Skimmer 47.
Hawaiian Monarch	1944	17807	640	72	16	ST(A)	ex Marine Dragon 65.
Hawaiian Motorist	1945	7901	492	70	16	ST	ex Hawaiian Fisherman 62, ex Sea Falcon 47.

To Han, ren. GRAND UNITY

Matson Navigation Co: MONTEREY

Messageries Maritimes: PASTEUR

Name	Date	Tons Gross	Length (feet)	Breadth (feet)	Speed (knots)	Engines	Former Names
Hawaiian Princess	1967	3874	338	52	14	M(2)(A)	
Hawaiian Progress	1970	17000	721	95	23	ST(A)	
Hawaiian Queen	1944	17504	640	72	16	ST(A)	ex Marine Devil 65.
Hawaiian Rancher	1944	7842	492	70	16	ST	ex Sea Ray 47.
Hawaiian Refiner ..	1944	7843	492	70	16	ST	ex Sea Fiddler 47.
Pacific Banker ..	1945	14161	544	70	16	ST(A)	ex Hawaiian Craftsman 67, ex Marguerite Le Hand 47.
Pacific Trader ..	1945	14246	544	70	16	ST(A)	ex Hawaiian Planter 67, ex Sea Pegasus 47.
Lurline	1974						
Matsonia							

Oceanic Steamship Company

Name	Date	Tons Gross	Length (feet)	Breadth (feet)	Speed (knots)	Engines	Former Names
Mariposa	1953	14812	564	76	19	ST	ex Pine Tree Mariner 56.
Monterey	1952	14799	564	76	19	ST	ex Free State Mariner 56.
Sonoma	1944	7741	492	70	16	ST	ex Hawaiian Pilot 61, ex Burleigh 47.
Ventura	1945	7870	492	70	16	ST	ex Hawaiian Wholesaler 61, ex Hanover 47.

MAVROLEON BROS. (SHIP MANAGEMENT) LTD.

Falaise S.S. Co. & Falaise Ore Carriers Ltd.

FUNNEL: *Yellow with red ' M ' on white over blue bands.*
HULL: *Black with white line.*

Name	Date	Tons Gross	Length	Breadth	Speed	Engines
Finnamore Meadow	1961	13057	535	70	14	M(A)

Traditional Traders Shipping Ltd.

Name	Date	Tons Gross	Length	Breadth	Speed	Engines
Victore	1963	19543	615	85	14	M(A)

(LIBERIA)
General Freighters Corporation

Name	Date	Tons Gross	Length	Breadth	Speed	Engines
Alessandra ..	1967	14845	595	75	15	M(A)
Nicola	1968	9034	463	67	14	M(A)
Syrie	1968	9024	463	67	14	M(A)

(LIBERIA)
Fairsail Carrier Corporation

Name	Date	Tons Gross	Length	Breadth	Speed	Engines
Carina	1969	9072	463	67	14	M(A)

GÉNÉRALE MARITIME   **(FRANCE)**
CIE. DES MESSAGERIES MARITIMES

FUNNEL: *Black*. PASTEUR *has white funnel, black top with house flag.*
LAOS *and* PACIFIQUE *have white funnel with house flag.*

HULL: *Black with white line and red boot-topping, or white with green boot-topping.*

ROUTES: **A.** *Round the world—Marseilles, Tahiti, New Caledonia and Australia via Panama and return via Cape of Good Hope.*
B. *Marseilles to E. Africa, Madagascar, Reunion and Mauritius.*
C. *Hamburg, Havre, Southampton to South America.*
D. *N. Europe and Algiers to Malaya, Indo-China, Philippines, Hong Kong, China and Japan.*
E. *Coastal services* **(a)** *Madagascar,* **(b)** *Australia to New Caledonia,* **(c)** *Saigon, Hong Kong, Japan.*

Name		Date	Tons Gross	Length (feet)	Breadth (feet)	Speed (knots)	Engines	Former Names
Aquilon	..	1968	8581	472	66	17	M	
Caledonien	..	1952	12712	549	68	17	M(2)	
Euphate	..	1955	7030	460	61	16	M(2)	
Gallieni	..	1954	4576	378	53	12½	M(A)	
Gange	..	1953	6929	461	61	16	M(2)	
Godavery	..	1955	6936	489	62	16	M	
Indus	..	1950	6919	476	61	15½	M(2)	
Iraouaddy	..	1953	6929	461	61	16	M(2)	
Jean Laborde	..	1952	10902	492	64	17	M(2)	
Kangourou	..	1970	26450	748	100	21½	ST(A)	
Kouang-Si	..	1957	6991	489	62	16	M	
Le Natal	..	1956	7051	489	62	16	M	
Malais	..	1959	7475	514	65	18	M	
Maori	..	1958	7474	514	65	18	M	
Marquisien	..	1959	7475	514	65	18	M	
Martiniquais	..	1960	7475	514	65	18	M	
Mauricien	..	1960	7475	514	65	18	M	
Moheli	..	1963	9384	515	65	16	M	ex Cheshire 68.
Moonie	..	1955	6936	489	62	16	M	
Mozambique	..	1959	8763	491	64	16	M	ex Chatwood 68.
Oyonnax	..	1965	4950	367	53	16	M(A)	
Pacifique	..	1952	13520	532	72	21	ST(2)	ex Viet Nam 67.
Pasteur	..	1966	17986	571	80	20½	M(2)	
Pierre Loti	..	1952	10945	492	64	17	M(2)	
Polynesie	..	1955	3709	344	49	14	M	
Si-Kieng	..	1957	6998	489	62	16	M	
Sindh*	..	1956	7051	489	62	16	M	
Tahitien	..	1953	12614	549	68	17	M(2)	
Tigre	..	1956	7051	489	62	16	M	
Vanoise	..	1960	7058	514	65	18	M	
Var	..	1964	7595	514	65	18	M	
Vaucluse	..	1965	7595	514	65	18	M	
Velay	..	1961	7508	514	65	18	M	
Ventoux	..	1960	7508	514	65	18	M	
Vienne	..	1964	7595	514	65	18	M	
Vivarais	..	1960	7504	512	65	18	M	
Vosges	..	1960	7508	514	65	18	M	
Yalou	..	1957	6998	489	62	16	M	
Yang-Tse	..	1958	6998	489	62	16	M	
Yarra	..	1957	7051	489	62	16	M	

Also smaller ships.   * Detained since 1967 in Suez Canal.

METCALFE SHG. CO. LTD.

Metcalfe, Son & Co.

FUNNEL: *Black with red " M " on white band.*

HULL: *Black with red boot-topping.*

Name			Date	Tons Gross	Length (feet)	Breadth (feet)	Speed (knots)	Engines	Former Names
Fidentia	..	..	1956	5568	469	59	13½	M	ex Kepwickhall 66.
Industria	..	..	1960	7774	452	60	12	M	ex Silverisle 65.

MICHALINOS & CO. LTD.

FUNNEL: *Black with white " M " on broad blue band.*

HULL: *Black with red boot-topping.*

Riverdore	..	..	1959	8080	456	60	13	M

United Merchants Shg. Co.

FUNNEL: *Black with white " UM " on broad blue band.*

Castledore		..	1956	7952	456	60	12	RT

(JAPAN)

MITSUI–O.S.K. LINES K.K.

FUNNEL: *Light red.*

HULL: *Grey or bright blue with red or green boot-topping.*

ROUTES:

A. *Japan, U.S. Pacific Coast, Panama, U.S. Atlantic Coast, New York.*

B. *Japan, U.S. Pacific Coast, Panama, Gulf of Mexico and Canada.*

C. *Japan, U.S. Pacific Coast, Panama, Brazil, Uruguay, Argentina, West and East Africa.*

D. *Japan, Hong Kong, Aden, Jeddah, Suez, Mediterranean ports, North Europe.*

E. *Japan, Hong Kong, Rabaul, New Zealand, Australia.*

F. *Japan, Bangkok, Malaya, Karachi, Persian Gulf.*

G. *Japan, Malaya, Saigon, Rangoon, Chittagong, Calcutta, Ceylon.*

Messageries Maritimes: MARQUISIEN

Mitsui-O.S.K.: RECIFE MARU

Name	Date	Tons Gross	Length (feet)	Breadth (feet)	Speed (knots)	Engines	Former Names
Arimasan Maru	1974	74500				M	Bulk
Acapulco Maru ..	1951	6493	503	64	16	M	ex Kyoei Maru 67.
Adelaide Maru ..	1954	6525	503	64	16	M	ex Kyotoku Maru 67.
Akagisan Maru ..	1951	6416	499	64	17	M	
Akashisan Maru ..	1951	6458	499	63	17	M	
Akibasan Maru ..	1952	6446	499	64	17	M	
America Maru ..	1968	16404	614	82	21	M(A)	
Andes Maru ..	1951	8231	473	62	15½	M	
en. Nippon **Argentina Maru***	1958	10970	513	67	16	M	
Arizona Maru ..	1956	9049	513	64	16	M	
Atlas Maru	1951	8075	473	62	15½	M	
Awajisan Maru ..	1952	6448	499	64	17	M	
Awobasan Maru ..	1952	6738	499	64	17	M	
Azuchisan Maru ..	1953	6758	452	58	17	M	
Azumasan Maru ..	1950	6993	453	59	14	M	
Barcelona Maru ..	1967	10463	545	76	20½	M	
Bengal Maru ..	1949	5429	401	54	12	M	ex Yoko Maru 60.
Bergen Maru ..	1966	10450	545	76	20½	M	
Bombay Maru ..	1958	7009	451	58	14	M	
Brazil Maru* ..	1954	10216	512	64	16	M	now a museum
Bremen Maru ..	1966	10430	545	76	20½	M	
Bristol Maru ..	1966	10428	545	76	20½	M	
Buenos Aires Maru	1956	8563	494	63	16	M	
Cape Town Maru ..	1957	4923	396	55	12½	M	ex Ginko Maru 61. To Pa... ASAN...
Caracas Maru ..	1969	6887	505	72	18	M(A)	
Chicago Maru ..	1959	9107	512	64	17	M	
Congo Maru ..	1954	6388	451	58	14	M	ex Tozai Maru No. 11—64.
Corinto Maru ..	1970	7300	511	72	18	M(A)	
Cristobal Maru ..	1969	6881	505	72	18	M(A)	
Curacao Maru ..	1969	7298	511	72	18	M(A)	
Durban Maru ..	1956	7228	446	59	13½	M	ex Tenko Maru 64.
Euphrates Maru ..	1968	7701	448	66	18	M	
Hague Maru ..	1961	9173	512	64	17¼	M	
Hagurosan Maru	1955	9619	514	65	18½	M	
Hakonesan Maru ..	1954	6499	504	63	17	M	
Hamburg Maru ..	1957	8807	494	63	16½	M	
Harunasan Maru	1954	6490	504	64	17	M	
Havana Maru ..	1957	9375	512	63	17¼	M	
Hawaii Maru ..	1952	9217	513	64	16½	M(2)	
Heiwa Maru ..	1963	12723	551	71	15	M(A)	
Hodakasan Maru ..	1955	9616	514	65	18½	M	
Hoeisan Maru ..	1954	6560	504	63	17¼	M	
Honolulu Maru ..	1958	9237	513	64	17¼	M	To Pan. ren. SEA CROWN
Honmoku Maru ..	1968	11161	500	71	15	M	
Houston Maru ..	1960	9132	512	64	17¾	M	
Hudson Maru ..	1960	9133	512	64	17¾	M	
Kasugasan Maru ..	1962	8192	492	63	17½	M	
Kinkasan Maru ..	1961	8221	492	63	17½	M	
La Plata Maru ..	1955	9390	496	63	16½	M	
London Maru ..	1953	8038	473	62	15½	M	
Madagascar Maru	1953	6623	447	58	14	M	ex Tozai Maru No. 8—64.
Madras Maru ..	1957	6339	451	58	14	M	
Manjusan Maru ..	1957	9455	514	65	17¼	M	
Matsudosan Maru	1959	9548	514	65	18	M	
Mayasan Maru ..	1958	9558	514	65	18	M	
Megurosan Maru	1958	9566	514	65	18	M	
Melbourne Maru ..	1956	6318	451	58	14	M	
Mexico Maru ..	1952	9229	513	64	16½	M(2)	
Mikagesan Maru ..	1956	9424	514	65	17½	M	
Mogamisan Maru ..	1956	9594	514	65	17¼	M	
Mombasa Maru ..	1958	7214	448	59	13¾	M	ex Toko Maru 61.
Momijisan Maru ..	1959	9503	514	65	18	M	To Pan., ren. SEA BRAVE
Montevideo Maru	1956	8825	494	63	16½	M	
Mont Blanc Maru	1974	27900				M	Cont.

Mitsui-O.S.K.: BARCELONA MARU

[*John G. Callis*

A. P. Moller: CHRISTIAN MAERSK at her home port, Copenhagen

[*F. W. Hawks*

A. P. Moller: THOMAS MAERSK

Name	Date	Tons Gross	Length (feet)	Breadth (feet)	Speed (knots)	Engines	Former Names
Musashisan Maru ..	1958	9584	514	65	18	M	to Pan, ren · SEA ADVENTURE
Nagaosan Maru ..	1960	6555	434	58	15½	M	
Narasan Maru ..	1958	5190	407	54	13	M	
Nikkohsan Maru ..	1961	5093	407	54	13½	M	
Norfolk Maru ..	1961	9173	512	64	18	M	
Panama Maru ..	1952	9191	513	64	16½	M(2)	
Philippine Maru ..	1955	9043	513	64	16½	M	
Port Elizabeth Maru	1952	7202	466	61	15	M	ex Kamagawa Maru 69.
Port Louis Maru ..	1952	7129	476	60	14	M	ex Wako Maru 66.
Recife Maru ..	1967	7772	459	62	15	M(A)	
Rio de Janeiro Maru	1965	7770	459	63	16	M(A)	
Rio Grande Maru ..	1967	7772	459	62	15	M(A)	
Rosario Maru ..	1965	7696	459	63	16	M(A)	
Sacramento Maru	1967	6743	510	71	18½	M	
Saint Louis Maru ..	1967	6751	511	72	18½	M(A)	
San Francisco Maru	1967	6750	510	71	18½	M	
Savannah Maru ..	1967	6750	510	71	18½	M	
Seattle Maru ..	1959	9107	532	64	17½	M	
Suez Maru ..	1954	8160	473	62	15½	M	
Tacoma Maru ..	1962	9171	512	64	17½	M	
Tigris Maru ..	1968	7616	441	66	15	M(A)	
Wakaosan Maru ..	1965	9753	459	72	18	M(A)	
Yoshinosan Maru ..	1956	8783	483	62	15	M	
Ohmuesan Maru	1974	124000				M	

* Owned by Nihon Ijusen K.K.
  Also tankers, ore carriers and other ships.

(DENMARK)

A. P. MOLLER

FUNNEL: *Black with 7-pointed white star on broad blue band.*

HULL: *Light blue with red boot-topping.*

Name	Date	Tons Gross	Length (feet)	Breadth (feet)	Speed (knots)	Engines	Former Names
Anette Maersk ..	1962	6497	500	67	17½	M(A)	
Bella Maersk ..	1968	15850	592	75	16	M	
Brigit Maersk ..	1968	15850	592	75	16	M	
Cecilie Maersk ..	1967	11000	560	80	22	M	
Charlotte Maersk	1967	11000	560	80	22	M	
Chastine Maersk ..	1968	10918	560	81	22	M	
Christian Maersk ..	1968	10918	560	81	22	M	
Clara Maersk ..	1968	11000	560	80	22	M	
Clifford Maersk ..	1969	10915	560	81	22	M	
Cornelia Maersk ..	1967	10928	560	81	22	M	To Yugosl · ren VDGE
Dragor Maersk ..	1961	3335	435	58	15	M	To Lib·
Effie Maersk ..	1955	7122	539	64	18½	M	
Estelle Maersk ..	1958	3651	412	54	13¾	M(A)	
Hans Maersk ..	1958	3656	412	54	13¾	M(A)	
Hartvig Maersk ..	1957	3646	412	54	13¾	M(A)	
Henriette Maersk ..	1962	6152	490	63	17½	M(A)	
Janecke	1961	23548	670	90	17	M(A)	ex Janecke Maersk 65.
Jens Maersk ..	1957	3913	445	54	14¾	M	
Jeppesen Maersk	1951	6740	478	64	17¼	M	To Somalia, ren · SouthSea
Jesper Maersk ..	1953	6472	485	63	17¼	M	ex Chastine Maersk 68.
Johannes Maersk ..	1953	6428	489	63	17½	M	To Liberia
Knud Maersk ..	1958	3913	448	54	14¾	M	
Lars Maersk ..	1956	3886	445	54	14¾	M	
Laura Maersk ..	1966	27074	696	94	16	M(A)	
Laust Maersk ..	1965	27042	696	94	16	M(A)	

Arnold Maersk 1975 con ti
Adrian Maersk 197 "
Margrethe Maersk 197 "
Axel Maersk 197 "

143

Name		Date	Tons Gross	Length (feet)	Breadth (feet)	Speed (knots)	Engines	Former Names
Marchen Maersk		1974	16000				M	cont.
Leda Maersk	..	1957	6420	497	64	17½	M	
Leise Maersk	..	1967	44905	839	107	16	M(A)	
Lexa Maersk	..	1957	6381	498	64	17½	M	
Lica Maersk	..	1956	6365	498	64	17½	M	
Louis Maersk	..	1967	44896	839	107	16	M(A)	
Luna Maersk	..	1957	6381	498	64	17½	M	
Magleby Maersk	..	1964	5926	486	64	18	M	
Marchen	..	1962	23539	670	90	17	M(A)	ex Jesper Maersk 65.
Maren Maersk	..	1953	6429	489	63	17½	M	
Marit Maersk	..	1956	7136	539	64	17	M	
Nelly Maersk	..	1961	1985	300	48	13½	M(A)	
Nicoline Maersk	..	1951	6740	478	64	17¼	M	
Niels Maersk	..	1961	1985	300	48	13½	M(A)	
Olga Maersk	..	1970	30030	718	100	16	M(A)	
Olivia Maersk	..	1969	30039	718	100	16	M(A)	
Ras Maersk	..	1957	3219	383	51	13	M(A)	
Rita Maersk	..	1955	6310	499	64	18¼	M	
Robert Maersk	..	1958	3217	383	51	13	M(A)	
Romo Maersk	..	1959	3228	383	51	13	M(A)	
Sally Maersk	..	1954	7168	539	64	18½	M	To Lib.
Susan Maersk	..	1954	6481	499	64	18½	M	
Svend Maersk	..	1957	3882	445	54	14¾	M	
Thomas Maersk	..	1962	9050	560	74	17½	M(A)	
Thuro Maersk	..	1964	5926	486	64	18	M	
Tobias Maersk	..	1963	9051	560	74	17½	M(A)	
Torben Maersk	..	1963	6152	490	63	17½	M(A)	
Trein Maersk	..	1962	9050	560	74	17½	M(A)	

Also tankers.

| Maersk Topper | 1974 | 850 |
| Maersk Trimmer | 1974 | 850 |

(U.S.A.)

MOORE-McCORMACK LINES INC.

FUNNEL: *Red ' M ' on white disc on green band between yellow and black top.*

HULL: *Grey with red boot-topping.* ARGENTINA *and* BRASIL *have white hulls.*

ROUTES: **A.** *East Coast United States and Canada to and from East Coast of South America and West Indian islands.*

B. *Great Lakes ports of United States and Canada to and from East Coast ports of South America and West Indian islands.*

C. *East Coast United States and Canada to and from Scandinavia, Russia, Northern Europe, Amsterdam and Rotterdam.*

D. *West Coast United States and Canada to and from Panama, Caribbean Islands, North and East Coast South America.*

E. *East Coast United States to and from the Caribbean (cruise service).*

F. *East Coast United States to and from South and East Africa and Indian Ocean islands.*

Argentina	..	..	1958	15257	618	84	23	ST(2)	
Brasil	..	..	1958	15257	618	84	23	ST(2)	To Holland America, ren. Vole
Mormacaltair	..	..	1965	10484	551	75	22	ST	
Mormacargo	..	..	1964	10484	551	75	22	ST	
Mormacbay	..	..	1960	9252	483	68	18½	ST	
Mormaccape	..	..	1961	9258	483	68	18½	ST	
Mormaccove	..	..	1961	9361	488	68	18½	ST	

Moore-McCormack: MORMACSKY   [*F. R. Sherlock*

Moore-McCormack: MORMACLYNX   [*F. W. Hawks*

MOORE-McCORMACK LINES INC. (continued)

Name		Date	Tons Gross	Length (feet)	Breadth (feet)	Speed (knots)	Engines	Former Names
Mormacdawn	..	1946	7667	492	70	17½	ST	
Mormacdraco	..	1965	10484	551	75	22	ST	
Mormacglen	..	1961	9258	483	68	18½	ST	
Mormacgulf	..	1946	7667	492	70	17	ST	
Mormacisle	..	1946	7667	492	70	17½	ST	
Mormaclake	..	1961	9259	483	68	18½	ST	
Mormacland	..	1946	7667	492	70	17½	ST	
Mormaclynx	..	1964	10484	551	75	22	ST	
Mormacmail	..	1946	7667	492	70	17½	ST	
Mormacpride	..	1960	9252	483	68	18½	ST	
Mormacrigel	..	1965	10484	551	75	22	ST	
Mormacrio	..	1945	7640	492	70	17½	ST	ex William Harris Hardy 47.
Mormacscan	..	1961	9259	483	68	18½	ST	
Mormacsea	..	1969	11757	602	90	23	ST(A)	
Mormacsky	..	1969	11757	602	90	23	ST(A)	_to Amer-Export, ren. G M_
Mormacstar	..	1969	11757	602	90	23	ST(A)	_Rep_
Mormacsun	..	1970	11757	602	90	23	ST(A)	
Mormactrade	..	1962	9259	483	68	18½	ST	
Mormacvega	..	1964	10484	551	75	22	ST	
Robin Goodfellow		1945	7694	492	70	17	ST	ex Sea Carp 47.
Robin Gray	..	1943	7702	492	70	17	ST	ex Fayette 47, ex Sea Hawk 43.
Robin Hood		1945	7669	492	70	17	ST	ex Sea Dolphin 47.
Robin Trent	..	1943	7741	492	70	17	ST	ex Ravager 48.

Tkr. Mormacstar 1975
Tkr. Mormacsun 1976

MOSS HUTCHISON LINE LTD.

FUNNEL: *Black with broad white band.*
HULL: *Black with red boot-topping.*

Amarna			1949	3422	367	52	14	M	ex Assyria 68, ex Amarna 67.
Assiout	..	..	1949	3422	367	52	14	M	_To Greece, ren. CHRYSSOULA_
Kantara	..	..	1947	3213	366	52	13	M	
Karnak	..	..	1948	3198	366	52	13	M	
Kypros	..	..	1950	3499	368	52	13½	M	ex Aurania 67, ex Kypros 67.
Memphis	..	..	1947	3575	365	52	13½	M	
Tabor	..	..	1952	3694	385	55	14½	M	

Also tanker—**Busiris** (Trident Tankers Ltd.).

(NORWAY)

A/S J. LUDWIG MOWINCKELS REDERI

FUNNEL: *Yellow with black top separated by red, white and blue bands.*
HULL: *Grey with red boot-topping.*

Egda 1974 25000 M bulk

Egda	..	..	1957	5403	436	58	17	M	
Heina	..	..	1970	16500	550	80	16	M(A)	
Horda	..	..	1955	5734	467	58	15	M	
Lista	..	..	1970	16500	550	80	16	M(A)	
Norma	..	..	1963	5854	469	61	17	M	
Palma	..	..	1955	3972	412	55	15	M	
Sygna	..	..	1967	30503	713	98	16	M(A)	

Also tankers.

CIA. NACIONAL DE NAVEGACAO

FUNNEL: *Black.*

HULL: *Grey with green boot-topping.*

ROUTES: **A.** *Lisbon, Madeira, Portuguese East and West Africa, Cape Town and Durban.*
        B. *Lisbon, Macau and Dili (Timor).*

Name			Date	Tons Gross	Length (feet)	Breadth (feet)	Speed (knots)	Engines	Former Names
Angola	..	..	1948	13078	550	67	17	M(2)	
Beira	..	..	1963	8701	531	70	18	M	
India		..	1951	7631	432	59	14½	M(2)	
Mocambique	..		1949	12976	550	67	17	M(2)	
Mocamedes		..	1947	5508	450	59	13½	M	
Nacala	..		1966	8966	488	67	16	M	ex Hunan 68.
Niassa	..		1955	10742	497	64	16	M	
Principe Perfeito	..		1961	19383	625	79	20	ST(2)	
Rovuma	..	..	1946	5500	450	59	13½	M	
S. Thome	..		1938	5335	441	56	12	M	
Timor	..	..	1951	7656	432	59	14½	M(2)	

Also smaller ships.

NAESS DENHOLM & CO. LTD.

FUNNEL: *Black with blue " N " on white diamond on broad red band.*

HULL: *Grey with green boot-topping.*

Anglo Pacific Shipping Co. Ltd.

Iron Clipper	..	1961	23794	670	91	14	M(A)	ex Naess Clipper 64.

Anglo-Norness Shipping Co. Ltd.

Iron Cavalier	..	1962	23811	670	91	14	M(A)	ex Naess Cavalier 66
Naess Talisman*	..	1966	40769	820	104	15½	M(A)	

* Owned by Nile S.S. Co. Ltd.

Favorita Shipping Co. Ltd.

Darius	..	..	1962	25157	669	91	14	M(A)	ex Naess Clarion 69.

Turnbull Scott Shipping Co. Ltd.

Naess Parkgate	..	1966	40767	820	104	15½	M(A)

National Shipping Corporation: SAFARAZ RAFIQI

[Fotoship

National Shipping Corporation: TARBELA

[John G. Callis

Inverness Shipping Co. (Bermuda) Ltd.

Name	Date	Tons Gross	Length (feet)	Breadth (feet)	Speed (knots)	Engines	Former Names
Naess Trader ..	1957	6853	425	57	13	M(A)	

Norness Shipping Co. (Bermuda) Ltd.

Naess Pioneer ..	1960	19797	637	80	14	M(A)	To Greece, ren · A G H105 NICOLAOS

Also tankers and other ships.

(PAKISTAN)

NATIONAL SHIPPING CORPORATION

FUNNEL: *Black with letters " NSC " in white circle on broad blue band between two narrow white bands.*

HULL: *Grey, red boot-topping.*

Name			Date	Tons Gross	Length	Breadth	Speed	Engines	Former Names
Abasin	..	..	1964	6329	508	65	15	M	ex Peshawar 64.
Aziz Bhatti	..	..	1966	7236	499	67	15	M(A)	
Chenab	..	..	1965	6314	508	64	15	M	
Harappa	..	..	1954	6745	525	63	17	ST	ex Leipzig 70.
Haringhata	..	..	1954	7003	512	61	16	M	ex Reichenfels 70, ex Willi Rickmers 69, ex Kybfels 66.
Jhelum	..	..	1960	5922	466	61	15	M	ex Kirriemoor 64.
Kaptai	..	..	1967	10216	505	67	18	M(A)	
Karanphuli	..	..	1959	7036	502	62	14½	M	ex Albert Janus 65.
Karotua	..	..	1958	9221	488	63	15½	M(A)	ex Weybridge 67, ex Rossetti 64, ex Weybridge 64.
Mainamati	..	..	1955	6342	510	61	17	M	ex Tubingen 70.
Meonjodaro	..	..	1968	8917	507	65	18	M	
Padma	..	..	1958	7036	502	62	14½	M	ex Albert Vogler 64.
Pussur	..	..	1965	6441	498	63	16	M	ex Teesta 65.
Rangamati	..	..	1968	9101	507	65	18	M	
Ravi	..	..	1958	5935	466	61	14½	M	ex Jedmoor 64.
Rupsa	..	..	1958	8525	477	62	14	M	ex La Falda 64, ex Montcalm 58.
Sarfaraz Rafiqi	..	..	1966	7236	499	67	18	M(A)	
Shalamar	..	..	1969	9147	506	64	18	M	
Sipsah	..	..	1959	5577	463	60	15	ST	ex Mary Holt 65.
Sunderbans	..	..	1968	8917	507	65	18	M	
Surma	..	..	1951	5890	456	58	11	SR	ex Ramillies 66, ex Seawall 55.
Sutlej	..	..	1957	6356	496	62	16	M	ex Kalliopi Pateras 65.
Swat	..	..	1958	9223	488	63	15½	M(A)	ex Wimbledon 68, ex Port Wimbledon 65, ex Wimbledon 60.
Tarbela	..	..	1968	10216	505	67	18	M(A)	
Taxila	..	..	1968	9101	507	65	18	M	
Warsak	..	..	1968	10216	505	67	18	M(A)	

Also smaller ships.

NEDERLAND LINE (ROYAL DUTCH MAIL)
N.V. Stoomv Maats " Nederland "

FUNNEL: *Yellow with black top. Ships sailing in Nedlloyd Lines have white bordered blue disc with white letters " NLL ".*

HULL: *Black with red boot-topping.*

ROUTES:
- **A.** *Europe to Br. North Borneo, Philippines, China and Japan.*
- **B.** *Europe via Pacific islands to New Zealand and direct to Europe.*
- **C.** *Pacific Coast U.S.A. and Canada to South Coast East Asia and Persian Gulf.*
- **D.** *(Nedlloyd Lines). Various services between Gulf of Mexico, U.S.A. Atlantic ports or Great Lakes to Persian Gulf, India, Pakistan or Far East, also U.S.A. to Africa and Far East to South America.*

Name	Date	Tons Gross	Length (feet)	Breadth (feet)	Speed (knots)	Engines	Former Names
Bali ..	1947	9646	520	63	15	M	
Balong	1956	8789	477	66	16½	M	ex Batang 56.
Banda	1956	8785	477	66	16¼	M	
Banggai	1957	8613	477	66	16¼	M	
Batjan	1956	8789	477	66	16½	M	
Batu ..	1957	8838	477	66	16¼	M	
Bawean	1953	9525	494	65	16	M	
Bengkalis	1953	9474	514	65	16	M	ex Banka 57.
Billiton	1951	7445	493	66	16½	ST	
Karachi	1958	10891	536	67	17	M	
Karakorum	1958	10891	536	67	17	M	
Karimata ..	1953	10614	531	67	16½	M	
Karimun ..	1953	10614	531	67	16½	M	
Neder Ebro	1960	10275	522	67	17½	M	
Neder Eems	1959	10275	522	67	17½	M	
Neder Elbe	1959	10275	522	67	17½	M	
Neder Lek	1967	9638	532	78	20½	M	
Neder Linge	1967	9638	532	78	20	M	
Neder Rhone	1962	9900	537	71	19	M	
Neder Rijn	1962	10300	537	71	19	M	
Neder Waal	1959	10897	536	67	17½	M	
Neder Weser	1960	10959	536	67	17½	M	
Radja ..	1946	8330	492	70	16½	ST	ex Noord Brabant 46.
Rondo	1946	8354	492	70	16½	ST	ex Gelderland.
Rotti	1946	8358	492	70	16½	ST	ex Holland 46.
Trident Amsterdam	1970	11500	538	77	20	M(A)	

NEDLLOYD DEJIMA

NEDLLOYD KIMBERLEY

Cont.

VAN NIEVELT, GOUDRIAAN & CO'S STOOMV. MAATS N.V.

FUNNEL: *Yellow with white star on broad blue band.*

HULL: *Black with yellow line and red boot-topping or grey.*

Name	Date	Tons Gross	Length (feet)	Breadth (feet)	Speed (knots)	Engines	Former Names
Alcor ..	1957	6735	496	64	16	M	
Algol ..	1957	6735	496	64	16	M	
Algorab ..	1960	6723	496	64	16	M	
Alioth ..	1950	5123	459	58	15	M	ex Black Hawk 67.
Alkes ..	1957	6735	496	64	16	M	
Asmidiske ..	1958	11396	541	67	15	M(A)	
Asterope ..	1958	11396	541	67	15	M(A)	

Also smaller ships.

Megrez   1961   1279

ex Silver Comet, Garda

Nederland Line: NEDER LINGE ⊗   *[R. J. Weeks*

Nigerian National Shipping Line: RIVER NIGER   *[R. J. Weeks*

N.Y.K. Line: YAMAGUCHI MARU   [F. R. Sherlock

N.Y.K. Line: VIRGINIA MARU   J. Mathieson

NIGERIAN NATIONAL SHIPPING LINE LTD.

FUNNEL: *Green with black top, black band and white ' N '.*
HULL: *Pale green with darker green boot-topping.*

Name	Date	Tons Gross	Length (feet)	Breadth (feet)	Speed (knots)	Engines	Former Names
Ahmadu Bello ..	1963	6127	465	63	14½	M	
Dan Fodio	1950	6183	464	60	14½	M	ex La Sierra 59.
El Kanemi	1956	5660	452	60	14	M	ex Silverdene 60.
Herbert Macaulay	1957	8449	460	60	13½	M	ex Sussex Trader 64.
King Jaja	1955	5869	451	58	12	M	ex Tyria 59.
Nnamdi Azikiwe	1963	6063	465	63	14½	M	
Oduduwa	1954	5571	454	59	12½	M	ex North Cornwall 59.
Oranyan	1953	6009	466	60	13½	M	ex La Hacienda 60.
River Benue ..	1968	8003	448	62	16½	M	
River Ethiope ..	1969	8003	448	63	16½	M	
River Niger ..	1968	8003	448	62	16½	M	
River Ogun ..	1968	8003	448	63	16½	M	

NIPPON YUSEN KAISHA
N.Y.K. Line

FUNNEL: *Black with broad white band containing two red bands.*

HULL: *Black with white line and red boot-topping.*

ROUTES: **A.** *Round the World westbound from Yokohama and Japanese ports.*

B. *Pacific Coast, Vancouver, San Francisco and Los Angeles via Panama to Liverpool and London.*

C. *Other services from Japan cover Mediterranean, Asian and Australian ports, N. and S. America, Tarakan (Borneo) and Honolulu.*

Aizu Maru	1953	7724	494	63	16	M	
Akagi Maru ..	1951	7592	494	63	16	M	
Aki Maru	1954	7588	495	62	16	M(2)	
Akita Maru ..	1952	7583	494	63	16	M	
Arima Maru ..	1952	7529	495	63	16	M(2)	
Arita Maru ..	1953	7589	495	63	16	M(2)	
Asama Maru ..	1953	7542	492	63	16	M	
Aso Maru	1951	7522	495	63	16	M(2)	
Astoria Maru ..	1952	7503	494	62	16	M	
Atami Maru ..	1952	7575	492	63	16	M	
Atsuta Maru ..	1954	7725	495	63	16	M(2)	
Awata Maru ..	1952	7601	495	62	16	M(2)	
Boston Maru ..	1962	9049	513	64	15	M	
Caledonia Maru ..	1957	7637	450	60	14	M	
Chigusa Maru† ..	1969	24115	635	97	15	M(A)	
Fushimi Maru ..	1970	10800	515	74	18	M(A)	
Fuso Maru	1970	10800	515	74	18	M(A)	
Gloria Maru ..	1958	8298	480	63	16	M	
Hikawa Maru	1976	24700				M	cont.
Chishima Maru	1974	6,400				M	
Jinyu Maru (autos)	1975						

153

NIPPON YUSEN KAISHA *(continued)*

Name	*Date*	*Tons Gross*	*Length (feet)*	*Breadth (feet)*	*Speed (knots)*	*Engines*	*Former Names*
Hakusan Maru	197						cont.
Hakata Maru	1974	30700				M	cont.
Hakone Maru ..	1968	16240	614	85	20	M(A)	
Hakozaki Maru ..	1969	23669	697	97	15	M(A)	
Hampton Maru ..	1961	9071	514	64	15	M	
Heiyo Maru ..	1951	6753	463	59	13½	M	
Hikokane Maru ..	1958	8402	472	62	14	M	
Hikone Maru † ..	1957	7213	448	59	13¼	M	To Lib., ren. MEDITERRANEAN DARBY
Hikoshima Maru	1953	6553	449	58	14	M	
Himeji Maru ..	1956	7209	448	59	13¼	M	To Lib. ren. ATLANTIC DARBY
Ibaraki Maru ..	1965	9486	510	72	18½	M	
Ise Maru	1965	9486	510	72	18½	M	
Iwaki Maru ..	1966	10087	513	72	20	M	
Iwashiro Maru ..	1966	9974	513	74	18½	M(A)	
Iwate Maru ..	1966	9490	510	72	18	M	
Iyo Maru	1965	9501	510	72	18½	M	
Izumi Maru ..	1966	10039	518	74	20	M	
Izumo Maru ..	1966	10094	513	73	20	M(A)	
Kaga Maru ..	1966	11379	560	76	20¾	M	
Kai Maru	1966	11381	560	76	20¾	M	
Kawachi Maru ..	1966	11386	560	76	20¾	M	
Kii Maru	1966	11380	560	76	20¾	M	
Manila Maru ..	1954	9358	494	63	16	ST	
Matsubara Maru ..	1969	9719	488	70	17	M(A)	
Matsue Maru ..	1964	8210	459	66	14	M(A)	
Matsumae Mary ..	1965	9210	463	76	14	M(A)	
Matsushiro Maru ..	1966	9336	472	71	14½	M(A)	
Matsuyama Maru	1968	10369	476	72	17	M(A)	
Miyagi Maru ..	1966	10143	466	68	17	M(A)	
Nagara Maru ..	1958	8245	470	61	14¼	M	
Nagato Maru ..	1957	8261	470	61	15	M	
New York Maru ..	1953	7715	492	62	16	M(2)	
Noshiro Maru ..	1968	9465	494	68	18	M(A)	
Noto Maru ..	1968	9463	494	68	18	M(A)	
Oceania Maru ..	1958	8803	496	64	16	M	
Olympia Maru ..	1952	7385	468	60	14	M	
Sado Maru ..	1956	9383	509	64	17¾	M	
Saga Maru	1959	9287	513	64	18	M	
Sagami Maru ..	1955	9415	509	64	17¾	M	
Saikyo Maru ..	1961	9241	513	64	20	M	
Saitama Maru ..	1959	9385	510	64	17½	M	
Sanuki Maru ..	1955	9096	514	64	17¾	M	
Sapporo Maru ..	1961	9607	510	64	18	M	
Satsuma Maru ..	1956	9339	514	64	17¾	M	
Seta Maru	1960	9271	513	64	18	M	
Settsu Maru ..	1957	9416	514	64	17½	M	
Shiga Maru ..	1958	9375	514	64	18	M	
Shimane Maru ..	1958	9264	514	64	18	M	
Shizuoka Maru ..	1958	9242	509	64	18	M	
Sitka Maru ..	1965	8576	424	60	17	M(A)	
Soei Maru	1960	7170	447	59	18	M	
Sumida Maru ..	1960	9291	513	64	18	M	
Suruga Maru ..	1957	9379	509	64	17½	M	
Victoria Maru ..	1953	7519	495	62	16	M(2)	
Virginia Maru ..	1955	7479	450	61	16	M	
Wakakusa Maru ..	1968	7657	454	61	18	M(A)	
Wakamatsu Maru	1967	8394	460	61	18	M	
Wakasa Maru ..	1962	7327	439	62	16	M(A)	
Wakato Maru ..	1960	6953	431	61	15	M(A)	
Wakaura Maru ..	1969	7673	454	62	18	M(A)	
Yamagata Maru ..	1965	10039	528	76	19½	M	
Yamaguchi Maru	1965	10023	528	76	19½	M	
Yamanashi Maru	1962	9676	528	68	16	M(A)	
Yamashiro Maru ..	1963	10032	528	76	18	M	

Also tankers, bulk/ore carriers and other ships.

† Jointly owned with Showa Yusen K.K.

Norddeutscher Lloyd: MOSEL EXPRESS   [R. J. Weeks

Norddeutscher Lloyd: NECKARSTEIN   [R. J. Weeks

Norddeutscher Lloyd: HOLSTENSTEIN in April 1969   [*WSS Collection*

Fred Olsen: BOSPHORUS   [*John G. Callis*

NORDDEUTSCHER LLOYD (N.D.L.)

FUNNEL: *Yellow.*

HULL: *Black with red boot-topping.*

ROUTES: *See Hamburg-America Line.*
(BREMEN and EUROPA): Bremerhaven to New York.
Also cruising.

Name		Date	Tons Gross	Length (feet)	Breadth (feet)	Speed (knots)	Engines	Former Names
Badenstein	..	1968	10481	532	74	21	M	
Barenstein	..	1953	5547	499	59	16½	M(A)	
Bartenstein	..	1956	5911	498	60	17½	M	
Bayernstein	..	1968	10481	532	74	21	M	
Bieberstein	..	1953	5547	498	59	16½	M	
Birkenstein	..	1955	5854	498	61	17½	M	
Bischofstein	..	1956	5856	498	61	17½	M	
Blankenstein	..	1956	5911	498	61	17½	M	
Bodenstein	..	1957	5911	498	61	17½	M	
Brandenstein	..	1952	5628	498	59	16½	M	
Breitenstein	..	1956	5856	498	61	17½	M	
Bremen	..	1938	32360	697	90	23	ST(4)	ex Pasteur 59.
Buchenstein	..	1958	6233	482	65	18	M(A)	
Buntenstein	..	1959	6230	482	65	17½	M	
Burgenstein	..	1958	6215	482	65	18	M(A)	
Europa	..	1953	21514	600	77	19	M(2)	ex Kungsholm 65.
Friesenstein	..	1967	10481	532	74	21	M	
Havelstein	..	1954	6903	549	63	19	M	To Somali, ren. NANKUO
Hessenstein	..	1967	10481	533	74	21	M	To Ecuador
Holstenstein	..	1967	10481	532	74	21	M	
Illstein	..	1959	3049	414	53	14½	M	
Isarstein	..	1954	6900	549	63	18	M	
Lindenstein	..	1954	4849	434	57	18	M	ex Clary Thorden 65
Mosel Express	..	1969	13396	560	81	20	M(A)	
Melbourne Express		1970	24800	715	95	23	ST(A)	
Moselstein	..	1954	6928	549	63	18	M	
Nabstein	..	1959	3660	428	53	14½	M	
Neckarstein	..	1953	6993	549	63	19	M	
Ravenstein	..	1947	8036	546	65	17¼	M(3)	ex Bastogne 55.
Regenstein	..	1960	7357	527	65	18	M	
Reifenstein	..	1946	8071	546	64	17¼	M(3)	ex Houffalize 55.
Riederstein	..	1960	7375	527	65	18	M	
Rothenstein	..	1946	8113	546	64	17¼	M(3)	ex Stavelot 55.
Sachsenstein	..	1968	10481	531	74	21	M	
Schwabenstein	..	1967	10481	533	74	21	M	
Tannstein	..	1955	5596	498	60	17½	M	
Torstein	..	1955	5597	498	60	17½	M	
Travestein	..	1954	7008	549	63	19	M	
Werrastein	..	1953	6905	549	63	19	M	
Weser Express	..	1968	13382	543	81	20	M(A)	
Weserstein	..	1953	6996	549	63	19	M	
Wiedstein	..	1959	3049	414	53	14½	M	

Also smaller ships. Fleet to be merged with Hamburg America Line.

NORSHIPS FREIGHTERS INC.

FUNNEL: *Yellow with blue " N " on broad white band between two narrow blue bands.*

HULL: *Black with white line, red boot-topping.*

Name		Date	Tons Gross	Length (feet)	Breadth (feet)	Speed (knots)	Engines	Former Names
Lord Byron	..	1957	9364	501	63	14	M	
N. Zografia†	..	1959	11299	530	68	15	M	ex Lord Gladstone 69.

† Operates under Greek flag.

(NORWAY)

NORWEGIAN AMERICA LINE
(Den Norske Amerikalinje A/S)

FUNNEL: *Yellow with blue band bordered by white and red bands.*

HULL: *Grey, orange boot-topping with white line (passenger ships have no orange boot-topping).*

ROUTES: **A.** *Norwegian and Danish ports to New York.*
B. *Norwegian and Danish ports to Canada and Great Lakes.*
C. *Cruises.*
D. *Scandinavian, U.K. and Continental ports to East Africa and Madagascar.*

		Date	Tons	Length	Breadth	Speed	Engines	
Altafjord	..	1962	8719	505	63	16½	M(A)	
Bergensfjord	..	1956	18739	578	72	20	M(2) *To S'pore, ren. RASA SAYA*
Idelfjord	..	1960	5537	424	54	16	M	
Kongsfjord	..	1951	5934	469	58	15	M *To S'pore*
Norefjord	..	1953	5246	443	58	15	M *to Greece, ren. NISSOS ITHAK*
Sagafjord	..	1965	24002	620	80	20	M(2)	
Sunndalsfjord	..	1955	4621	433	57	15	M	ex Bow Plate 64.
Topdalsfjord	..	1959	5748	424	54	15	M	
Tyrifjord	..	1953	5243	443	58	15	M	
Vigrafjord	..	1963	6301	462	63	16½	M(A)	
Vindafjord	..	1959	8742	467	61	15	M	ex Thorscarrier 68.
Vistafjord	..	1960	7131	501	64	15	M	

Also smaller ships.

(NORWAY)

FRED OLSEN & CO.

FUNNEL: *Yellow with white and blue houseflag.*

HULL: *Grey with green boot-topping.*

		Date	Tons	Length	Breadth	Speed	Engines	
Baghdad	..	..	1956	2581	374	50	15	M	
Balblom	..	..	1948	1420	277	42	11	M(A)	
Baldrain	..	..	1947	1419	277	42	11	M(A)	
Balduin	..	..	1955	2224	290	43	10½	M(A)	
Balkis	..	..	1955	4212	374	50	15	M	
Balzac	..	..	1955	3614	346	48	15	M(A)	
Bandeirante	..	..	1960	5368	472	61	16	M(A)	
Bayard	..	..	1951	2374	346	46	15	M *to France, ren. Capitaine La*
Belgrano	..	..	1952	5986	433	54	18	M	ex Carib 69, ex Arawak 64.

Fred Olsen: BUFFALO

[John G. Callis

Oregon Steamship Co: LONDONER

[Malcolm Cranfield

FRED OLSEN & CO. (continued)

Name			Date	Tons Gross	Length (feet)	Breadth (feet)	Speed (knots)	Engines	Former Names
Bencomo	..	..	1950	2797	386	53	16	M	
Bergerac	..	..	1955	3607	346	48	15	M	
Black Prince†	..	..	1966	9500	465	67	22	M(2)	
Black Watch*	..	..	1966	9500	465	67	22	M(2)	
Blenheim	..	..	1970	10300	490	66	23	M(2)	
Bohemund	..	..	1950	2421	346	46	15	M(A)	*ToSpore, ren Kota Juvan*
Bolinas	..	..	1956	6735	508	66	17	M	
Bonanza	..	..	1953	7148	511	64	17	M	
Bonnard	..	..	1958	3640	349	50	16	M	
Borealis	..	..	1948	2919	376	53	14	M	
Borgland	..	..	1953	5658	469	58	15	M	ex Concordia Borgland 65, ex Borgland 65.
Bosphorus	..	..	1956	4027	378	52	15	M	
Botticelli	..	..	1959	3410	349	50	16	M	
Brabant	..	..	1956	2194	290	43	15	M(A)	
Braemar	..	..	1952	4766	374	53	16	M	
Braque	..	..	1958	3647	349	50	16	M	
Briseis	..	..	1957	2566	379	52	15½	M	
Bruno	..	..	1948	2752	383	53	17	M	
Buffalo	..	..	1953	6963	508	63	16½	M	
Burrard	..	..	1956	6737	508	65	17	M	

Borgny Dolphin 1974 M drilling rig

Also tankers and smaller ships.

† When operated by Bergen Line known as **Venus.**

* Jointly owned by Bergen Line and operates as **Jupiter** by that Company.

Borgen 1975 5000 M ferry

(NORWAY)

OLSEN & UGELSTAD

FUNNEL: *Black with ' OU ' monogram interrupting two white bands.*
HULL: *Grey with red boot-topping.*

Name			Date	Tons	Length	Breadth	Speed	Engines	Former Names
Dovrefjell	..	..	1967	26644	667	96	15	M(A)	
Filefjell	..	..	1968	26645	667	96	15	M(A)	
Gjendefjell	..	..	1961	12921	546	67	15	M(A)	ex Angeline 68.
Haukefjell	..	..	1962	3876	355	52	16	M	
Holtefjell	..	..	1965	23859	663	94	16	M(A)	
Makefjell	..	..	1959	4905	453	59	16	M	
Norefjell	..	..	1966	23864	663	94	16	M(A)	
Ornefjell	..	..	1955	4973	438	58	15	M	ex Havhok 65.
Sirefjell	..	..	1962	3876	355	52	16	M(A)	
Sognefjell	..	..	1967	23660	663	94	16	M(A)	
Varangfjell	..	..	1956	10774	520	63	12½	M	

Jotunfjell

Also tankers.

OREGON STEAMSHIP CO. LTD.

FUNNEL: *Green with white ' O ' on black diamond.   Black top.*
HULL: *Black.*

Name			Date	Tons	Length	Breadth	Speed	Engines	Former Names
Laurentian	..	..	1970	14809	575	75	15	M(A)	
Londoner	..	..	1961	6951	499	63	15	M	
Lutetian	..	..	1967	7880	512	66	15	M	

OVERSEAS CONTAINERS LTD.

(CONTAINER FLEETS LTD.)

(A Container Consortium formed by British & Commonwealth Group, Ocean S.S. Co Ltd., Furness Withy & Co. Ltd., and Peninsular & Oriental S.N. Co. Ltd.)

FUNNEL: *Green with ' O.C.L. ' insignia in white.*

HULL: *Mid-brunswick green.*

Furness Withy & Co. Ltd.

Name		Date	Tons Gross	Length (feet)	Breadth (feet)	Speed (knots)	Engines	Former Names
Botany Bay	..	1969	26876	746	100	$21\frac{1}{2}$	ST(A)	

P. & O. Steam Navigation Co. Ltd.

Name		Date	Tons Gross	Length (feet)	Breadth (feet)	Speed (knots)	Engines	Former Names
Discovery Bay	..	1969	26876	746	100	$21\frac{1}{2}$	ST(A)	
Moreton Bay	..	1969	26876	746	100	$21\frac{1}{2}$	ST(A)	

Ocean Steam Ship Co. Ltd.

Name		Date	Tons Gross	Length (feet)	Breadth (feet)	Speed (knots)	Engines	Former Names
Flinders Bay	..	1969	26756	746	100	$21\frac{1}{2}$	ST(A)	

Scottish Shire Line (Cayzer Irvine & Co. Ltd.)

Name		Date	Tons Gross	Length (feet)	Breadth (feet)	Speed (knots)	Engines	Former Names
Encounter Bay	..	1969	26756	746	100	$21\frac{1}{2}$	ST(A)	

Shaw Savill & Albion Co. Ltd.

Name		Date	Tons Gross	Length (feet)	Breadth (feet)	Speed (knots)	Engines	Former Names
Delphic ..	..	1949	10690	510	66	16	M(2)	
Jervis Bay ..	..	1970	26750	746	100	$21\frac{1}{2}$	ST(A)	

New Zealand Shipping Co. Ltd. (Managers)

Name		Date	Tons Gross	Length (feet)	Breadth (feet)	Speed (knots)	Engines	Former Names
Devon ..	..	1946	7237	495	65	16	ST	

Overseas Containers Ltd: MORETON BAY passing the uncompleted Opera House at Sydney, New South Wales   [*J. Mathieson*

Pacific Steam Navigation Co: OROYA—since renamed PACIFIC RANGER   [*Malcolm Cranfield*

PACIFIC STEAM NAVIGATION COMPANY
Furness Withy & Co. Ltd.

FUNNEL: *Yellow.*
HULL: *Black with green boot-topping.*
ROUTE: *Liverpool, London, Hull, Glasgow and Continental ports to Bermuda, Bahamas, U.S. Gulf ports and W. Coast of S. America.*

Name		Date	Tons Gross	Length (feet)	Breadth (feet)	Speed (knots)	Engines	Former Names
Chandeleur	..	1959	5217	386	54	14½	M	ex Cienfuegos 68.
Cotopaxi	.. ..	1954	8559	513	66	16	ST	
Eleuthera	.. ..	1959	5407	386	54	14½	M	
Kenuta	.. ..	1950	8494	513	66	16	ST	
Orcoma†	.. ..	1966	10300	509	70	18	M	
Orita	.. ..	1957	6311	475	64	17	M	ex Afric 68. TO HK, NH. HONG KONG ISLAND
Pacific Exporter	..	1957	6311	475	64	17	M	ex Oropesa 70, ex Aramaic 68.
Pacific Ranger	..	1956	6311	475	64	17	M	ex Oroya 70, ex Arabic 68.
Pizarro	.. ..	1955	8564	513	66	16	ST	
Potosi	.. ..	1955	8564	513	66	16	ST	
Somers Isle	..	1959	5515	396	54	14½	M	

† Owned by Nile S.S. Co. Ltd.

PALM LINE LTD.

FUNNEL: *Green with black top and green palm tree on white disc and band*
HULL: *Dark grey with red boot-topping.*

Name		Date	Tons Gross	Length	Breadth	Speed	Engines
Africa Palm	..	1953	5410	452	58	10½	M
Akassa Palm	..	1958	5797	473	62	13½	M
Andoni Palm	..	1958	5802	473	62	13¼	M
Badagry Palm	..	1956	5051	447	58	15	M
Bamenda Palm	..	1956	5154	447	58	13½	M
Elmina Palm	..	1957	5505	455	60	13¾	M
Enugu Palm	..	1958	5328	455	60	13½	M
Ibadan Palm	..	1959	5799	460	63	15	M
Ikeja Palm	..	1961	5816	460	63	15	M
Ilesha Palm	..	1961	5816	460	63	14	M
Ilorin Palm	..	1960	5658	460	63	15	M
Kano Palm	..	1958	8515	500	63	14½	M
Katsina Palm	..	1957	8510	500	63	14¼	M
Lagos Palm	..	1961	5927	474	63	16	M
Lobito Palm	..	1960	5923	474	63	16	M
Matadi Palm	..	1970	9500	485	69	16	M(A)

P. & O.
Peninsular and Oriental S.N. Co.

FUNNEL: *Yellow for* ARCADIA, IBERIA, HIMALAYA, CHUSAN, ORCADES, ORIANA, ORONSAY, ORSOVA *and* "STRATHS", *others black.* CANBERRA *has twin uptakes aft.*

Pacific Steam Navigation Co: ELEUTHERA [John G. Callis

Palm Line: BADAGRY FALM [R. J. Weeks

Palm Line: LOBITO PALM

[F. R. Sherlock

Palm Line: ELMINA PALM in May 1968

[John G. Callis

Strathnaver 1962 9890 M ex Jumna   Strathairn 1963 9874 M ex Koh...
Strathtay 1962 7277 M ex Trebartha   Strathnevis 1963 8380 M ex Nu...
Strathtevot 1961 7277 M ex Trefusis   Strathnewton 1959 8388 M ex Nur...
Strathtr... 1963 6975 M ex Treneglos

P. & O. (continued)

HULL: *White with green or red boot-topping for ships with yellow funnels, black with white line and red boot-topping for the remainder.*

ROUTES: **A.** *Southampton to Australia via Las Palmas, Capetown, etc. Some vessels continue from Australia to Honolulu, San Francisco and Vancouver.*

B. *Cruising mainly from Southampton.*

C. *"Strath" Service—London via Cape Town to Hong Kong, Kobe, and Yokohama, returning via Panama Canal to Rotterdam, Hamburg and London.*

D. *"Pando" Service—London to Malaysia, Singapore, Philippines, Taiwan, Hong Kong and Japan.*

Bison 1975
Buffalo 1975

Tkr. Post Endeavour 1974 151,700 M

Strathduns 197
Strathdyce 197

Name	Date	Tons Gross	Length (feet)	Breadth (feet)	Speed (knots)	Engines	Former Names
Arcadia	1954	29871	721	91	22½	ST(2)	
Canberra	1961	44807	819	103	27½	TE(A)(2)	
Cannanore	1949	6845	485	63	14½	M	
Chusan	1950	24318	673	85	22	ST(2)	
Himalaya	1949	27989	709	91	22	ST(2)	
Iberia	1954	29614	719	91	22½	ST(2)	
Orcades	1948	28472	709	94	22	ST(2)	
Oriana	1960	41910	804	97	27½	ST(2)	
Oronsay	1951	28117	709	94	22	ST(2)	
Orsova	1954	29091	723	91	22½	ST(2)	
Pando Cape	1954	8800	527	69	18	ST	ex Ballarat 68.
Pando Cove	1951	9236	523	69	17	ST	ex Comorin 68, ex Singapore 64.
Pando Gulf	1957	8753	520	69	17½	ST	ex Woodarra 68. to Ben Lin ren. Bena
Pando Head	1948	8925	522	67	17	ST	ex Surat 68.
Pando Point	1957	8753	520	69	17½	ST	ex Waroonga 68. to Ben Li ren. Ben
Pando Sound	1954	8777	527	69	18	ST	ex Bendigo 68.
Pando Strait	1952	9235	523	69	17	ST	ex Sunda 68.
Patonga	1953	10070	500	65	16	ST	
Strathardle	1967	12539	563	79	21	M	
Strathbrora	1967	12539	563	79	21	M	
Strathconon	1967	12539	563	79	21	M	

Meynell (bulk) 1974 69,900 M

See also Hain-Nourse Ltd., Overseas Containers Ltd. and Trident Tankers Ltd.

Sun Princess 1975 18,000
⊗ Island Princess 1972 20,000   ex Spirit of London
Strathardle 1974 9,200 M   to Ellerman, ren. CITY OF...
Strathdevon 1975 9,200 M
Strathdick 197
Strathdoon 197
Strathnaird ex Nigaristan 1970
Stratharlick ex Tabaristan 1969 ... 9630 M

(POLAND)

POLISH OCEAN LINES

FUNNEL: *Yellow with red band and device.*

HULL: *Black or grey, red or green boot-topping.*

Name	Date	Tons Gross	Length (feet)	Breadth (feet)	Speed (knots)	Engines
Adam Asnyk	1974	9631				
Adolf Warski	1959	6718	505	64	16	M
Aleksander Zawadzki	1966	5730	501	64	16	M
Andrzej Strug	1963	6919	505	64	16	M
Beniowski	1960	7299	517	66	16	M
Boleslaw Bierut*	1957	6674	505	64	16	M
Boleslaw Chrobry	1967	5527	477	62	16	M
Boleslaw Smialy	1967	5527	477	62	16	M
Chopin	1959	6987	502	62	16	M(2)
Boleslaw Prus	1974	9800				M

P & O: CANBERRA passing a Sandringham flying-boat which operates between Sydney and
Lord Howe Island
[J. Y. Freeman

P & O: IBERIA   [Bert Moody

P & O: CHITRAL (Transferred to Eastern & Australian Steamship Co. Ltd.) [*John G. Callis*

P & O: STRATHARDLE [*F. R. Sherlock*

P & O: ORCADES

Polish Ocean Lines: STEFAN BATORY

Polish Ocean Lines: WYSPIANSKI   [R. J. Weeks

Port Line: PORT HUON   [J. Y. Freeman

Name	Date	Tons Gross	Length (feet)	Breadth (feet)	Speed (knots)	Engines	Former Names
Czacki	1965	5576	478	61	16	M	
Djakarta*	1961	6915	505	64	16	M	
Domeyko	1962	5697	478	61	16	M	
Emilia Plater	1959	6718	505	64	16	M	
Florian Ceynowa	1957	6784	505	64	15	M	
Francesco Nullo	1964	5668	501	63	16	M	
General Bem	1940	5307	439	56	12	M	ex Dona Aniceta 50.
General Sikorski	1957	6785	505	64	15	M	
Grunwald	1968	6380	504	65	16	M	
Gwardia Ludowa	1968	5621	501	62	16	M	
Hanka Sawicka	1962	6944	506	64	16	M	
Hanoi	1960	6914	505	64	16	M	
Hel	1969	10970	546	77	16	M(A)	
Henryk Jendza	1966	5581	478	61	16	M	
Heweliusz	1962	5700	479	61	16	M	
Jan Matejko	1959	6748	505	64	16	M	
Janek Krasicki	1960	6904	505	64	16	M	
Jozef Conrad	1961	5752	487	63	16	M	
Jozef Wybicki	1966	5713	501	64	17	M	
Jurata	1970	11000	546	77	16	M	
K. I. Galczynski	1964	5584	478	61	16	M	
Kapitan Kosko	1957	6629	505	64	15½	M	
Kilinski *[handwritten: Kalinowski]*	1944	7697	455	62	16	ST	ex Mexico Victory 47.
Kochanowski	1962	5731	487	63	16	M	
Konin	1968	6283	505	68	16	M	
Konopnicka	1961	9660	505	64	16	M	
Kosciuszko *[handwritten: KWidzyn 1974 3400 / Kopalnia Sosnowiec 1974 8600]*	1939	7707	515	63	10	RT / M	ex Admiral Nachimov 47, ex Rhein-*[handwritten: built]*fels 46.
Kraszewski	1963	7151	503	67	16	M	
Lelewel	1962	7817	505	64	16	M	
Leningrad	1965	5730	501	64	16	M	
Lenino	1964	5667	501	64	16	M	
Ludwik Solski	1960	6904	505	64	16	M	
Merceli Nowotko	1956	6660	505	64	15	M	
Mieszko I	1967	5513	477	62	16	M	
Moniuszko	1960	6947	502	62	16	M(A)	
Norwid	1962	5512	463	63	16	M	
Nowowiejski	1962	7088	503	62	16	M(A)	
Olesnica	1959	5384	407	54	15½	M	
Paderewski	1960	7230	501	62	16	M	
Pawel Szwydkoj	1965	5578	478	61	16	M	
Pekin	1960	6914	505	64	16	M	
Phenian	1961	6923	505	64	16	M	
Piotr Dunin	1966	7000	501	64	16	M	
Przyjazn Narodow	1937	8876	479	59	12	M(2)	ex Marchen Maersk 51, ex Perida 46, ex Caldera 41, ex Marchen Maersk 41.
Pulkownik Dabek	1970	8650	502	64	16	M	
Reymont	1958	6608	505	64	16	M	
Romer	1964	5587	479	61	16	M	
Sienkiewicz	1959	5264	455	59	16	M	
Slowacki	1924	5262	392	50	10	M(2)	ex Rena 56, ex Fordefjord 37, ex Emma Maersk.
Smolny	1968	5726	501	64	16	M	
Sniadecki	1963	5701	479	61	15	M	
Stanislaw Dubois	1965	5729	501	63	16	M	
Staszic	1963	5702	478	61	16	M	
Stefan Batory	1952	15024	503	69	16½	ST	ex Maasdam 68.
Stefan Czarniecki	1967	6500	504	65	16	M	
Stefan Okrzeja	1957	6620	505	64	16	M	
Szymanowski *[handwritten: Syn Pulku 1974 20600]*	1961	7178	503	62	16	M(2)	

Name		Date	Tons Gross	Length (feet)	Breadth (feet)	Speed (knots)	Engines	Former Names
Traugutt	.. ..	1964	5667	501	64	16	M	
Warynski	.. ..	1936	4361	425	56	10	M	ex General Brusiloff 47, ex Athen 46.
Westerplatte	..	1967	8700	504	65	16½	M	
Wieniawski	..	1962	7099	501	62	16	M(A)	
Wladyslaw Broniewski	..	1963	6919	504	64	16	M	
Wyspianski	..	1962	5731	487	63	15½	M	
Zabrze	..	1969	6576	444	58	16	M	
Zakopane	..	1968	6576	444	58	16	M	
Zambrow	..	1969	6576	444	58	16	M	
Zamenhof	..	1959	6698	502	62	16	M(A)	
Zamosc	..	1968	6588	444	58	16	M	
Zawichost	..	1970	6581	444	58	16	M	
Zawiercie	..	1969	6581	444	58	16	M	
Zeromski	.. ..	1960	5309	455	59	15½	M	

Uniwersytet Wroclawski 30700   1974   M

Also other ships.   * Detained since 1967 in Suez Canal.

PORT LINE LTD.

FUNNEL: *Red with black top and thin black rings.*

HULL: *Grey with red boot-topping.*

ROUTES: *U.K. ports to Australia and New Zealand.*
Montreal, New York to Australia and New Zealand via Panama Canal.

Name		Date	Tons	Length	Breadth	Speed	Engines	
Port Adelaide	..	1951	7828	490	65	15½	M	
Port Albany*	..	1965	8362	489	68	18	M	
Port Alfred	..	1961	10487	500	68	17	M	
Port Auckland	..	1949	10200	560	70	17	M(2)	
Port Brisbane	..	1949	10176	560	70	17	M(2)	
Port Burnie	..	1966	8374	489	68	18	M	
Port Caroline	..	1968	12398	612	81	21½	M(2)	
Port Chalmers	..	1968	12398	612	81	21½	M(2)	
Port Huon*	..	1965	8362	489	68	18	M	
Port Invercargill†		1958	10463	490	66	15½	M	
Port Launceston	..	1957	10468	491	66	15½	M	
Port Lincoln	..	1946	7249	488	62	15	M	
Port Lyttelton	..	1947	7413	488	64	15	M	
Port Melbourne‡		1955	10205	533	70	17	M(2)	To Garras, Greece, ren. D
Port Montreal	..	1954	8548	469	64	16	M	
Port Nelson	..	1951	8184	490	65	15½	M	
Port New Plymouth		1960	11194	561	74	18	M(2)	
Port Nicholson	..	1962	11711	574	76	18	M(2)	
Port Phillip	..	1942	9947	524	68	16	M(2)	
Port Pirie	..	1947	10537	529	68	16	M(2)	
Port St. Lawrence		1961	8297	500	68	17	M	
Port Sydney	..	1955	9189	533	70	17	M(2)	to Garras, Greece, ren.
Port Townsville	..	1951	8170	489	65	15½	M	
Port Victor*	..	1943	10390	529	68	16	M(2)	
Port Vindex	..	1943	10480	524	68	16	M(2)	
Port Wellington	..	1946	10569	529	68	16	M(2)	

* Owned by Cunard S.S. Co. Ltd.
† Detained in Suez Canal since 1967, abandoned to Insurers.
‡ Operated by Compass Line between Australia and South Africa.

Port Line: PORT CHALMERS near Dunedin, New Zealand [*Malcolm Cranfield*

Port Line: PORT NEW PLYMOUTH [*F. W. Hawks*

Prince Line: LANCASTRIAN PRINCE   [F. R. Sherlock

Ropner Shipping Co: STONEPOOL   [J. Y. Freeman

POWER S.S. CO. LTD.

O. Gross & Sons Ltd.

FUNNEL: *Black " OG " on yellow with black top.*

HULL: *Black with red boot-topping.*

Name	Date	Tons Gross	Length (feet)	Breadth (feet)	Speed (knots)	Engines	Former Names
Huntsland	1954	6515	477	64	15	M	

PRINCE LINE LTD.

Furness Withy & Co. Ltd.

FUNNEL: *Dark red with black top, black base and black band, and white Prince of Wales' feathers.*

HULL: *Grey with red boot-topping.*

ROUTE: *U.K. and Continent to Mediterranean, and general trading.*

Name	Date	Tons Gross	Length (feet)	Breadth (feet)	Speed (knots)	Engines	Former Names
African Prince† ..	1955	3596	372	53	13½	M	ex Pinemore 65.
Black Prince ..	1955	3597	372	53	13½	M	
Chiltern Prince ..	1970	1570	285	47	15	M(A)	
Lancastrian Prince	1960	4800	372	53	13½	M	
Malvern Prince ..	1969	1570	284	48	15	M(A)	
Mendip Prince ..	1970	1590	285	47	13½	M(A)	
Southern Prince ..	1956	7731	467	61	14	M	ex Medic 60, ex Southern Prince.
Western Prince ..	1955	7726	467	61	14	M	ex Manchester Trader 69, ex Western Prince 63, ex Zealandic 60, ex Western Prince 57.

† Owned by Johnston Warren Lines Ltd.

PURVIS SHIPPING CO. LTD.

The Aviation & Shipping Co. Ltd.

FUNNEL: *Black with red " P " on broad white band.*

HULL: *Black, white bulwark line and red boot-topping.*

Name	Date	Tons Gross	Length (feet)	Breadth (feet)	Speed (knots)	Engines	Former Names
Avisfaith	1962	7868	461	60	14	M	

(WESTERN GERMANY)
RICKMERS-LINIE G.m.b.H.

FUNNEL: *Black with houseflag on broad white band.*

HULL: *Black.*

RICKMERS-LINIE G.m.b.H. (continued)

Name		Date	Tons Gross	Length (feet)	Breadth (feet)	Speed (knots)	Engines	Former Names
Mai Rickmers	..	1957	10631	516	67	15	M	ex Erik Blumenfeld 65.
Paul Rickmers	..	1955	7910	483	61	14¾	M	
Peter Rickmers	..	1962	9572	524	67	16	M	
R. C. Rickmers	..	1957	8127	494	61	15	M	*To Somalia, ren · MALTIN*

SIR R. ROPNER & CO. LTD.

Ropner Shipping Co. Ltd.

FUNNEL: *Green with red and white check square.*
HULL: *Green, some with white line and light green boot-topping.*

Name		Date	Tons Gross	Length	Breadth	Speed	Engines	
Stonepool	.. ..	1966	27049	718	90	16	M(A)	
Wandby	.. ..	1959	11545	519	67	14	M(A)	*To Greece, ren · Sea Ranger*
Ruby		*1971*	*57250*					
Iron Somersby		*1971*	*57250*					

Pool Shipping Co. Ltd.

Name		Date	Tons	Length	Breadth	Speed	Engines
Bridgepool	..	1962	11428	522	68	14½	M(A)

(NETHERLANDS)

ROYAL INTEROCEAN LINES

Koninklijke Java—China Paketvaart Lijnen N.V. & Koninklijke Paketvaart Maats.

FUNNEL: *Black with crown on white diamond on red and blue panel.*
HULL: *Black with red boot-topping. (Some TJI... ships have white hulls).*
ROUTES:
A. *Japanese ports, Hong Kong, Singapore, Mauritius, Lourenco Marques, Durban, Cape Town, Rio de Janeiro, Santos, Montevideo, Buenos Aires.*
B. *Japanese ports, Hong Kong, Singapore to East, South and West Africa.*
C. *East and South African ports to Australian and New Zealand ports.*
D. *Bombay, Colombo, Singapore, to Australian ports.*
E. *Melbourne, Sydney, Brisbane, Japanese ports, Hong Kong, Sydney, Melbourne.*
F. *Hong Kong, Singapore, Lautoka/Suva, Auckland, Napier, Wellington, Lyttelton, Dunedin.*
G. *Singapore, Brisbane, Sydney, Melbourne.*

Name		Date	Tons	Length	Breadth	Speed	Engines
Hollands Brink*	..	1970	16170	576	75	15½	M(A)
Hollands Burcht*		1965	16575	612	75	15	M(A)
Hollands Diep*	..	1961	9631	509	64	13½	M
Hollands Dreef*	..	1962	9645	501	64	13½	M

Royal Interocean Lines: STRAAT ADELAIDE, since renamed SAFOCEAN ADELAIDE
[J. Mathieson

Royal Interocean Lines: STRAAT LAGOS, owned by Koninklijke Paketvaart Maatschappij
(Royal Packet Co)   [Fotoship

Royal Interocean Lines: STRAAT CHATHAM

[V. H. Young

Royal Netherlands Steamship Co: NEPTUNUS

[R. J. Weeks

Name	Date	Tons Gross	Length (feet)	Breadth (feet)	Speed (knots)	Engines	Former Names
Hollands Duin* ..	1961	9645	501	64	$13\frac{1}{2}$	M	
Straat Agulhas ..	1969	10484	528	76	20	M	
Straat Algoa* ..	1969	10484	528	76	20	M	
Straat Bali ..	1953	8079	518	69	$16\frac{1}{2}$	M	
Straat Banka ..	1952	9138	472	64	17	M	
Straat Chatham ..	1962	5434	455	62	17	M	
Straat Clarence ..	1959	5424	455	62	17	M	
Straat Clement ..	1959	5251	455	62	17	M	
Straat Colombo ..	1962	7553	455	62	17	M	
Straat Cook ..	1956	5082	439	60	16	M	
Straat Cumberland	1960	5434	455	62	17	M	
Straat Fiji ..	1966	9129	514	67	20	M	
Straat Florida ..	1966	9126	514	67	20	M	
Straat Franklin* ..	1963	9118	515	67	20	M	
Straat Frazer* ..	1963	9069	515	67	20	M	
Straat Freetown ..	1963	9094	515	67	20	M	
Straat Fremantle..	1964	9130	515	67	20	M	
Straat Fushimi ..	1965	9102	514	67	20	M	
Straat Futami ..	1965	9104	514	67	20	M	
Straat Hobart* ..	1968	10217	531	72	20	M	
Straat Holland* ..	1967	10184	531	72	20	M	
Straat Hong Kong	1968	10184	531	72	20	M	
Straat Honshu ..	1968	10217	531	72	20	M	
Straat Johore ..	1957	5446	455	62	16	M	
Straat Lagos* ..	1958	6867	478	57	$14\frac{1}{2}$	M	ex Van der Hagen 67
Straat Le Maire* ..	1958	7029	478	57	$14\frac{1}{2}$	M	ex Van Heemskerck 66.
Straat Lombok* ..	1957	5087	439	60	16	M	
Straat Luanda* ..	1958	7073	478	57	$14\frac{1}{2}$	M	ex Van Linschoten 67.
Straat Luzon* ..	1958	6863	478	57	$14\frac{1}{2}$	M	ex Van Spilbergen 67.
Straat Madura* ..	1956	5082	439	60	16	M	
Straat Magelhaen	1958	7047	506	67	16	M	
Straat Mozambique	1954	8072	518	69	$16\frac{1}{2}$	M	
Straat Rio ..	1960	7041	506	67	17	M	
Straat Singapore ..	1957	5292	455	62	16	M	
Straat Torres ..	1956	5076	439	60	16	M	
Straat Towa ..	1957	6740	490	63	17	M	ex Towa 66.
Straat van Diemen	1959	7142	506	67	$16\frac{1}{2}$	M	
Tjibantjet	1952	8098	472	62	16	M	
Tjiliwong	1959	3674	326	52	15	M	
Tjiluwah	1951	8978	479	63	$16\frac{1}{2}$	M(2)	
Tjimanuk	1959	3674	326	52	15	M	
Tjinegara	1951	9067	472	64	17	M	ex Straat Makassar 56.
Tjipondok	1945	7646	455	62	15	ST	ex Hillsdale Victory 46.
Tjitarum	1959	3674	326	52	15	M	
Tjiwangi	1951	9000	479	63	$16\frac{1}{2}$	M(2)	

Also smaller ships.   * Owned by Royal Packet Company (K.P.M.).

(NETHERLANDS)
Zodiac Shipping Co. Ltd.

Safocean Adelaide	1968	10484	528	76	20	M	ex Straat Adelaide 70.
Safocean Amsterdam ..	1968	10484	528	76	20	M	ex Straat Amsterdam 70.

(SOUTH AFRICA)
Capricorn Lines (Pty) Ltd.

Name	Date	Tons Gross	Length (feet)	Breadth (feet)	Speed (knots)	Engines	Former Names
Safocean Albany ..	1968	10484	528	76	20	M	ex Straat Accra 70.
Safocean Auckland	1968	10484	528	76	20	M	ex Straat Auckland 70.

ROYAL MAIL LINES LTD.
Furness Withy & Co. Ltd.

FUNNEL: *Yellow.*

HULL: *Black or white.*

ROUTES: **A.** *U.K. ports to West Indies and Central American ports.*
B. *U.K. ports to South America.*
C. *U.K. ports and Continental ports to North Pacific coast ports via Panama Canal.*
D. *Cruising* (ANDES).

Name			Date	Tons	Length	Breadth	Speed	Engines	Former Names
Albany	..	..	1957	7299	445	59	14	M	
Andes	..		1939	25895	669	84	21	ST(2)	
Derwent	..	..	1949	11207	561	72	17	ST(2)	ex Persic 69.
Douro	..	..	1946	9706	480	66	15	M(2)	ex Hornby Grange 69.
Loch Loyal		..	1957	10405	503	68	16	M	To Taiwan
Lombardy	..		1958	8105	460	60	14	M	ex Manchester Freighter 69, ex Cairnforth 65.
Picardy	..		1957	7102	445	59	14	M	
Reina del Mar*	..		1956	20747	601	78	18	ST(2)	
Thessaly	..		1957	7083	445	59	14	M	

* On charter to Union Castle Mail S.S. Co.

ROYAL NETHERLANDS STEAMSHIP CO. LTD.
Koninklijke Nederlandsche Stoomboot Maatschappij N.V.

FUNNEL: *Black with two white bands widely separated.*

HULL: *Black or grey, red boot-topping.*

Name			Date	Tons	Length	Breadth	Speed	Engines
Achilles	..	..	1959	6134	424	58	16	M
Archimedes		..	1960	6235	457	58	16	M
Ares ..	..	..	1959	6135	457	58	16¼	M
Aristoteles		..	1962	6230	457	58	16	M
Ceres	..		1959	6235	457	58	16¼	M

Name		Date	Tons Gross	Length (feet)	Breadth (feet)	Speed (knots)	Engines	Former Names
Diogenes	.. ..	1960	6236	457	58	16¼	M	
Ganymedes	.. ..	1961	6236	457	58	16	M	
Hercules	.. ..	1963	6170	457	58	16	M	
Hermes	.. ..	1962	6170	457	58	16	M	
Mercurius	.. ..	1966	5153	477	64	18	M	
Neptunus	.. ..	1967	5163	477	64	18	M	
Oranje Nassau	..	1957	7537	432	57	15½	M	
Palamedes	.. ..	1961	6150	457	58	16¼	M	
Pericles	.. ..	1960	6236	457	58	16	M	
Prins der Nederlanden	..	1957	7552	432	57	15½	M	
Socrates	.. ..	1960	6155	457	58	16	M	
Ulysses	.. ..	1962	6155	456	58	16	M	

And a large fleet of smaller ships.

(NETHERLANDS)
ROYAL ROTTERDAM LLOYD
Koninklijke Rotterdamsche Lloyd N.V.

FUNNEL: *Black. Ships sailing in Nedlloyd Lines have white bordered blue disc with white letters " NLL ".*

HULL: *Silver grey with white line, orange boot-topping.*

ROUTES: **A.** *Rotterdam and Antwerp to Singapore and Indonesia.*

B. *Pacific ports of N. America to Philippines, Indonesia, Malaya, India, Pakistan, East and South Africa.*

Name		Date	Tons	Length	Breadth	Speed	Engines	
Abel Tasman								cont.
Ampenan	..	1950	9947	529	67	17	ST	
Bengalen	..	1956	9817	598	66	16	ST	
Blitar	..	1949	9384	515	63	16	M(2)	to Indonesia
Garoet	..	1948	9823	515	63	16	M(2)	
Leuve Lloyd	..	1966	9603	532	78	21	M	
Limburg	..	1946	8374	492	70	16½	ST	
Loire Lloyd	..	1967	9649	532	78	21	M	
Maas Lloyd	..	1956	9706	529	66	18	M	
Madison Lloyd	..	1960	9733	528	66	18	M	
Main Lloyd	..	1962	9735	529	66	18	M	
Marne Lloyd	..	1957	9723	529	66	18	M	
Mersey Lloyd	..	1959	9732	529	66	18	M	
Merwe Lloyd	..	1957	9709	529	66	18	M	
Mississippi Lloyd		1958	9723	529	66	18	M	
Musi Lloyd	..	1957	9723	529	66	18	M	
Overijsel	..	1946	8364	492	70	16½	ST	
Schelde Lloyd	..	1958	8328	545	70	17½	M	
Schie Lloyd	..	1959	8321	545	70	17½	M	
Seine Lloyd	..	1961	8244	545	70	17½	M	
Utrecht	..	1947	8346	492	70	16½	ST	
Wonogiri	..	1953	7569	508	66	16	M	
Wonorato	..	1954	7512	508	66	16	M	
Wonosari	..	1952	7583	508	66	16	M	
Wonosobo	..	1954	7502	508	66	16	M	
Zeeland	..	1946	8372	492	70	16½	ST	

Royal Rotterdam Lloyd: MARNELLOYD [*F. W. Hawks*

Sven Salen: SINGO in the Bristol Channel [*Malcolm Cranfield*

SVEN SALEN A/B

Salenrederierna A/B

FUNNEL: *Blue with white ' S ' and white brackets above and below.*

HULL: *White.*

Name			Date	Tons Gross	Length (feet)	Breadth (feet)	Speed (knots)	Engines	Former Names
Antigua	..	..	1960	8283	493	62	18½	ST	
Argonaut	..	..	1964	8247	490	62	19	M	
Atitlan	..	..	1960	8066	488	62	18½	M	
Atlantide	..	..	1960	8069	488	62	18½	M	
Ballade	..	..	1962	6929	450	60	19	ST	
Barcarolle	..	..	1962	6933	450	60	19	ST	
Biskopso	..	..	1956	13685	536	71	15	M(A)	To Cyprus, ren · ATHANASIA COMNINOS
Bjorno*	..	..	1955	4473	360	52	12	M(A)	
Bolero	..	..	1961	6932	450	60	19	ST	
Cayman	..	..	1956	6185	444	57	18½	M	
Hispaniola	..	..	1956	6194	444	56	18½	M	
Husaro	..	..	1961	4531	410	57	15	M(A)	
Ledaro*	..	..	1955	8885	489	59	15	M(A)	ex Vindafjord 64.
San Benito	..	..	1968	6412	489	64	20	M	
San Blas	..	..	1967	6415	489	64	20	M	
San Bruno	..	..	1967	6414	489	64	20	M	
Segero	..	..	1962	6671	410	57	15	M(A)	
Singo*	..	..	1962	4822	360	52	13	M(A)	
Snowstorm			1972	11422	569	81	22	M	

Also tankers.   * Ore/oil carrier.

CHR. SALVESEN LTD.

FUNNEL: *Red with narrow white band and blue top.*

HULL: *Black with red boot-topping.*

Inverleith	..	..	1961	15628	598	75	15	M(A)	ex Cressington Court 66, ex Hector Halcyon 62.
Salambria	..	..	1964	5903	485	62	15	M	
Salmela	..	..	1961	6033	487	62	15	M	
Salvada	..	..	1961	5954	485	62	15	M	
Salvina	..	..	1963	5954	485	62	15	M	
Soutra (drilling ship)			1958	6733					

Also smaller ships.

SCINDIA S.N. CO. LTD.

FUNNEL: *Black with broad yellow band.*

HULL: *Black with white line and red boot-topping.*

Sven Salen: SAN BENITO   [L. R. Mugridge

Scindia S.N. Co: JALARASHMI   [Malcolm Cranfield

Name	Date	Tons Gross	Length (feet)	Breadth (feet)	Speed (knots)	Engines	Former Names
Jaladhan	1956	6527	509	64	17	M	
Jaladhanya ..	1957	6527	509	64	17	M	
Jaladharati ..	1957	6527	509	64	17	M	
Jaladharma ..	1957	6527	509	64	17	M	
Jaladhir	1957	6527	509	64	17	M	
Jaladhruv ..	1956	6527	509	64	17	M	
Jaladuhita ..	1958	6036	480	63	17	M	ex Lucie 59.
Jaladurga ..	1960	6286	505	64	17	M	
Jaladuta ..	1959	6288	505	64	17	M	
Jalaganga ..	1958	5869	453	60	14	M	ex Silverlake 63.
Jalagirija ..	1963	10694	510	69	15	M	ex Rosewood 68.
Jalagomati ..	1958	6487	499	62	14½	M	ex Jalasiltonhall 63.
Jalagopal ..	1955	6805	497	63	14	M	ex Sitanja 59.
Jalagouri ..	1957	5869	453	60	14	M	ex Silverforce 64.
Jalajaya ..	1966	8305	520	68	16	M	
Jalajyoti ..	1966	8302	520	68	16	M	ex Apj Ambar 66.
Jalakala ..	1964	6482	502	66	16¾	M	
Jalakanta ..	1965	6526	502	67	16½	M	
Jalakendra ..	1965	9379	502	66	16½	M	
Jalakirti ..	1961	6901	502	66	16¾	M	
Jalakrishna..	1960	6888	502	66	16¾	M	
Jalamadhuri ..	1955	4486	438	57	13	ST	ex Lannion 64.
Jalamani ..	1970	9300	497	67	—	M	
Jalamanjari ..	1956	4486	438	56	13	ST	ex Meudon 64.
Jalamayur ..	1970	9350	497	67	—	M	
Jalamoti ..	1955	4486	438	56	13	ST	ex Gaillon 64.
Jalapalaka ..	1961	9292	497	62	16	M	ex Clan Fraser 65.
Jalapankhi ..	1961	9242	497	62	16	M	ex Clan Ferguson 65.
Jalarajan ..	1966	11323	525	71	16	M(A)	
Jalarashmi ..	1966	11323	525	71	16	M(A)	
Jalaratna ..	1967	11323	525	71	16	M(A)	
Jalatarang ..	1963	12089	540	70	15	M(A)	ex Bente Brovig 69.
Jalaveera ..	1958	5074	476	58	12	M	
Jalavihar ..	1955	5086	476	58	12	M	ToGreece, ren. Katerina
Jalavijaya ..	1955	5085	476	58	12	M	
Jalavikram* ..	1958	5067	476	58	14	M	
Jalavishnu ..	1956	5078	476	58	12	M	
Jalazad ..	1955	6199	499	61	14	M	
Jaljawahar ..	1955	6199	499	61	14	M	
Narottam Morarjee	1967	29966	730	94	15	M(A)	ex Orm Jarl 69.

Also smaller ships.

SEABRIDGE SHIPPING LTD.

(This bulk carrier consortium formed by the undermentioned companies operates the ships on long-term charter on general bulk carrying.)

Bibby Brothers & Company

(BRITAIN STEAMSHIP CO. LTD.)

Atlantic Bridge ..	1968	44842	810	106	15½	M(A)	
Ocean Bridge ..	1970	66150	850	134	15½	M(A)	
Pacific Bridge ..	1967	44795	810	106	15½	M(A)	
Westminster Bridge	1968	42202	805	106	15½	M(A)	

Bowring S.S. Company Ltd.

Name		Date	Tons Gross	Length (feet)	Breadth (feet)	Speed (knots)	Engines	Former Names
Forth Bridge	..	1967	28467	674	98	16	M(A)	
London Bridge	..	1967	28467	674	98	16	M(A)	
Sydney Bridge	..	1970	34000	735	106	15½	M(A)	

H. Clarkson & Company Ltd.

Gallic Bridge	..	1967	42774	805	106	15	M(A)	
Jersey Bridge	..	1966	22490	657	85	16	M(A)	
Spey Bridge	..	1969	66126	850	134	15	M(A)	

Furness Withy & Co. Ltd.
(HOULDER BROS. & CO. LTD.)

Furness Bridge	..	1971	81000	965	145	15½	M(A)	
Orotava Bridge	..	1968	28880	716	92	15½	M(A)	ex Orotava 69.
Clyde Bridge	..	1967	24024	662	92	15	M(A)	ex Clydesdale 68.

Hunting & Son Ltd. & Silver Line Ltd.

(U.S.A.)

SEATRAIN LINES INC.
(HUDSON WATERWAYS CORPORATION)

FUNNEL: *White, with two blue arrows in form of " S ".*
HULL: *Black, with 'Seatrain Lines' in white.*

Transcolumbia	..	1945	12420	520	72	16	ST(A)	ex Marine Lynx 67.
Transcolorado	..	1945	10014	523	72	16	ST(A)	ex Marine Adder 67.
Transglobe	..	1944	11278	523	72	16	ST(A)	ex Marine Wolf 61.
Transhawaii	..	1945	13489	633	72	16	ST(A)	ex General J. H. McRae 69.
Transidaho	..	1945	13489	633	72	16	ST(A)	ex General W. F. Hase 69.
Transindiana	..	1945	13489	633	72	16	ST(A)	ex General W. C. Langfitt 69.
Transoregon	..	1945	13489	633	72	16	ST(A)	ex General W. G. Haan 69.

Scarsdale Shipping Co.
(MANAGERS J. & J. DENHOLM (MANAGEMENT) LTD.)

| **Euroliner** | .. | .. | 1971 | — | 792 | 100 | 25 | GT(A) | |
| **—** | .. | .. | 1971 | — | 792 | 100 | 25 | GT(A) | |

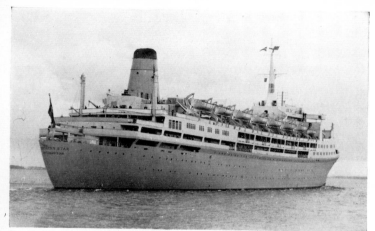

Shaw Savill: NORTHERN STAR [Bert Moody

Shaw Savill: AKAROA, formerly AMAZON [John G. Callis

SHAW SAVILL LINE
Shaw Savill & Albion Co. Ltd.

FUNNEL: *Buff with black top.* NORTHERN STAR *has black star on funnel.*

HULL: *Black, light grey or white, red boot-topping.*

ROUTES:
  A. *Passengers only:* SOUTHERN CROSS *and* NORTHERN STAR— *Southampton to Australia and New Zealand.*
  B. *Passengers and cargo:* ARANDA, AKAROA *and* ARAWA— *London to Australia and New Zealand.*
  C. *U.K. and Continental ports to Australia and New Zealand.*
  D. *Cruising.*

Name	Date	Tons Gross	Length (feet)	Breadth (feet)	Speed (knots)	Engines	Former Names
Akaroa	1959	18565	584	78	17½	M(2)	ex Amazon 68.
Alaric	1958	6692	473	64	17	M	
Amalric§	1960	7791	458	64	17	M	
Aranda	1960	18575	584	78	17½	M(2)	ex Aragon 69.
Arawa	1960	18595	584	78	17½	M(2)	ex Arlanza 68.
Britannic	1967	12228	546	74	19	M	
Canopic‡	1954	11166	512	69	17½	M(2)	
Carnatic	1956	11144	512	69	17	M(2)	
Cedric‡	1952	11232	512	69	17	M(2)	
Ceramic	1948	15067	561	72	17	ST(2)	
Cretic	1955	11151	512	69	17	M(2)	
Cymric	1953	11182	512	69	17	M(2)	
Delphic†	1949	10690	510	66	16	M(2)	
Iberic	1961	11043	510	70	17	M	
Icenic	1960	11042	513	70	17	M	
Illyric	1960	11256	513	70	17	M	
Ionic	1959	10978	513	70	17	M	
Langstone	1958	3441	406	54	17	M	ex Saracen 70.
Laurentic	1965	7964	481	66	18	M	
Majestic	1966	12277	540	74	19	M	*TO N.Z.. ren. NZ AORA*
Medic	1963	11120	538	71	18	M(2)	*SOLD*
Megantic	1962	11120	538	71	18	M(2)	
Mystic* *SOLD*	1959	6656	480	64	17	M	
Northern Star	1962	23983	650	84	20	ST(A)(2)	
Ocean Monarch	1957	24467	640	85	21	ST(2)	ex Empress of England 70.
Southern Cross	1955	19313	604	79	20	ST(A)(2)	*TO Greece, ren. CALYF*
Suevic	1950	13350	561	72	17	ST(2)	
Zealandic	1965	7946	481	66	18	M	

* On charter from Johnston Warren Lines.
‡ Owned by Cairn Line of Steamships Ltd.
† Owned by Overseas Containers Ltd.
§ Operated by Crusader Shipping Co. Ltd.

Crusader Shipping Co. Ltd.

(*These vessels are jointly owned by Blue Star Line, New Zealand S. Co., Port Line and Shaw, Savill & Albion and managed by last-named company.*)

FUNNEL: *Yellow with Crusader shield and sword on large black shield.*

HULL: *Eau-de-nil.*

Name	Date	Tons Gross	Length (feet)	Breadth (feet)	Speed (knots)	Engines	Former Names
Amalric	1960	7791	458	64	17	M	
Crusader	1957	3461	406	54	17	M	ex Edith Thorden 57.
Turakina	1960	7707	455	62	17	M	

Shaw Savill: MAJESTIC

[Malcolm Cranfield

Shaw Savill-Crusader Shipping: AMALRIC   [F. W. Hawks

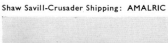

Handwritten annotations:

VISHVA PRAYAS
HARSHA VARDHANA   1974   9.400   17 M
TKr. JAINARAYAN VYAS   1975   14.100   M
TKr. RAFI AHMED KIDWAI   1974   14.100   M
TKr. BHAGAT SINGH   1974   12000   m
Kanishka   1964   21635   M   (bulk)

SHIPPING CORPORATION OF INDIA

FUNNEL: *Black two gold bands and blue disc with white edge.*

Jhansiki Rani   1975   42800   M (bulk)

HULL: *Black.*

Handwritten: State of Himachal Pradesh 1971 9816   M   ex Jolandia
Laxmi   1963   21.635   (bulk carr.)   M   ex Akbar Jayanti

Name	Date	Tons Gross	Length (feet)	Breadth (feet)	Speed (knots)	Engines	Former Names
Bharata	*1963*	*21,252*				*M*	
Ajanta	1968	23395	635	91	14¾	M(A)	*ex*
Bailadilla*	1970	45000	842	106	15	M(A)	
Barauni*	1970	45752	842	106	15	M(A)	
Bellary*	1969	45000	842	106	15	M(A)	
Nalanda	1968	23607	635	91	14¾	M(A)	
Sanchi	1968	23372	635	91	14¾	M(A)	
Vishva Anand	1958	3864	375	49	15	M(A)	ex Sturmfels 68, ex Nortropic 58.
Vishva Bhakti	1968	9332	505	64	17	M	
Vishva Bindu	1969	8120	477	62	17	M	
Vishva Chetana	1969	8119	477	62	17	M	ex Zygmunt August 69.
Vishva Darshan	1971	9330	510	64	16	M	
Vishva Dharma	1969	9330	493	64	17	M	
Vishva Jyoti	1959	9173	505	64	17	M	ex Jala Vishva Jyoti 61
Vishva Kalyan	1966	8955	510	64	16	M	
Vishva Kanti	1956	7055	492	64	14½	M	ex Angela Fassio 64.
Vishva Kaushal	1966	9655	479	66	15	M(A)	
Vishva Kirti	1960	9167	505	64	16	M	
Vishva Kusum	1955	3156	315	46	13	M(A)	ex Adria 68.
Vishva Lalita	1957	3936	374	49	15½	M(A)	ex Sternenfels 68, ex Norprado 57.
Vishva Mahima	1966	8956	501	64	15	M	
Vishva Mangal	1963	9165	505	64	17	M	
Vishva Maya	1963	9150	505	64	17	M	
Vishva Nidhi	1961	6209	509	64	17	M	
Vishva Prabha	1959	9457	490	62	14½	M	
Vishva Pratap	1957	7055	492	64	14½	M	ex Elettra Fassio 64.
Vishva Pratibha	1957	3903	376	49	15½	M(A)	ex Stolzenfels 68, ex Norcastle 57.
Vishva Prem	1962	9150	505	64	17	M	
Vishva Raksha	1966	8956	501	64	17	M	
Vishva Sandesh	1969	8119	477	62	16	M	ex Zygmunt Stary 69.
Vishva Seva	1968	9360	502	66	16	M	
Vishva Shakti	1969	9360	505	64	16	M	
Vishva Shobha	1969	9337	505	64	16	M	
Vishva Siddhi	1968	9330	505	64	16	M	
Vishva Sudha	1959	10447	527	66	15	M(A)	ex Westfalia 62.
Vishva Tej	1967	9367	502	66	16	M	
Vishva Tilak	1966	9655	479	66	16	M	
Vishva Tirth	1967	9360	502	66	16	M	
Vishva Usha	1960	8186	496	61	14	M(A)	
Vishva Vandana	1959	10411	518	65	14	M(A)	ex Madame Butterfly 68.
Vishva Vibhuti	1966	8959	501	64	16	M	
Vishva Vijay	1966	9655	479	66	16	M	
Vishva Vikas	1968	8422	477	62	17	M	ex Wladyslaw Jaglello 68.
Vishva Vikram	1970	9350	505	64	16	M	
Vishva Vir	1957	7055	492	64	14	M	ex Carmela Fassio cont. 64.
Vishva Apurva	*1974*	*11200*				*M*	
Vishva Vivek	1959	10843	522	66	14½	M	ex Figaro 68.
Vishva Ami Tabh	*1974*	*11000*				*M*	

Also many smaller ships.   * Bulk/ore/oil carriers.

Handwritten:

TKr   Vivekananda   1974   57500   190   M
MV   Abul Kalam Azad   1974   62500*   M
MV   Gautama Buddha   1974   69.000   M   bulk
TKr   Rajendra Prasad   1974   62.000   M
TKr MV   B.R. Ambedkar   1974   57.500   M

Shipping Corporation of India: VISHVA VIKAS [J. Mathieson

Shipping Corporation of India VIVSHA KIRTI [John G. Callis

SHIPPING & COAL CO. LTD.

FUNNEL: *Black with blue diamond on broad white band between two narrow red bands.*

HULL: *Black.*

Name			Date	Tons Gross	Length (feet)	Breadth (feet)	Speed (knots)	Engines	Former Names
Foreland	..	..	1967	23007	673	90	15	M(A)	

Also smaller ships.

SICULA OCEANICA S.A. (SIOSA)
Grimaldi Line

FUNNEL: *Blue with narrow black top and white ' S ' in white ring.*

HULL: *White or black.*

Caribia	..	..	1928	24496	631	80	19	M(2)	ex Vulcania 65.
Fides	..	..	1964	16100	635	76	15	M(A)	
Irpinia	..	..	1929	13204	537	67	15	M(2)	ex Campana 55, ex Rio Jackal 46, ex Campana 43.

" SITMAR "
Soc. Italiana Trasporti Marittimi S.p.A.
(VARIOUS COMPANIES)

FUNNEL: *Yellow with blue ' V '.*

HULL: *White.*

ROUTE: *Southampton to Australia and New Zealand returning via Singapore or Panama.*

Castel Felice		..	1930	10952	493	64	17	ST(2)	ex Keren 52, ex Kenya 51, ex Fairstone 50, ex Kenya 49, ex Keren 49, ex Kenya 49.
Fairland	..	..	1956	21947	608	80	20	ST(2)	ex Carinthia 68.
Fairsky	..	..	1942	12464	492	70	17	ST	ex Castel Forte 58, ex Attacker 52, ex Barnes, ex Steel Artisan.
Fairstar	..	..	1957	21619	609	78	18	ST(2)	ex Oxfordshire 64.
Fairwind	..	..	1957	22017	608	80	20	ST(2)	ex Sylvania 68.

Shipping Corporation of India: VISHVA RAKSHA

[Fotoship

Sicular Oceanica: IRPINIA leaves Naples

[Malcolm Cranfield

Sitmar: CASTEL FELICE recently broken up

[L. R. Mugridge

Sitmar: FAIRSKY

[F. W. Hawks

SILVER LINE LTD.

FUNNEL: *Black with two white diagonal stripes on blue square with white border.*

HULL: *Black or grey, red boot-topping.*

Name		Date	Tons Gross	Length (feet)	Breadth (feet)	Speed (knots)	Engines	Former Names
Chelsea Bridge	..	1967	57318	820	134	15	M(A)	ex Sigsilver 70.
Silvercove ..	..	1967	12843	516	74	15	M(A)	

St. Helen's Shipping Co. Ltd.

Silvercape ..	..	1967	12669	516	74	15½	M(A)	

Silver Isle Navigation (Bermuda) Ltd.

Silverbeach	..	1962	11276	526	67	13	M(A)	ex Totem Star 64, ex Norse Coral 63.
Silversea ..	..	1963	11276	526	67	13	M(A)	ex Totem Queen 64, ex Norse Reef 63.

Bishopsgate Shipping Co. Ltd.

Silvermain	..	1969	17500	535	85	15	M(A)	
Silversand ..	..	1958	10887	503	70	12	M(A)	
Silvershore ..	..	1960	12718	525	70	14	M(A)	ex Aldersgate 69.

Nile Steam Ship Co. Ltd.

Silverhawk	..	1969	6750	427	66	15	M(A)	

I. M. SKAUGEN & CO.

FUNNEL: *Yellow, black top with white diamond, blue and red border and black 'S'.*

HULL: *White.*

Skauborg	..	..	1961	18280	650	75	14½	M(A)	
Skaufast*	..	..	1968	57204	855	134	16	M(A)	
Skaumor	..	..	1958	17407	621	74	16	ST(A)	ex Alcides.
Skaustrand	..	..	1962	18275	650	75	16	M(A)	
Skausund	..	..	1966	20430	614	86	16	M(A)	

* Owned by Norwegian Bulk Carriers.

Royal Caribbean Cruise Lines A/S

Song of Norway ..	1969	17500	552	79	22	M(2)	

OVE SKOU

FUNNEL: *Black with white ' S 'on broad blue band.*

HULL: *White or grey with blue line.*

Name		Date	Tons Gross	Length (feet)	Breadth (feet)	Speed (knots)	Engines	Former Names
Atlantic Skou	..	1968	15761	613	75	17	M(A)	
Benny Skou	..	1966	4832	451	60	17½	M	
Birgitte Skou	..	1960	5133	453	59	16½	M	
Dinna Skou	..	1969	6582	513	65	18	M(A)	
Ditta Skou	..	1969	6582	513	65	18	M(A)	
Dorte Skou	..	1968	6582	513	65	18	M(A)	*ren SYNE* *roGree*
Else Skou	..	1951	4248	418	56	17	M	ex Benny Skou 66.
Grete Skou	..	1959	4211	416	57	17	M	*To Lebanon, ren. Master To*
Hanne Skou	..	1958	4213	416	57	17	M	
Helle Skou	..	1962	4207	416	57	16½	M	
Inger Skou	..	1964	4262	428	57	16½	M	
Jytte Skou	..	1965	4829	451	60	17	M	
Kirsten Skou	..	1964	4259	428	57	16½	M	
Lotte Skou	..	1966	4829	451	60	17½	M	
Mads Skou	..	1961	4207	416	57	17	M	
Maren Skou	..	1961	5184	453	59	16½	M	
Marie Skou	..	1962	4206	416	57	16½	M	
Mette Skou	..	1963	4262	428	57	16½	M	
Pacific Skou	..	1968	15761	613	75	17	M(A)	
Petra Skou	..	1954	4427	431	57	17	M	ex Susanne Skou 67 *TOGr ren.*
Susanne Skou	..	1967	4571	451	60	17½	M	
Dolly Skou		*1974*	*6600*				*M*	

Also smaller ships.

CHRISTEN SMITH SHIPPING CO.

Belships Co. Ltd. Skibs A/S

FUNNEL: *Blue with blue ' CS ' monogram and anchor on white disc.*

HULL: *Grey with red boot-topping.*

Name			Date						
Belblue	..	..	1968	11362	530	68	16	M(A)	*To Cyprus, ren 'LAMANT*
Belcargo	..	..	1966	11468	543	68	16	M(A)	
Belevelyn	..	..	1957	6520	407	59	13	M(A)	
Belforest	..	..	1947	6125	418	62	12	M(A)	ex Christen Smith 68.
Belkarin	..	..	1954	6550	407	59	13	M(A)	
Bellully	..	..	1955	6528	407	59	13	M(A)	ex Bellis 67.
Belnippon	..	..	1964	6313	455	60	15	M	*To E. Germany, ren JOHN*
Belocean	..	..	1968	11344	544	68	16	M(A)	
Beloro			*1974*	*43000*					

Also tankers.

Silver Line: SILVER BEACH   [*John G. Callis*

Ove Skou: SUSANNE SKOU   [*F. R. Sherlock*

Christen Smith Shipping Co: BELOCEAN

[*John G. Callis*

Reardon Smith Line: WELSH CITY

[*R. J. Weeks*

SIR WILLIAM REARDON SMITH & SONS LTD.

Reardon Smith Line Ltd. & Leeds Shg. Co. Ltd.

FUNNEL: *Dark red with black top and black ' S '.*
HULL: *Black with red boot-topping.*

Name		Date	Tons Gross	Length (feet)	Breadth (feet)	Speed (knots)	Engines	Former Names
Atlantic City	..	1967	27029	668	95	15	M(A)	
Cardiff City	..	1962	10089	500	67	14½	M	
Chiyoda	..	1965	18460	639	80	15	M(A)	ex Eastern City 70.
Cornish City	..	1969	10800	500	72	16	M(A)	
Devon City	..	1960	10141	510	67	14½	M	
Fresno City	..	1970	16650	630	84	15	M(A)	
Houston City	..	1963	10089	500	67	·14½	M	
Indian City	..	1967	27018	668	95	15	M(A)	
Orient City	..	1960	10300	510	67	14½	M	*To S'pore, ren. TONG SIT*
Prince Rupert City	..	1970	16644	630	84	15	M(A)	
Vancouver City	..	1969	16644	630	84	15	M(A)	
Victoria City	..	1970	16644	630	84	15	M(A)	
Welsh City	..	1968	10790	500	72	16	M(A)	
Wilkawa *ren. Chikuwa*	..	1964	18461	639	80	15	M(A)	ex Australian City 69.

W. A. SOUTER & CO. LTD.

Sheaf Steam Shg. Co. Ltd.

FUNNEL: *Black with yellow wheatsheaf on blue band.*
HULL: *Grey with red boot-topping.*

Sheaf Crest	..	1968	9392	462	72	14½	M(A)	*To Greece, ren. Father Panos*
Sheaf Mount	..	1965	21996	646	85	15	M(A)	
Sheaf Tyne *Sheaf Field*	..	1967	29037	709	96	15	M(A)	

Bamburgh Shg. Co. Ltd.

FUNNEL: *Black with red castle on blue over yellow band.*

Bamburgh Castle	..	1959	11894	512	70	12	M(A)
Cheviot	..	1961	13082	525	70	12	M(A)
Dunstanburgh Castle	..	1969	57024	855	134	15	M(A)
Lindisfarne	..	1960	12733	525	70	12	M(A)
Longstone	..	1960	13062	525	70	12	M(A)

Reardon Smith Line: EASTERN CITY, since renamed CHIYODA [J. Y. Freeman

W. A. Souter & Co: SHEAF TYNE [R. J. Weeks

SOUTH AFRICAN MARINE CORPORATION LTD.

FUNNEL: *Grey with black top and narrow blue and white and wide orange bands.*

HULL: *Grey or white with red or green boot-topping.*

Name	Date	Tons Gross	Length (feet)	Breadth (feet)	Speed (knots)	Engines	Former Names
S.A. KAAPLAND	1960	9773					ex KAAPLAND
S.A. Alphen ..	1966	10571	551	75	20	M	
S.A. Constantia ..	1968	10592	551	75	21	M	
S.A. Drakenstein ..	1964	6837	520	69	17	M	ex Drakenstein 66.
S.A. Hexrivier ..	1966	10059	521	69	18	M	
S.A. Huguenot ..	1966	10571	551	75	20	M	
S.A. Langkloof ..	1963	6898	521	69	17	M	ex Langkloof 66.
S.A. Letaba ..	1963	6827	520	69	17	M	ex Letaba 66.
S.A. Merchant ..	1955	9517	491	63	15	M	ex South African Merchant 66.
S.A. Morganster ..	1969	10596	551	75	20	M	
S.A. Nederburg ..	1967	9535	542	75	20	M	
S.A. Oranje* ..	1948	27513	747	84	22	ST(2)	ex Pretoria Castle 66.
S.A. Pioneer ..	1952	9518	491	63	15	ST	ex South African Pioneer 66, ex Sira 57.
S.A. Trader ..	1954	9518	491	63	15	ST	ex South African Trader 66, ex Sjoa 58.
S.A. Transporter ..	1953	9518	491	63	15	ST	ex South African Transporter 66, ex Simoa 58.
S.A. Tzaneen ..	1964	6837	520	69	17	M	ex Tzaneen 66.
S.A. Vaal* ..	1961	30212	760	90	23½	ST(2)	ex Transvaal Castle 66.
S.A. Van der Stel..	1966	9502	542	75	20	M	
S.A. Vergelegen ..	1969	10600	551	75	20	M	
S.A. Weltevreden..	1966	9496	542	75	20	M	
S.A. Zebediela ..	1968	6490	521	69	18	M(A)	

* Operates in conjunction with Union Castle Mail S.S. Company's Mail Service.

Springbok Shipping Co. (South Africa) Ltd.

Name	Date	Tons Gross	Length	Breadth	Speed	Engines	Former Names
S.A. Shipper ..	1954	7898	503	66	17	ST	ex South African Shipper 66, ex Rooibok 61, ex Uzinto 60, ex Clan Robertson 59.
S.A. Statesman ..	1950	8405	512	66	17	ST	ex South African Statesman 66, ex Boskob 61, ex Clan Sinclair 60.

South African Sugar Carriers (Pty.) Ltd.

Name	Date	Tons Gross	Length	Breadth	Speed	Engines	Former Names
S.A. Sugela ..	1965	16405	584	76	16	M(A)	ex Sugela 65.

STAG LINE LTD.

Joseph Robinson & Sons (Management) Ltd.

FUNNEL: *Black with white stag on broad red band.*

HULL: *Black with red boot-topping.*

Name			Date	Tons Gross	Length (feet)	Breadth (feet)	Speed (knots)	Engines	Former Names
Camellia	..	..	1953	6161	435	56	12	M(A)	
Gloxinia	..	..	1958	7665	480	60	13	M(A)	
Ixia	..	..	1964	15910	595	75	14	M(A)	
Photinia	..	..	1961	7676	480	60	13	M(A)	
Zinnia	..	..	1968	16122	598	75	14½	M(A)	

(U.S.A.)

STATES MARINE LINES INC.

FUNNEL: *Dark red with white star on broad blue band between narrow white bands.*

HULL: *Grey or black with red boot-topping.*

Name		Date	Tons	Length	Breadth	Speed	Engines	Former Names
Aloha State	..	1943	7870	492	70	16½	ST	ex Edward Luckenbach 59, ex Sea Snipe 45.
Bay State	..	1944	8162	459	63	15	ST	ex Julie Luckenbach 59, ex Tate 47.
Bayou State	..	1944	8162	459	63	15	ST	ex Mary Luckenbach 59, ex Waukesha 47
Blue Grass State	..	1944	8121	459	63	15	ST	ex Edgar F. Luckenbach 59, ex Tolland 47.
Buckeye State	..	1943	7868	492	70	16½	ST	ex George Luckenbach 59, ex Sea Star 49.
Constitution State		1943	7774	492	70	16½	ST	ex Steel Recorder 69, ex Knox 47.
Copper State	..	1943	7838	492	70	16½	ST	ex Harry Luckenbach 59, ex Sea Devil 49.
Gopher State	..	1944	7870	492	70	16½	ST	ex Mathew Luckenbach 59, ex Sea Perch 47.
Green Mountain State	..	1945	7641	455	62	15	ST	ex Flagstaff Victory 49.
Keystone State	..	1945	10781	520	72	18	ST(A)	ex Marine Filer 55.
Old Dominion State	1963	10567	509	68	15	M	ex Norbeth 68.
Palmetto State	..	1945	7604	455	62	15	ST	ex Margaret Brown 57, ex Fisk Victory 51.
Pine Tree State	..	1943	7950	492	63	16	ST	ex Green Port 67, ex Mormacport 64, ex Mormacsun 63, ex P. & T. Pathfinder 57, ex Sea Hound 47.
Rainer	..	..	1970	12300	—	—	18	M	

Stag Line: GLOXINIA

F. C. Strick & Co: GORJISTAN

Name		Date	Tons Gross	Length (feet)	Breadth (feet)	Speed (knots)	Engines	Former Names
Sooner State	..	1945	8292	460	63	15	ST	ex Santa Victoria 60, ex Oregon 57, ex Wild Hunter 47, ex Expounder.
Sunshine State	..	1963	10435	508	68	15	M(A)	ex Vikara 69.
Volunteer State	..	1945	7689	455	62	15¼	ST	ex Alice Brown 57, ex Genevieve Peterkin 57, ex St. John's Victory 51.
Wolverine State	..	1945	10508	520	72	18	ST(A)	ex Marine Runner 55.

Global Bulk Transport Inc.

Empire State	..	1945	8263	460	63	15	ST	ex Sparkling Wave 46.
Evergreen State	..	1943	7959	492	70	16½	ST	ex L. J. Luckenbach 59, ex Lamar 49.
Hoosier State	..	1945	10508	520	72	18	ST(A)	ex Marine Arrow 55.

FRANK C. STRICK & CO. LTD.

FUNNEL: *Alternate red and blue chevrons on broad white band on black funnel.*

HULL: *Grey with red boot-topping.*

Strick Line Ltd.

Albistan	..	1948	5516	441	57	11	SR	
Armanistan	..	1965	8531	486	63	16	M	ex Elysia 68. TO P&O, ren
Baharistan	..	1959	8121	511	64	15	M	TO P&O, ren. STRATHBARC
Baluchistan	..	1956	8385	510	63	15	M	
Farsistan	..	1959	9400	501	63	14½	M	TO P&O, ren STAATHADDIE
Floristan	..	1965	9296	503	68	16	M	TO P&O, ren STRATHALVIE
Gorjistan	..	1961	9449	501	63	16	M	" " " STRATHATLOU
Karaghistan	..	1957	7150	478	59	13	M	To CYPRUS, ren CONSTAN-
Khuzistan	..	1955	7145	478	59	13	M	
Kohistan	..	1960	9665	501	63	16	M	TO P&O, ren STRATHAJLAK
Nigaristan	..	1970	9630	510	70	16	M	TO P&O, ren. STRATHAIRD
Registan	..	1966	9069	503	64	17½	M	" " " STRATHANNA
Serbistan	..	1966	8985	503	64	16	M	TO P&O, ren STRATHANG
Tabaristan	..	1969	9627	511	70	17½	M	TO P&O, ren. STRATHARU
Tangistan	..	1950	7222	478	59	12½	RT	
Turkistan	..	1963	9270	503	66	16	M	TO P&O, ren STRATHASSY

Shahristan Steamship Co. Ltd.

Baltistan	..	1953	7489	478	59	13	M	
Shahristan	..	1965	9280	503	68	16	M	TO P&O, ren STRATHAPPI

Sugar Line: CRYSTAL DIAMOND   [*John G. Callis*

Swedish America Line: GRIPSHOLM   [*F. R. Sherlock*

SUGAR LINE LTD.

FUNNEL: *Black with three silver coloured bands separated by two blue bands.*

HULL: *Black with red boot-topping.*

Name	Date	Tons Gross	Length (feet)	Breadth (feet)	Speed (knots)	Engines	Former Names
Crystal Crown ..	1957	8671	461	61	12¼	M(A)	
Crystal Diamond	1957	8670	461	61	12¼	M(A)	
Crystal Gem ..	1956	8674	461	61	12	M(A) *To Nicaragua, ren · VANDA*
Crystal Sapphire ..	1960	11688	559	65	14½	M(A)	
Sugar Crystal ..	1967	13894	550	74	15½	M(A)	
Sugar Exporter* ..	1960	11687	559	65	14½	M(A)	ex Athelprincess 66.
Sugar Importer* ..	1959	11687	559	65	14½	M(A)	ex Athelprince 66.
Sugar Producer ..	1968	13894	550	74	15½	M(A)	
Sugar Transporter	1970	13894	550	73	15½	M(A)	
Sugar Trader	*1974*	*17800*				*M*	

* Owned by Albion Co. Ltd. Bermuda.

SUISSE-ATLANTIQUE SOC. D' ARM. MAR. S.A.

FUNNEL: *Grey with yellow and red houseflag interrupting two yellow bands.*

HULL: *Grey with red boot-topping.*

Name	Date	Tons Gross	Length (feet)	Breadth (feet)	Speed (knots)	Engines	Former Names
Bregaglia	1962	14112	559	73	14	M(A)	
Castasegna ..	1958	8871	504	62	15	M	ex Cruzeiro do Sul 65.
Celerina	1959	8840	503	62	15½	M	
Corviglia ..	1958	8871	504	62	15	M	
General Guisan ..	1957	9054	502	62	15	M	
Lavaux	1959	9018	500	62	14	M	
Romandie ..	1965	21449	630	85	15	M(A)	
St. Cerque ..	1962	14112	559	73	14	M(A)	ex Bariloche 66.

SWEDISH AMERICAN LINE
Svenska Amerika Linien

FUNNEL: *Yellow with three yellow crowns on blue disc.*

HULL: *White with red boot-topping.*

ROUTES: **A.** *Gothenburg to New York.*
B. *Cruises.*

Name	Date	Tons Gross	Length (feet)	Breadth (feet)	Speed (knots)	Engines	Former Names
Gripsholm	1957	23215	631	82	19	M(2)	*To Karageorgis Lines*
Kungsholm ..	1966	26678	660	87	22	M(2)	*To Flagship Cruises*

See also Atlantic Container Line.

SWEDISH ATLANTIC LINE

FUNNEL: *Yellow with three yellow crowns on blue disc.*
HULL: *White with red boot-topping.*

Name		Date	Tons Gross	Length (feet)	Breadth (feet)	Speed (knots)	Engines	Former Names
Blankaholm	..	1962	6403	442	58	17	M	
Odensholm	..	1962	6401	442	58	17	M	
Sagaholm	..	..	1963	6916	442	57	16	M	
Stureholm	..	..	1957	6543	491	63	17	M	
Svaneholm	..	1960	5749	482	62	17	M	
Vingaholm	..	1962	7494	450	61	$15\frac{1}{2}$	M(A)	ex Felis 67.
Vasaholm	..	1955	5868	482	62	17	M	
Vretaholm	..	1962	6398	442	58	17	M	

SWEDISH EAST ASIATIC COMPANY

A/B Svenska Ostasiatiska Kompaniet

FUNNEL: *Yellow with three crowns on blue disc.*
HULL: *White.*

Name			Date	Tons	Length	Breadth	Speed	Engines	Former Names
Burma	..	..	1952	6989	508	65	$17\frac{1}{2}$	M(2)	
Ceylon	..	..	1950	6960	508	65	$17\frac{1}{2}$	M(2)	
Hainan	..	..	1946	4743	462	59	16	M	
Hakone	..	..	1967	7328	512	70	$18\frac{1}{2}$	M(A)	
Hirado	..	..	1967	7327	512	70	$18\frac{1}{2}$	M(A)	
Hokkaido	..	..	1966	7326	512	70	$18\frac{1}{2}$	M(A)	
Hondo	..	..	1966	7335	511	70	$18\frac{1}{2}$	M(A)	
Indus	..	..	1969	6149	458	71	$16\frac{1}{2}$	M(A)	
Isfahan	..	..	1969	6149	459	71	$16\frac{1}{2}$	M(A)	
Japan	..	..	1950	6960	508	65	$17\frac{1}{2}$	M(2)	
Kyoto	..	..	1955	6021	482	62	17	M	
Mandalay	..	..	1960	5779	482	62	17	M	
Minikoi	..	..	1955	6031	482	62	17	M	
Nagasaki	..	..	1961	6256	521	68	$17\frac{1}{2}$	M	
Nara	..	..	1964	6294	521	68	$17\frac{1}{2}$	M	
Nicobar	..	..	1963	6290	521	68	$17\frac{1}{2}$	M	
Sabang	..	..	1955	5914	482	62	17	M	
Sudan	..	..	1953	7222	508	65	$17\frac{1}{2}$	M(2)	
Tamara	..	..	1960	6073	467	61	$14\frac{1}{2}$	M	ex Tigris 67, ex Anjan 63.

Nippon is detained in Suez Canal and abandoned to Insurers.

SWEDISH LLOYD

Svenska Lloyd Rederi A/B

FUNNEL: *White, black top with gold star on blue disc.*
HULL: *Grey or white.*

Swedish Atlantic Line: SAGAHOLM [*F. W. Hawks*

Swedish Lloyd: HISPANIA [*F. R. Sherlock*

Name			Date	Tons Gross	Length (feet)	Breadth (feet)	Speed (knots)	Engines	Former Names
Dalmatia	..	..	1962	4321	398	48	15	M(A)	
Gallia	..	..	1961	4315	398	48	15	M(A)	
Hispania	..	..	1966	7772	463	69	18	M(2)	ex Svea 69.
Industria	..	..	1964	4315	398	48	15	M(A)	
Italia	..	..	1961	4325	398	48	15	M(A)	
Patricia	..	..	1967	8897	463	69	18	M(2)	
Saga	..	..	1966	7927	463	69	18	M(2)	
Scania	..	..	1962	4315	398	48	15	M(A)	
Valencia	..	..	1964	4316	398	48	15	M(A)	ex Hispania 68.

Many smaller ships.

(SWEDEN)

SWEDISH ORIENT LINE
Svenska Orient Linien

FUNNEL: *Yellow with red and black bands and AB superimposed.*
HULL: *White.*

Name			Date	Tons	Length	Breadth	Speed	Engines
Birkaland	..	..	1969	5988	459	71	17	M(A)
Boreland	..	..	1969	6150	458	71	17	M(A)
Tavastland		..	1955	3652	393	54	15	M(A)
Thebeland	..	..	1961	4179	442	58	16	M
Thuleland	..	..	1955	3659	393	54	15	M(A)
Timmerland		..	1956	3716	393	54	15	M(A)
Tundraland		..	1958	3714	393	54	15	M(A)
Tyrusland	..	..	1963	4169	442	58	16	M
Vidaland	..	..	1954	4302	429	58	16	M
Vikingland	..	..	1951	4272	429	58	16	M
Vingaland	..	..	1950	4367	429	58	16	M

W. J. TATEM LTD.
Atlantic Shipping & Trading Co. Ltd.

FUNNEL: *Black with white " T " on broad red band.*
HULL: *Grey with red boot-topping.*

Name			Date	Tons	Length	Breadth	Speed	Engines
Exning	..	..	1965	7184	516	71	15	M
Landwade	..	..	1961	7657	461	60	14	M

(SWEDEN)

TIRFING S.S. COMPANY
Angf. A/B Tirfing

FUNNEL: *Yellow, three narrow red bands with AB in white.*
HULL: *Grey.*

Swedish Orient Line: TYRUSLAND   [*Fotoship*

W. J. Tatem Ltd: EXNING off Gravesend   [*Malcolm Cranfield*

Tirfing S.S. Co: TROJALAND

Transatlantic Rederi: TALARAH

Transatlantic Rederi: WAITARA [J. Y. Freeman

Transatlantic Espanola: BEGONA [R. J. Weeks

Name	Date	Tons Gross	Length (feet)	Breadth (feet)	Speed (knots)	Engines	Former Names
Atland	1956	12737	583	70	15	M(A)	
Lake Eyre†	1961	8303	489	62	18½	M	
Lappland	1959	12963	583	70	15½	M(A)	
Nordland	1965	27229	708	95	16	M(A)	
Sydland	1960	6312	473	60	15	M(A)	
Traneland†	1957	3712	393	54	15	M(A)	
Trojaland†	1962	4176	442	58	16	M	
Uppland	1963	16141	597	75	15½	M(A)	
~~Atland (OBO)~~	1974	84000				M	

† Operated by Swedish Orient Line.

Lappland (OBO)   1974   84000
TKr. Hemland   1975

(SWEDEN)

TRANSATLANTIC REDERI A/B

FUNNEL: *Yellow, blue top.*
HULL: *Grey.*

Name	Date	Tons Gross	Length (feet)	Breadth (feet)	Speed (knots)	Engines
Alabama	1962	5979	472	65	17½	M
Arizona	1961	6308	472	65	17½	M
Australic	1965	8002	490	62	19	M
Bullaren	1943	3188	381	52	14½	M(2)
Cirrus	1960	7796	526	66	19½	M(2)
Cooranga	1955	3645	397	54	17	M
Cumulus	1950	7807	526	66	19½	M(2)
Elgaren	1957	5362	470	63	17	M
Goonawarra	1962	8164	513	68	17¾	M
Hallaren	1960	6725	468	65	17	M
Hjelmaren	1946	3851	423	58	16½	M
Indiana	1956	5382	459	61	17½	M
Kirribilli	1956	7457	511	68	17½	M
Lommaren	1952	4207	429	58	16½	M
Mangarella	1945	4907	432	57	14	M
Minnesota	1949	6049	473	59	19	M(2)
Mirrabooka	1961	8160	513	68	17½	M
Nimbus	1947	6749	494	62	19½	M(2)
Paralla	1970	13460	648	94	20	M(A)
Parrakoola	1962	8156	513	68	17½	M(A)
Stratus	1948	6750	494	62	19½	M(2)
Sunnaren	1948	4149	423	58	16½	M
Talarah	1967	10724	512	70	19	M(A)
Vikaren	1954	4507	426	58	14	M
Vingaren	1960	6702	468	65	17	M
Waitara	1966	10715	512	70	19	M(A)
Woollahra	1967	10728	511	70	19	M(A)
Yarrawonga	1941	4879	432	57	14	M

See also Atlantic Container Line.
Killara is detained in Suez Canal and abandoned to Insurers.

(SPAIN)

CIA. TRASATLANTICA ESPAÑOLA S.A.

FUNNEL: *Black.*
HULL: *Black with red boot-topping and white line.*
ROUTES: **A.** *Southampton, Bilbao, Santander, La Coruna, Vigo, Cadiz, Las Palmas, Teneriffe, Venezuela and the Caribbean.*
       B. *Bilbao, Santander, Vigo, Cadiz, San Juan, Vera Cruz, New York.*

Name			Date	Tons Gross	Length (feet)	Breadth (feet)	Speed (knots)	Engines	Former Names
Almudena ..		..	1956	3886	371	48	15	M	ex Iberico 61.
Begona		..	1945	10139	455	62	17½	ST	ex Castel Bianco 57, ex Vassar Victory 47.
Covadonga		..	1953	10226	487	62	16½	M	ex Monastero de la Rabida.
Guadalupe ..		..	1953	10226	487	62	16½	M	ex Monastero de la Guadalupe.
Montserrat		..	1945	9008	455	62	17½	ST	ex Castel Verde 57, ex Wooster Victory 50.
Satrustegui		..	1948	6615	401	55	17	M(2)	ex Explorador Iradier 52.
Virginia De Churruca		..	1949	6518	401	55	18	M(2)	ex Conde de Argelejo 52.

TURNBULL SCOTT SHG. CO. LTD.

FUNNEL : *Black with white " TS " on white bordered red shield.*
HULL : *Black with red boot-topping.*

Name		Date	Tons Gross	Length (feet)	Breadth (feet)	Speed (knots)	Engines	Former Names
Flowergate*	..	1969	58589	830	131	15	M(A)	To Sweden, ren. PORSUS
Naess Parkgate†	..	1966	40767	820	104	15½	M(A)	
Redgate	..	1969	1426	254	39	11	M(A)	
Saltersgate	..	1969	1426	254	39	11	M(A)	
Waynegate	..	1970	1426	254	39	11	M(A)	
Eskdalegate	..	1969	2587					M	ex Bruni & Fredericksy

Handwritten annotations: "Iron" at left margin; "To Sweden, ren. PORSUS" in Flowergate row; "ex Bruni & Fredericksy" in Eskdalegate row.

* Ore/oil carrier. † Managed by Naess Denholm & Co.

(RUSSIA)

U.S.S.R.

FUNNEL : *White or black with yellow hammer and sickle on red band.*
HULL : *White or black.*

(Note:- The merchant fleet of the U.S.S.R. is very large and owing to limitations in space it is not possible to list all the ships, but the following are the principal passenger carrying vessels.)

Name			Date	Tons Gross	Length (feet)	Breadth (feet)	Speed (knots)	Engines	Former Names
Admiral Nakhimov			1925	15286	549	69	14	SR(2)	ex Berlin 47.
Adsharia	..	..	1964	5261	401	53	18	M(2)	
Alexandr Pushkin		..	1965	19861	578	77	20	M(2)	
Armeniya	..	..	1963	5261	401	53	18	M(2)	
Asia ..	..	..	1924	12019	490	66	12	SR(2)	ex Der Deutsche 46, ex Sierra Morena 34.
Baikal	..	..	1962	5245	401	53	18	M(2)	
Baltika	..		1940	7494	445	60	16	TE(2)	ex Vyacheslav Molotov 57.
Bashkiriya ..			1964	5261	401	53	18	M(2)	
Estonia	..	..	1960	4871	401	53	18	M(2)	
Felix Dzerjinsky		..	1958	4871	401	53	18	M(2)	
Grigory Ordjonikidze		..	1959	4871	401	53	18	M(2)	
Gruzia	..		1939	11030	511	67	16	M(2)	ex Sobieski 50.
Ilyich	..	..	1933	12049	524	66	13	M(2)	ex Caribia 46.
Ivan Franko		..	1964	19861	578	77	20	M(2)	

U.S.S.R.: ALEXANDR PUSHKIN

[*Southern Photos*

U.S.S.R.: NADESHDA KRUPSKAJA

[*A. P. Oakden*

U.S.S.R.: BALTIKA

[F. W. Hawks

U.S.S.R.: LITVA

[Fotoship

Name		Date	Tons Gross	Length (feet)	Breadth (feet)	Speed (knots)	Engines	Former Names
Khabarovsk	..	1962	5235	401	53	18	M(2)	
Krim ..	..	1928	5008	380	51	12	M(2)	
Latvia	..	1960	4871	401	53	18	M(2)	
Litva ..	..	1960	4871	401	53	18	M(2)	
M. Uritzkij	..	1959	4871	401	53	18	M(2)	
Maria Ulyanova	..	1960	4871	401	54	18	M(2)	
Mikhail Kalinin	..	1958	4871	401	53	18	M(2)	
Nadeshda Krupskaja		1963	5261	401	53	18	M(2)	
Nikolaevsk ..	..	1962	5230	401	53	18	M(2)	
Petropavlovsk	..	1961	4871	401	53	18	M(2)	
Pobeda	..	1928	9829	505	61	12	M(2)	ex Iberia 46, ex Magdalena 34.
Rossia	..	1938	17870	562	74	15	DE(2)	ex Empire Welland 46, ex Patria 45.
Russ ..	..	1933	12931	498	66	15	M(2)	ex Cordillera 49.
Shota Rustaveli	..	1968	19861	578	77	20	M(2)	
Sovetsky Sojus	..	1923	23009	673	72	15	ST(2)	ex Hansa 50, ex Albert Ballin 35.
Taras Shevchenko		1965	19549	578	77	20	M(2)	
Turkmenia	..	1961	5230	401	53	18	M(2)	
Ukraina	..	1938	6406	433	58	18	M(2)	
Vazlav Vorovsky	..	1959	4871	401	53	18	M(2)	
Vladivostok	..	1960	4871	401	53	18	M(2)	

UNION CASTLE MAIL S.S. CO. LTD.

Cayzer, Irvine & Co. Ltd.

FUNNEL: *Red with black top.*

HULL: *Lilac grey with brown boot-topping. Some cargo vessels have a black hull with a white line.*

ROUTES: **A.** *Southampton via Madeira or Las Palmas to Capetown, Port Elizabeth, East London and Durban. (Operated in conjunction with South African Marine Corp.)*
B. *U.K. ports to South Africa.*
C. *Cruising.*

Name		Date	Tons Gross	Length	Breadth	Speed	Engines	Former Names
Edinburgh Castle	..	1948	27489	747	84	$22\frac{1}{2}$	ST(2)	
Good Hope Castle		1965	10538	593	77	$22\frac{1}{2}$	M(2)	
Kinnaird Castle†	..	1956	7737	503	66	16	ST	ex South African Scientist 62, ex Clan Ross 61.
Pendennis Castle		1958	28453	763	84	$22\frac{1}{2}$	ST(2)	
Reina del Mar*	..	1956	20747	601	78	18	ST(2)	
Richmond Castle		1944	7477	474	63	$15\frac{1}{2}$	M	
Riebeck Castle	..	1946	7755	474	63	$15\frac{1}{2}$	M	
Rotherwick Castle		1959	9360	520	66	$16\frac{1}{2}$	M	
Rothesay Castle	..	1960	9360	520	66	$16\frac{1}{2}$	M	
Rowallan Castle	..	1943	7474	474	63	$15\frac{1}{2}$	M	
Roxburgh Castle	..	1945	7514	474	63	$15\frac{1}{2}$	M	
Rustenburg Castle		1946	7767	474	63	$15\frac{1}{2}$	M	
Southampton Castle		1965	10538	593	77	$22\frac{1}{2}$	M(2)	
Tantallon Castle	..	1954	7218	495	66	$15\frac{1}{2}$	M	
Tintagel Castle	..	1954	7430	495	66	$15\frac{1}{2}$	M	
Windsor Castle	..	1960	36123	783	93	$23\frac{1}{2}$	ST(2)	

* On charter from Royal Mail Lines Ltd.
† Owned by King Line Ltd.

Union Castle Line: ROTHERWICK CASTLE [*F. W. Hawks*

Union Castle Line: REINA DEL MAR, on charter from Royal Mail Lines [*Bert Moody*

Union S.S. Co of New Zealand: SEAWAY KING

[J. Y. Freeman

Union S.S. Co of New Zealand: MAHENO

[J. Mathieson

UNION S.S. CO. OF NEW ZEALAND LTD.

FUNNEL: *Red with black top and black rings.*
HULL: *Green with yellow line and red boot-topping.*
ROUTES: A. *Auckland and Wellington to Sydney and other Trans-Tasman services,*
         B. *Auckland to Suva and other Pacific islands.*
         C. *New Zealand ports to Singapore, Rangoon, Calcutta and Colombo.*
         D. *Australian ports to Tasmania.*
         E. *Many New Zealand coastal services.*

Name	Date	Tons Gross	Length (feet)	Breadth (feet)	Speed (knots)	Engines	Former Names
Hawea	1967	2926	366	56	16½	M(2)	
Kaimiro	1956	3722	345	50	12	M	
Kaitoke	1948	3551	345	51	11¼	M	
Kaituna	1956	3722	345	50	12½	M	
Karepo	1964	3222	326	48	14	M	
Karetu	1964	3222	326	48	14	M	
Katea	1958	3790	345	51	12½	M	
Kawaroa	1950	3532	345	51	11½	M	
Kawerau	1955	3698	345	50	12	M	
Koraki	1957	3790	345	51	12½	M	
Koranui	1956	3722	345	50	12	M	
Kowhai	1952	3528	345	50	11½	M	
Kurutai	1952	3528	345	51	11	M	
Maheno	1969	4560	430	63	18	M(2)(A)	
Maori	1953	7490	456	64	21	TE(2)	*To HK,*
Marama	1969	4700	430	63	18	M(2)	
Ngahere	1966	4548	367	54	12½	M(A)	
Ngakuta	1962	4576	367	54	12½	M(A)	
Ngapara	1966	4548	367	54	12½	M(A)	
Ngatoro	1962	4576	367	54	12½	M(A)	
Risdon	1959	4125	360	52	12½	M	
Seaway King	1964	2961	371	52	17	M(A)(2)	
Seaway Queen	1964	2961	371	52	17	M(A)(2)	
Taveuni	1945	2820	374	52	15½	M(2)	ex Argentinean Reefer 68.
Tofua	1951	5299	391	55	14½	M(2)	
Waikare	1958	3839	345	51	12½	M	
Waimate	1951	3506	346	50	10½	M	
Waimea	1953	3657	345	51	11½	M	
UNION WELLINGTON	1973	2638				M	

Many smaller ships.

(NETHERLANDS)

UNITED NETHERLANDS STEAMSHIP CO.
Vereenigde Nederlandsche S.M.N.V.

FUNNEL: *Black with broad orange band.*
HULL: *Black or grey with red boot-topping.*
ROUTES: A. *Amsterdam, Antwerp, Southampton, Las Palmas, Teneriffe, Cape Town, Port Elizabeth, East London, Durban.*
         B. *Rotterdam and Amsterdam to Mediterranean ports, Suez, Persian Gulf, India, Malaya, Hong Kong, China, Japan, and Australia.*

United Netherlands Steamship Co: WAALEKERK   [J. Y. Freeman

United Netherlands Steamship Co: WESTERKERK   [F. R. Sherlock

United Netherlands Steamship Co: GIESSENKERK   [R. J. Weeks

United States Line: AMERICAN LYNX   [F. R. Sherlock

Name		Date	Tons Gross	Length (feet)	Breadth (feet)	Speed (knots)	Engines	Former Names
Abbekerk	..	1946	8324	492	70	16½	ST	ex Friesland 47.
Abel Tasman	..	1971	29200	743	101	21½	ST(A)	
Amerskerk	..	1952	8235	495	70	16½	ST	
Annenkerk	..	1947	7904	523	63	16	M(2)	
Arendskerk	..	1948	7916	523	63	17	M(2)	
Bovenkerk	..	1960	8670	491	66	16¼	M	
Dahomeykust	..	1959	4561	380	53	13½	M	
Giessenkerk	..	1956	8329	495	63	16	M	
Kloosterkerk	..	1964	7779	541	69	18	M	
Koudekerk	..	1964	7779	541	69	18	M	
Laarderkerk	..	1958	8766	479	66	15	M	
Leiderkerk	..	1959	8766	479	66	15	M	
Lelykerk	..	1958	8766	479	66	15	M	
Nijkerk	..	1958	6347	496	63	16	M	
Oldekerk	..	1955	7001	493	63	16	M	
Ommenkerk	..	1956	8986	493	63	17	M	TO Costa Line, ren GIOVANNA C,
Oostkerk	..	1954	7008	493	63	16	M	" " " - LUISA C.
Ouwerkerk	..	1954	7007	493	63	16½	M	
Randfontein	..	1958	13694	585	70	18	M(2)	
Schiekerk	..	1962	8289	593	69	18	M	
Serooskerk	..	1960	9662	528	69	18	M	
Servaaskerk	..	1962	8288	593	69	18	M	
Simonskerk	..	1961	9671	528	69	18	M	
Sinoutskerk	..	1962	8287	593	69	18	M	
Sloterkerk*	..	1961	9811	528	69	18	M	
Spaarnekerk	..	1962	8288	593	69	18	M	
Steenkerk	..	1961	8290	593	69	18	M	
Streefkerk	..	1961	8309	593	69	18	M	
Waalekerk	..	1967	10710	547	75	20	M(A)	
Westerkerk	..	1967	10710	547	75	20	M(A)	
Willemskerk	..	1967	10710	547	75	20	M(A)	
Wissekerk	..	1967	10710	547	75	20	M(A)	
Zaankerk	..	1957	9049	508	66	17	M	
Zonnekerk	..	1957	9079	508	66	17	M	
Zuiderkerk*	..	1957	9197	507	66	17	M	

Also smaller ships.   * On charter from N.V. Neder. Tank & Pakety. Maats.

(U.S.A.)

UNITED STATES LINES

FUNNEL: *Dark red with white band and blue top.* UNITED STATES *has two funnels.*

HULL: *Black with red boot-topping.*

ROUTES: **A.** *E. Coast U.S.A. (New York, Boston, Baltimore, Philadelphia and Hampton Roads) to U.K. and N. Europe ports between Bilbao and Hamburg.*
B. *E. Coast U.S.A. to China, Japan, Philippines.*

American Apollo	..	1971	18876	701	90	23	ST	
American Astronaut		1969	18876	701	90	23	ST	
American Challenger	..	1962	11105	561	75	20	ST	
American Champion		1963	11105	561	75	20	ST	
American Charger		1962	11105	561	75	20	ST	
American Chieftain		1963	11105	561	75	20	ST	

Name	Date	Tons Gross	Length (feet)	Breadth (feet)	Speed (knots)	Engines	Former Names
American Corsair	1963	11105	561	75	20	ST	
American Courier	1963	11105	561	75	20	ST	
American Lancer ..	1968	18764	701	90	23	ST	
American Lark ..	1969	18876	701	90	23	ST	
American Legion ..	1968	18764	701	90	23	ST	
American Liberty	1968	18876	701	90	23	ST	
American Lynx ..	1968	18876	701	90	23	ST	
Pioneer Commander ..	1963	11105	561	75	20	ST	ex American Commander 68.
Pioneer Contender	1963	11164	561	75	20	ST	ex American Contender 66.
Pioneer Contractor	1963	11164	561	75	20	ST	ex American Contractor 66.
Pioneer Crusader	1963	11164	561	75	20	ST	ex American Crusader 67.
Pioneer Main ..	1953	8964	564	76	18	ST	ex Cotton Mariner 56.
Pioneer Mart ..	1954	8964	564	76	18	ST	ex Sunflower Mariner 56.
Pioneer Mill ..	1954	8964	564	76	18	ST	ex Show Me Mariner 56.
Pioneer Ming ..	1954	8964	564	76	18	ST	ex Silver Mariner 56.
Pioneer Minx ..	1953	8964	564	76	18	ST	ex Gopher Mariner 56.
Pioneer Mist ..	1954	8964	564	76	18	ST	ex Peninsular Mariner 56.
Pioneer Moon ..	1962	11164	561	75	20	ST	ex American Challenger 62, ex Pioneer Moon 62.
Pioneer Moor ..	1953	8964	564	76	18	ST	ex Mountain Mariner 56.
Pioneer Myth ..	1954	8964	564	76	18	ST	ex Pelican Mariner 56.
United States ..	1952	50924	990	102	30	ST(4)	

(DENMARK)
THE UNITED STEAMSHIP CO. LTD.
Det Forenede Dampskibs—Selskab A/S

FUNNEL: *Black with broad red band, white Maltese cross on blue disc.*

HULL: *Black or light grey with bright red boot-topping.*

Name			Date	Tons Gross	Length	Breadth	Speed	Engines	
Dana Regina			*1974*	*12,200*					
Aalborghus	..	..	1969	7698	410	63	20	M(2)	
Akershus	..	..	1965	5012	357	57	17½	M(2)	*To Mexico, ren. Mazatlan*
Alabama	..	..	1957	5506	451	59	15	M	
Alberta	..	..	1966	4507	463	62	19	M	
Athos	..	..	1961	2661	362	51	14	M	*To Lebanon*
England	..	..	1964	8221	459	63	22	M(2)	
Freesia	..	..	1961	2863	362	51	14	M	
Kong Olav V	..	..	1968	7956	410	63	22	M(2)	
Labrador	..	..	1967	4430	463	61	19	M	*To S'pore, ren. C. RA*
Magnolia	..	..	1963	2359	351	50	14	M	
Manitoba	..	..	1966	4507	463	61	19	M	
Michigan	..	..	1966	4503	463	62	19	M	
Missouri	..	..	1966	4508	463	62	19	M	
Nebraska	..	..	1966	4505	463	62	19	M	

United States Line: AMERICAN ASTRONAUT [*Fotoship*

United Steamship Co: MICHIGAN [*John G. Callis*

Van Ommeren: ZWIJNDRECHT

[R. J. Weeks

Vascongada: ARRAIZ, dating from 1925

[Malcolm Cranfield

Name	Date	Tons Gross	Length (feet)	Breadth (feet)	Speed (knots)	Engines	Former Names
Ohio..	1956	2812	355	50	14	M	
Oklahoma ..	1956	2806	356	50	14	M	
Ontario	1966	4423	463	62	19	M	
Petunia	1963	2383	351	50	14	M	To S'pore, ren. C. JOYCE
Prinsesse Margrethe	1968	7956	410	63	22	M(2)	
Prinsessen ..	1957	5061	397	53	20	M(2)(A)	ex Princesse Margrethe 68.
Skyros	1962	2661	362	51	14	M	To Lebanon, ren. BERYTE
Trekroner ..	1970	7698	404	63	20	M(2)	
Winston Churchill	1967	8658	461	67	22	M(2)	
Wisconsin ..	1966	4508	463	61	19	M	

Also a large fleet of coastal and short sea vessels.

(NETHERLANDS)
PHS. VAN OMMEREN N.V.

FUNNEL: *Black with white 'V' inside white ring.*

HULL: *Black with red boot-topping.*

Name	Date	Tons Gross	Length (feet)	Breadth (feet)	Speed (knots)	Engines	Former Names
Deltadrecht	1966	24698	658	95	15	M(A)	
Dordrecht ..	1965	24599	646	95	15	M(A)	
Duivendrecht	1965	24699	658	95	15	M(A)	
Holendrecht	1958	11931	541	68	14	M(A)	
Katendrecht	1961	8517	473	66	16	M	
Meerdrecht	1959	11931	541	68	14	M(A)	
Moordrecht	1962	15593	584	75	15	M(A)	ex Fruen 69, ex Hoegh Transporter 65.
Ossendrecht	1958	13871	612	68	14	M(A)	
Papendrecht	1961	8947	500	65	15	M	ex Holsworthy Beacon 68.
Pendrecht ..	1963	8998	500	65	15	M	ex Hurley Beacon 68
Pooldrecht	1962	9003	500	65	15	M	ex Brecon Beacon 68
Sliedrecht ..	1950	13066	557	69	14½	M(A)	
Thuredrecht	1960	13732	612	70	14½	M(A)	
Waardrecht	1962	10442	516	66	14½	M	
Wieldrecht	1963	10442	516	66	14½	M	
Woensdrecht	1964	10450	516	66	14½	M	
Zwijndrecht	1958	11946	540	68	14¼	M(A)	

(SPAIN)
CIA. NAVIERA VASCONGADA

FUNNEL: *Black with monogram composed of a red 'V' and blue 'N' on broad white band.*

HULL: *Black.*

Name	Date	Tons Gross	Length (feet)	Breadth (feet)	Speed (knots)	Engines	Former Names
Adriana	1969	4267	387	54	14	M(A)	
Alejandro Zubizarreta	1959	8224	474	61	13	M(A)	
Arraiz	1925	4537	385	56	9	SR	ex Queenswood.
Valentina Frias	1960	6366	474	61	13	M(A)	

O. WALLENIUS
VARIOUS COMPANIES

FUNNEL: *Yellow with yellow ' OW 'on broad green band.*

HULL: *Light grey with red boot-topping.*

Name			Date	Tons Gross	Length (feet)	Breadth (feet)	Speed (knots)	Engines	Former Names
Aida ..	..	..	1966	2274	326	49	13½	M(A)	
Andreas U*		..	1966	18803	609	75	15	M(A)	
Axel U*	..	..	1967	18669	609	79	15	M(A)	
Carmen	..	..	1963	17956	600	75	16	M(A)	
Citadel*	..	..	1966	18781	609	75	15	M(A)	
Johan U*	..	..	1966	18798	609	75	16	M(A)	
Madame Butterfly			1969	23360	661	91	16	M(A)	
Medea	..	..	1963	17959	600	75	16	M(A)	
Mignon	..	..	1970	2800	—	—	14	M	
Otello			1967	2274	325	49	13½	M(A)	
Rigoletto	..	..	1968	23361	661	91	16	M(A)	
Soya-Atlantic†	..		1954	15975	596	75	15	ST(A)	
Soya-Baltic†	..		1964	37792	788	108	17	ST(A)	
Traviata	..	..	1969	23360	660	91	16	M(A)	
Otello									

† Ore/oil carriers.   * Chartered vessels.   Also tankers and smaller ships.

Wallenius Bremen G.m.b.H.

Boheme	..	..	1968	9866	441	69	22	M(2)	
Tosca	..	..	1963	17836	627	81	15	M(A)	ex Donau 68.
Undine	..	..	1966	2179	312	49	13½	M(A)	

Also smaller ships.   See also Atlantic Container Line.

WATERMAN STEAMSHIP CORP.

FUNNEL: *Yellow, some with black ' W ' on white diamond on broad blue band.*

HULL: *Grey or black with red boot-topping.*

Jeff Davis		1962	12800					ex China Bear, ex Canad
Andrew Jackson	..	1945	6065	469	63	16	ST	
Carrier Dove	..	1944	8027	492	70	16	ST	ex Java Mail 69, ex Grafton 47, ex Sea Sparrow 44.
Citrus Packer	..	1945	7917	492	70	16	ST	ex American Mail 69, ex Sea Adder 47.
City of Alma	..	1945	6065	469	63	16	ST	
De Soto	..	1944	6065	469	63	16	ST	
Fairport	..	1946	6065	469	63	16	ST	
Joseph Hewes		1953	9300					ex President Jackson, Vol Mo

ex President Buchanan,

Wallenius: AXEL U

[*F. R. Sherlock*

Waterman Steamship Corporation: MADAKET

[*B. Reeves*

Westfal-Laesen: FJELLANGER

[Malcolm Cranfield

Westfal-Larsen: MALMANGER

[John G. Callis

Name			Date	Tons Gross	Length (feet)	Breadth (feet)	Speed (knots)	Engines	Former Names
Fanwood	..	..	1944	8178	459	63	16	ST	ex A. & J. Doctor Max 64, ex Fanwood 64, ex Hawaiian Banker 61, ex Sierra 61, ex Stokes 47.
Hastings	..	..	1944	6149	469	63	16	ST	
Hurricane	..		1943	7995	492	70	16½	ST	ex President Fillmore 68, ex President Harrison 66, ex Calloway 48, ex Sea Mink 48.
Iberville	..	..	1945	6065	469	63	16	ST	
Jeff Davis	..	..	1945	7948	492	70	17	ST	ex New York 68, ex Pacific Transport 60, ex Sea Scorpion 47.
John B. Waterman			1946	6165	469	63	16	ST	
Kyska	..	..	1945	6065	469	63	16	ST	
Lafayette	..	..	1944	7970	492	70	16	ST	ex California Mail 68, ex Canada Mail 63, ex Goshen 47, ex Sea Hare.
La Salle	..	..	1943	7995	492	70	16½	ST	ex President Johnson 68, ex Clay 48, ex Sea Carp 43.
Madaket	..	..	1945	6065	469	63	16	ST	
Morning Light	..		1941	7771	491	70	16	ST	ex Michigan 69, ex Washington 59, ex American Transport 58, ex Hawaiian Shipper 48, ex Empire Fulmar 42, ex Hawaiian Shipper 42.
Noonday	..	..	1945	7886	493	70	16½	ST	ex Bengal Mail 69, ex Oregon Mail 64, ex Sea Satyr 47.
Topa Topa	..		1945	6065	469	63	16	ST	
Wild Ranger		..	1946	8229	460	63	16	ST	
Yaka	..	..	1944	6065	469	63	16	ST	
Robert E. Lee			1974	32,300				ST	(LASH)
ex Canada Bear			1962	12,800					ex CANADA BEAR
Nathaniel Greene			1962	12,800					ex PHILIPPINE BEAR

(NORWAY)

WESTFAL-LARSEN & CO. A/S

FUNNEL: *Yellow with narrow black top and two narrow black bands. (Those ships operated jointly with Star Shg. Company have 2 stars on white plate between black top and bands.)*

HULL: *Grey with green boot-topping.*

Name			Date	Tons	Length	Breadth	Speed	Engines	
Berganger			1974	35500	bulk			M	To Lib, ren. KARANA AMPAT
Brimanger	..		1960	5604	413	56	17	M	
Davanger	..		1968	18470	564	85	15¾	M(A)	
Evanger	..		1955	7143	443	58	15½	M	
Falkanger	..		1965	16707	577	75	15	M(A)	To India, ren. ALEXANDRA N.
Fauskanger	..		1965	8999	476	62	17	M	
Fjellanger	..		1962	15649	561	72	15	M(A)	ex Silja 65.
Fossanger	..		1965	16683	577	75	15	M(A)	To India, ren. CHARISMA N.
Evanger								M	
Falkanger								M	

WESTFAL-LARSEN & CO. A/S (continued)

Name			Date	Tons Gross	Length (feet)	Breadth (feet)	Speed (knots)	Engines	Former Names
Heranger	..	..	1968	18469	564	85	15¾	M(A)	
Hosanger	..	..	1958	9709	497	63	14¾	M	
Hoyanger	..	..	1959	9477	511	64	17½	M	*to Bruusgard, ren. Her*
Malmanger	..	..	1968	18470	564	85	15¾	M(A)	
Moldanger	..	..	1950	8055	485	61	17	M	
Porsanger	..	..	1958	7285	443	60	16½	M	
Ravnanger	..	..	1963	8999	476	62	16½	M	
Risanger	..	..	1951	8044	485	61	17	M	
Siranger	..	..	1960	7128	444	58	16½	M	
Taranger	..	..	1969	18470	564	85	15¾	M(A)	
Villanger	..	..	1958	6647	505	64	17	M	*To Norway. ren. RYTTI*

Also tankers.

WEST HARTLEPOOL S. N. CO. LTD.

FUNNEL: *Yellow with black top and black " G ".*
HULL: *Black with red boot-topping.*

Grantleyhall	..		1962	9455	463	61	12½	M(A)	ex Skycrest 68.

(NORWAY)

WILH. WILHELMSEN

FUNNEL: *Black with two light blue bands close together.*
HULL: *Black with white line and red boot-topping.*

Name			Date	Tons Gross	Length	Breadth	Speed	Engines	Former Names
Tagaytay	..	..	1958	6147	524	66	17	M	
Tagus	..	..	1953	6397	499	64	17	M	
Taiko	..	..	1967	8811	552	80	21	M(A)	
Taimyr	..	..	1968	8817	552	80	21	M(A)	
Tai Ping	..	..	1958	6147	524	66	17	M	
Takara	..	..	1968	35955	735	104	16	M(A)	
Talabot	..	..	1967	8811	552	80	17	M	
Talisman	..	..	1952	6785	504	64	16	M	
Talleyrand	..	..	1949	6126	479	61	16	M	
Tamerlane	..	..	1967	7250	498	68	19½	M(A)	
Tampa	..	..	1959	6722	496	64	16	M	ex Alamak 69.
Tanabata	..	..	1968	35955	735	104	16	M(A)	
Tancred	..	..	1948	6133	479	61	16	M	
Tarantel	..	..	1960	6143	524	66	17	M	
Tarn	..	..	1961	7178	510	68	17½	M(A)	
Taronga	..	..	1967	7345	500	68	19½	M(A)	
Tatra	..	..	1959	6427	475	62	15	M	ex Sistina 66. *To Spore*
Tema	..	..	1960	3400	403	54	16	M	ex Brookville 63.
Temeraire	..	..	1957	6017	499	64	18	M	
Tennessee	..	..	1960	6723	496	64	16	M	ex Alnitak 69. *To Chma, re*
Terrier	..	..	1954	5231	459	60	16½	M	
Texas	..	..	1960	6723	496	64	16	M	ex Aludra 69. *To China, ren*
Theben	..	..	1953	7010	510	65	17½	M	
Themis	..	..	1953	7022	510	65	17½	M	
Thermopylae	..	..	1949	7262	520	65	17	M(2)	
Tiber	..	..	1954	6438	499	64	17	M	
Tijuca	..	..	1959	5999	490	64	17	M	
Tirranna	..	..	1967	10060	498	68	19½	M(A)	
Titania	..	..	1958	3396	403	54	16	M	ex Crestville 61.
Tachibana	..	..	1974	36300				M	*bulk*

Tender Carrier   1974   1500

West Hartlepool S.N. Co GRANTLEYHALL [*Malcolm Cranfield*

Wilh. Wilhelmsen: TARONGA [*F. R. Sherlock*

Wilh. Wilhelmsen: TAIKO

Wilh. Wilhelmsen: TENERIFFA since sold   [A. P. Oakden

Zim Israel Navigation Co: MEZADA   [John G. Callis

Name			Date	Tons Gross	Length (feet)	Breadth (feet)	Speed (knots)	Engines	Former Names
Toledo	..	..	1960	7161	510	68	18	M	
Tonsberg	..	..	1960	7151	510	68	17½	M(A)	
Toreador	..	..	1954	6005	472	62	17	M	
Toro	..	..	1969	8256	453	66	18	M(A)	
Toronto	..	..	1956	5506	466	60	16½	M	
Torrens	..	..	1967	7345	500	68	19½	M(A)	
Tortugas	..	..	1959	6723	496	64	16	M	ex Alchiba 69. *roChina, r*
Toulouse	..	..	1962	5013	449	60	17	M(A)	*toS'pore* *GUANG*
Trafalgar	..	..	1949	5466	464	62	16½	M	
Traviata	..	..	1959	6180	524	66	18	M	
Trianon	..	..	1961	7178	510	68	18	M(A)	
Tricolor	..	..	1960	7054	510	68	18	M(A)	
Trinidad	..	..	1968	8825	552	80	21	M(A)	
Troubadour	..	..	1954	6006	472	62	17	M	*ToEngland*
Tugela	..	..	1954	6988	510	65	17½	M	
Tulane	..	..	1956	6374	492	63	15	M	
Tungsha	..	..	1952	5461	464	62	16½	M	*ToGreece. ren .FANEROM*
Turandot	..	..	1957	5895	490	64	17	M	
Tyr	..	..	1968	5491	453	66	21	M(A)	
Tysla	..	..	1958	8736	467	61	17	M	ex Bay Master 65.

Also tankers.

IDWAL WILLIAMS & CO. LTD.
Garth Shipping Co. Ltd.
Graig Shipping Co. Ltd. and
Glynafon Shipping Co. Ltd.

FUNNEL: *Red "G" on white over green bands separating white from black top.*

HULL: *Green with dark green boot-topping.*

Glyntaf	..	..	1966	16329	573	75	15	M(A)	ex East Breeze 66.
Graigffion	..		1968	18453	611	83	15	M(A)	
Graigwerdd		..	1964	18618	611	83	15	M(A)	

(SPAIN)

YBARRA & CIA. S.A.

FUNNEL: *Black with white AV superimposed.*

HULL: *White or Grey.*

Cabo Del Pinar	..	1948	2542	292	43	12	SR	ex Villafranca 63.
Cabo Penas		1949	2544	292	43	12	SR	ex Villahueva 63.
Cabo San Roque	..	1957	14491	556	69	20	M(2)	
Cabo San Vicente		1959	14293	556	69	20	M(2)	
Cabo Santa Marta		1957	4972	431	57	16½	M	ex Pedro de Valdivia 64.
Cabo Santa Pola	..	1948	10142	487	62	16½	M	ex Monte Urbasa 69, ex Escorial 48.

Also smaller ships.

236

ZIM ISRAEL NAVIGATION CO. LTD.

FUNNEL: *White with seven gold stars between two blue bands.*

HULL: *Passenger and Refrigerated vessels—white with green boot-topping.*
Cargo vessels—Black with red boot-topping or grey with green boot-topping.

Name			Date	Tons Gross	Length (feet)	Breadth (feet)	Speed (knots)	Engines	Former Names
Alon	..	..	1960	5838	418	59	16	M(A)	
Ampal	..	..	1958	7915	516	68	16	M	
Beer Sheva		..	1961	5603	473	62	15	M	
Besor	..	..	1967	35121	742	104	16	M(A)	
Dahlia	..	..	1961	9378	463	61	16	M(A)	
Deganya	..	..	1960	5624	473	62	15½	M	
Elat	..	..	1960	19234	676	74	16	M(A)	
En Gedi	..	..	1964	23537	643	89	16	M(A)	
Eshel	..	..	1961	5828	418	59	16	M(A)	
Eshkol	..	..	1964	4219	444	58	18	M	
Etrog	..	..	1964	4219	444	58	18	M	
Galila	..	..	1967	4925	405	55	16	M(A)	ex Cinnamon Bay 67.
Gedera	..	..	1960	5624	473	62	15½	M	
Geffen	..	..	1959	2958	312	45	14	M(A)	ex Amal 69.
Hadar	..	..	1964	4219	444	58	18	M	
Mazal	..	..	1964	5000	455	60	17	M	
Mezada	..	..	1960	19247	676	74	16	M(A)	
Negba	..	..	1958	7913	517	68	16	M	
Nogah	..	..	1964	5000	455	60	17	M	*ren. Golden Beetle, To Lib.*
Nurith	..	..	1961	6982	463	61	16	M(A)	
Qeshet	..	..	1964	5000	455	60	17	M	*To Lib, ren. GOLDLEAF*
Sahar	..	..	1963	4899	451	61	17	M	*To Lib, ren. GOLD STREAM*
Shavit	..	..	1963	4895	451	61	17	M	
Shigma	..	..	1961	5836	418	59	16	M(A)	
Shomron	..	..	1955	5329	415	54	17	M	*to Cyprus, ren. AIDA*
Tamar	..	..	1967	5485	423	58	13½	M(A)	
Teverya	..	..	1961	5603	473	62	15½	M	
Timna	..	..	1961	19235	676	74	16	M(A)	
Tsedek	..	..	1963	4907	451	61	16	M	
Yafo	..	..	1964	4219	444	58	18	M	
Rimon			1967	5389				M	*ex Opal*
Avedat (bulk)			1964	23,537					
ex LILAC (cont.)			1956	6,233					

Zim Israel Navigation Co: ESKOL

CLASSIFIED NAMES

(Passenger Liners and Cargo Ships Section)

Names beginning					Company
ACT——	..	..	..	..	Assoc. Contr. Transportation
AL——	..	..	..	..	Nievelt Goudriaan
AMERICAN X——		..	..	..	U.S. Lines
AMSTEL——		..	..	..	Amsterdam
ATLANTIC X——	..	..	..	..	Atlantic Container Line
B——	..	..	..	..	Fred Olsen
BARON X——	..	..	..	..	Hogarth
BEAVER——	..	..	..	..	Canadian Pacific
BEL——	..	..	..	..	Christen Smith
BEN——	..	..	..	..	Ben Line Steamers
BLACK X——	..	..	..	..	Herlofson
BULK X——	..	..	..	..	Herlofson
CABO X——	..	..	..	..	Ybarra
CAP X——	..	..	..	..	Hamburg South America
CAPE X——	..	..	..	..	Lyle
CITY OF X——	..	..	..	..	Ellerman
CLAN X——	..	..	..	..	Clan
CLARK——	..	..	..	..	Clarkson (Denholm)
CONCORDIA X——	..	..	..	..	Haaland
CRYSTAL X——	..	..	..	..	Sugar
EASTERN X——	..	..	..	..	Indo-China
EMPRESS OF X——	..	..	..	..	Canadian Pacific
EX——	..	..	..	..	American Export Isbrandtsen
EXPORT X——	..	..	..	..	American Export Isbrandtsen
FAIR——	..	..	..	..	Sitmar
FERN——	..	..	..	..	Fearnley & Eger
FINN——	..	..	..	..	Finnlines
FLYING X——	..	..	..	..	American Export Isbrandtsen
FORT X——	..	..	..	..	French Line
GLEN——	..	..	..	..	Glen
HAWAIIAN X——	..	..	..	..	Matson
HELLENIC X——	..	..	..	..	Hellenic Lines
HOEGH X——	..	..	..	..	Hoegh
HUNTS——	..	..	..	..	Power
INDIAN X——	..	..	..	..	India
IRISH X——	..	..	..	..	Irish Shg.
IRON X——	..	..	..	..	Vallum (Common Bros.) or Naess
JAG X——	..	..	..	..	Great Eastern
JALA——	..	..	..	..	Scindia
JAMAICA X——	..	..	..	..	Jamaica Banana (Kaye)
KING X——	..	..	..	..	King Line (Clan)
LA X——	..	..	..	..	Buries Markes
LAKE X——	..	..	..	..	Australian National
LONDON X——	..	..	..	..	London & Overseas Freighters
MA—— (Indian names)		..	..	..	Cunard (Brocklebank)
MANCHESTER X——	..	..	..	..	Manchester Liners
MONTE X——	..	..	..	..	Aznar
MORMAC——	..	..	..	..	Moore-McCormack
NEDER X——	..	..	..	..	Nederland
OR——	..	..	..	..	P. & O.
ORE——	..	..	..	..	Ore Carriers (Houlder)
PACIFIC X——	..	..	..	..	Furness Withy
PANDO X——	..	..	..	..	P. & O.
PIONEER X——	..	..	..	..	United States Lines
POLAR X——	..	..	..	..	Hamburg S. America
PORT X——	..	..	..	..	Port Line
PRESIDENT X——	..	..	..	..	American President
RIVER X——	..	..	..	..	Nigerian National
S.A. X——	..	..	..	..	South African Marine Corp.
SAL——	..	..	..	..	Salvesen

Names beginning					Company
SANTA X——	..	..	..	..	*Grace or Ham. South America*
SHEAF X——	..	..	..	..	*Souter*
SILVER——	..	..	..	..	*Silver*
SIR X—— ..	..	..	..	..	*Min. of Defence*
SKAU—— ..	..	..	..	..	*Skaugen*
STRAAT X——	..	..	..	..	*Royal Inter-Ocean*
SUGAR X——	..	..	..	..	*Sugar*
T——	..	..	..	..	*Wilhelmsen*
THORS——	..	..	..	..	*Dahl*
TJI—— ..	..	..	..	..	*Royal Inter-Ocean*
TRANS—— ..	..	..	..	..	*Seatrain Lines*
TRE—— ..	..	..	..	..	*Hain-Nourse*
VISHVA X——	..	..	..	..	*Shg. Corp. of India*

Names ending					Company
——ANGER	..	..	..	..	*Westfal Larsen*
——BANK ..	..	..	..	..	*Bank*
—— BAY ..	..	..	..	..	*Overseas Contrs Line*
—— BEACON	..	..	..	..	*Van Ommeren*
——BRIDGE	..	..	..	..	*Seabridge*
——BURY ..	..	..	..	..	*Houlder (Alexander)*
——BY ..	..	..	..	..	*Ropner*
—— C ..	..	..	..	..	*Costa*
—— CASTLE	..	..	..	..	*Union Castle*
—— CITY ..	..	..	..	..	*C. Hill (Bristol) or Reardon Smith*
—— DAM ..	..	..	..	..	*Holland America*
—— DAN ..	..	..	..	..	*Lauritzen*
——DRECHT	..	..	..	..	*Van Ommeren*
——DYK ..	..	..	..	..	*Holland America*
——FELS ..	..	..	..	..	*Hansa*
——FIELD ..	..	..	..	..	*Hunting*
——FJELL ..	..	..	..	..	*Olsen & Ugelstad*
——FJORD ..	..	..	..	..	*Norwegian America*
——GARTH	..	..	..	..	*Cory*
——GATE ..	..	..	..	..	*Turnbull Scott*
—— GRANGE	..	..	..	..	*Houlder*
—— HEAD ..	..	..	..	..	*Heyn*
——HOLM ..	..	..	..	..	*Swedish America or Swedish Atlantic*
——IA	..	..	..	..	*Cunard or Anchor*
——IA (flowers)	..	..	..	..	*Stag*
——IAN ..	..	..	..	..	*Ellerman*
——IC ..	..	..	..	..	*Shaw Savill*
——ISTAN ..	..	..	..	..	*Strick*
——KERK ..	..	..	..	..	*United Netherlands*
——LAND ..	..	..	..	..	*Swedish Orient or Tirfing*
—— (DE) LARRINAGA	..	..	..	..	*Larrinaga*
—— LAURO ..	..	..	..	..	*Lauro*
—— L.D. ..	..	..	..	..	*Dreyfus*
—— LEONHARDT	..	..	..	..	*Leonhardt*
—— LLOYD ..	..	..	..	..	*Royal Rotterdam Lloyd*
—— LYKES ..	..	..	..	..	*Lykes Bros.*
—— MAERSK	..	..	..	..	*Moller*
—— MARU ..	..	..	..	..	*Japanese (possibly N.Y.K. or Mitsui-O.S.K.)*
——MORE ..	..	..	..	..	*Johnston Warren*
——MOOR ..	..	..	..	..	*Anchor*
—— PALM ..	..	..	..	..	*Palm*

Names ending					Company
——PARK	..	..	..	..	*Denholm*
——POOL	..	..	..	..	*Ropner*
—— PRINCE	..	..	..	..	*Prince*
—— REEFER	..	..	..	..	*Lauritzen*
—— RICKMERS	..	..	..	..	*Rickmers*
—— RIVER	..	..	..	..	*Black Star*
——SHIRE (English)		..	..	..	*Bibby*
——SHIRE (Scottish)		..	..	..	*Scottish Shire (Clan)*
——SHIRE (Welsh)		..	..	..	*Glen*
—— SKOU	..	..	..	..	*Skou*
——STAN	..	..	..	..	*Common Bros. or Strick*
—— STAR	..	..	..	..	*Blue Star*
—— STATE	..	..	..	..	*States Marine*
——STEIN	..	..	..	..	*Norddeutscher Lloyd*
——TON	..	..	..	..	*Chapman & Willan*
—— TORM	..	..	..	..	*Andersen*
—— TRADER	..	..	..	..	*Trader Nav. Co.*
——VILLE	..	..	..	..	*Klaveness*
——WOOD	..	..	..	..	*France Fenwick or Jacobs*
——WORTH	..	..	..	..	*Dalgliesh*

Names and Themes				Company
CHINESE	..	..	..	*China Nav. Co.*
" CITY " MARU	..	..	..	*Mitsui-O.S.K.*
COUNTIES (English)	..	..	..	*Federal*
COUNTRIES	..	..	..	*East Asiatic or Johnson*
EGYPTIAN TOWNS	..	..	..	*Moss Hutchison*
GERMAN TOWNS	..	..	..	*Hamburg America*
GREEK MYTHOLOGY	..	..	..	*Blue Funnel*
INDONESIAN	..	..	..	*Nederland or Royal Rotterdam Lloyd*
IRISH COUNTIES	..	..	..	*Avenue*
NEW ZEALAND NAMES	..	..	..	*Federal (New Zealand Shg. Co.) or Union S.S. Co. of N.Z.*
POETS, AUTHORS, ARTISTS, Etc.			..	*Lamport & Holt*
RIVERS (Central & S. American)			..	*Fyffes*
SAINTS—MALE CHRISTIAN NAMES			..	*Booth*
SPANISH NAMES BEGINNING WITH P—— or V——		..	..	*MacAndrews*
TRADES & PROFESSIONS		..	..	*Harrison*
WEST AFRICAN PLACES		..	..	*Elder Dempster*

Gulf Oil Corporation: UNIVERSE IRELAND, one of a group of six tankers which are at present the largest in the world, is eased towards terminal jetty

[Gulf Oil (G.B.) Ltd

PART TWO

Tankers

BRITISH GOVERNMENT

Ministry of Defence
(Navy Department)

FUNNEL: *Grey with black top.*

HULL: *Black or grey.*

Name	Date	Tons Gross	Tons Dwt	Length (feet)	Breadth (feet)	Speed (knots)	Engines	Former Names
Bayleaf*	1955	12123	17930	557	71	14½	M	ex London Integrity 59.
Black Ranger ..	1941	3440	3489	366	47	13½	M	
Blue Ranger ..	1941	3475	3543	366	47	13½	M	
Blue Rover ..	1970	7500	7060	461	63	18	M	
Brambleleaf* ..	1954	12123	18706	557	71	14	M	ex London Loyalty 59.
Brown Ranger..	1941	3462	3631	366	47	14	M	
Derwentdale*	1964	42343	72550	799	118	16	M	ex Halcyon Breeze 67.
Dewdale*	1965	35642	63588	775	108	15½	M	ex Edenfield 67.
Gold Ranger ..	1941	3324	3788	355	48	14	M	
Green Rover ..	1969	7503	7060	461	63	18	M	
Grey Rover ..	1969	7450	7060	461	63	18	M	
Olmeda ..	1965	18586	22270	648	84	18	ST	
Olna	1966	18582	22000	648	84	18	ST	
Olwen	1965	18604	22350	648	84	18	ST	ex Olynthus 67.
Orangeleaf* ..	1955	12481	17475	556	71	15	M	ex Southern Satellite 59.
Pearleaf* ..	1960	12353	18500	568	72	15	M	
Plumleaf* ..	1960	12459	18562	560	72	15	M	
Tideflow ..	1956	12980	18297	583	71	17	ST	ex Tiderace 58.
Tidepool ..	1963	14130	17400	584	71	17	ST	
Tidereach ..	1965	12965	18292	583	71	17	ST	
Tidespring ..	1963	13543	18918	584	71	17	ST	
Tidesurge ..	1956	13732	16800	583	71	17	ST	ex Tiderange 58.
Wave Baron ..	1946	8364	11423	491	64	14½	ST	ex Empire Flodden 46.
Wave Chief ..	1946	8322	11226	493	64	14½	ST	ex Empire Edghill 46.
Wave Prince ..	1946	8447	11257	494	64	14½	ST	ex Empire Herald 46.
Wave Ruler ..	1946	8386	11335	491	64	14½	ST	ex Empire Evesham 47.

* On charter.   Also small tankers.

ALVA S.S. CO. LTD.

FUNNEL: *Yellow with blue " V ".*

HULL: *White with green or red boot-topping.*

Name		Date	Tons Gross	Tons Dwt	Length	Breadth	Speed	Engines
Alva Star	..	1970	113933	228100	1090	150	15½	ST

Ministry of Defence (Naval): PLUMLEAF [*D. Clegg*

Ministry of Defence (Naval): BRAMBLELEAF [*Malcolm Cranfield*

Alvion Steamship Corporation: ALMIZAR

[R. J. Weeks]

[R. J. Weeks

Bergenske (Bergen Line): VEGA

Various Corporations under Liberian flag

Name		Date	Tons Gross	Tons Dwt	Length (feet)	Breadth (feet)	Speed (knots)	Engines	Former Names
Alchiba ..	..	1969	17000	26800	631	81	15	ST	
Alkaid ..	..	1953	15805	23790	603	77	14	M	
Alkor ..	..	1953	15805	23820	603	77	14	M	
Almak ..	..	1952	12618	19050	559	72	14	M	
Almizar..	..	1964	30599	57100	760	105	15	ST	
Alnair ..	..	1964	31330	55800	775	107	15	ST	
Altanin ..	..	1964	44935	83400	870	120	16½	ST	
Alvega ..	..	1956	21789	31816	663	87	14½	ST	

AMPOL PETROLEUM LTD.

FUNNEL: *Pale yellow, blue top and houseflag.*
HULL: *Grey.*

Name		Date	Tons Gross	Tons Dwt	Length	Breadth	Speed	Engines
Leslie J. Thompson	..	1959	16205	24700	615	77	15	M
P. J. Adams	..	1962	33979	54000	804	88	15½	ST
William G. Walkley	..	1954	12614	19050	556	72	13	M

CIE. AUXILIAIRE DE NAVIGATION

FUNNEL: *Black with broad band of red and white stripes.*
HULL: *Black with red boot-topping.*

Name		Date	Tons Gross	Tons Dwt	Length	Breadth	Speed	Engines	Former Names
Bethsabee	..	1952	21121	31174	665	85	15	M(2)	
Dahla	..	1954	21807	32853	663	87	16	ST	Torrance
Esmeralda	..	1957	27990	43099	724	98	16	ST	
Fabiola ..	..	1959	32125	50474	772	101	16½	M(2)	
Fausta ..	..	1961	32177	50577	772	101	16½	M(2)	
Gilda ..	..	1970	67280	—	—	—	16½	ST	
Gwenola	..	1966	57514	101130	919	123	16½	M	

ODD BERG

FUNNEL: *Black with black " B " silhouette on white disc.*
HULL: *Black.*

Name		Date	Tons Gross	Tons Dwt	Length	Breadth	Speed	Engines
Kollbryn	..	1966	51396	91800	840	128	16	ST
Kollbris	..	1960	12808	19775	560	72	15	M

Bergesen: BERGEHAVEN, whose port of registration is Stavanger

[R. J. Weeks

249

DET. BERGENSKE D/S. (BERGEN LINE)

FUNNEL: *Black with three white rings widely separated.*

HULL: *Grey with red boot-topping.*

Name	Date	Tons Gross	Tons Dwt	Length (feet)	Breadth (feet)	Speed (knots)	Engines	Former Names
Vega	1963	12678	19600	557	72	15½	M	

Also ocean, short-sea and coastal ships.

SIGVAL BERGESEN

FUNNEL: *Black with black anchor on broad white band.*

HULL: *Black.*

Name	Date	Tons Gross	Tons Dwt	Length	Breadth	Speed	Engines	Former Names
Barfonn† ..	1969	7000	7100	414	60	16	M	
Frostfonn†	1965	4183	4883	364	50	16	M	
Isfonn† ..	1966	14986	14400	581	80	16	M	
Rimfonn ..	1963	50677	86760	869	122	16	ST	
Stolt Vestfonn ..	1958	13409	19554	560	72	14	M	ex Vestfonn 65.
Sydfonn†	1965	4180	4888	364	50	16	M	
Tindfonn ..	1961	30992	51412	754	98	15½	ST	

Also cargo ships.   † Liquefied gas carrier.

SIG. BERGESEN d.y. & COMPANY

FUNNEL: *White with black top having diagonal light green stripe and house flag.*

HULL: *Light green.   Some vessels have green superstructure.*

Name	Date	Tons Gross	Tons Dwt	Length	Breadth	Speed	Engines	Former Names
Berge Bergesen	1963	52734	96140	869	122	17	M	
Berge Commander	1968	103178	202250	1065	159	16	M	
Berge Edda ..	1970	83168	162100	956	135	16	M	
Berge King ..	1970	142000	277800	1125	170	16	M	
Berge Odel ..	1963	31831	55025	734	194	17	M	
Berge Sigval ..	1967	54334	100885	865	128	15½	M	
Berge Tasta ..	1969	79969	156400	956	135	16	M	
Bergebig ..	1966	78785	149513	915	145	16	M	
Bergeborg ..	1966	78778	149634	915	145	16	M	
Bergebragd ..	1968	80003	156680	956	135	16	M ToGreece,ren .DARING
Bergehaven ..	1966	78785	149556	915	145	16	M	
Bergehus ..	1967	103194	202557	1065	159	15¾	M	
Bergeland ..	1965	52121	96170	869	122	16	M	
Bergetun ..	1967	57729	109545	881	122	16	M	
Bergevik ..	1969	54282	100000	865	128	16	M	
Bergevanga	1974							

Also cargo ships.

Berge Septimus 1974 139800   M

BIBBY LINE LTD.

FUNNEL: *Pink, black top.*

HULL: *Black, red boot-topping.*

Name	Date	Tons Gross	Tons Dwt	Length (feet)	Breadth (feet)	Speed (knots)	Engines	Former Names
Yorkshire	1975						M	
Wiltshire†	1968	10036	12320	498	70	16	M	
Devonshire †	1974	32100					M	

† Liquefied gas carrier.

BIORN BIORNSTAD & CO.

FUNNEL: *Black " B " on yellow with narrow black top.*

HULL: *Light grey, red boot-topping.*

Name		Date	Tons Gross	Tons Dwt	Length (feet)	Breadth (feet)	Speed (knots)	Engines	Former Names
Beau	..	1964	34137	59750	775	106	16	M	
Beaufort	..	1966	40852	74480	785	121	16	M	
Beau Geste	..	1963	31331	49660	750	102	16	ST	
Beaumont	..	1966	40850	74480	785	121	16	M	
Beauregard	..	1965	41007	74480	785	121	16	M	
Beauval	..	1967	48429	85750	846	128	16	M	

BLANDFORD SHG. CO. LTD.

FUNNEL: *Blue with white form (having diagonal green line) and red " B " over thin yellow cross (X).*

HULL: *Black with red boot-topping.*

Name		Date	Tons Gross	Tons Dwt	Length (feet)	Breadth (feet)	Speed (knots)	Engines	Former Names
Bamford	..	1967	54090	103700	889	128	16	ST	
Bedford	..	1967	54066	103785	889	128	16	ST	
Bideford	..	1969	107924	173500	1072	158	16	ST	
Boxford	..	1970	113081	215000	1069	158	16	ST	
Bulford	..	1968	105095	210822	1067	158	16	ST	

Bredford Co. Inc.

Name		Date	Tons Gross	Tons Dwt	Length (feet)	Breadth (feet)	Speed (knots)	Engines	Former Names
Blankenberg	..	1967	43122	87786	810	128	16	M	

Biornstad: BEAUREGARD

BP Tanker: BRITISH SIGNAL

BP TANKER CO. LTD.

FUNNEL: *Red with black top and large white square with BP shield.*
HULL: *Black.*

Name	Date	Tons Gross	Tons Dwt	Length (feet)	Breadth (feet)	Speed (knots)	Engines	Former Names
British Adventure ..	1951	18259	30218	643	82	15½	ST	
British Ambassador ..	1958	27114	44929	710	95	16½	ST	
British Argosy	1966	62427	112786	921	128	16	ST	
British Bombardier	1962	32128	54116	760	97	16	ST	
British Bulldog	1951	18380	30048	643	81	15½	ST	
British Captain	1965	38053	67944	816	108	16	ST	
British Cavalier	1962	32184	54557	760	97	16	ST	
British Centaur	1965	37832	67697	816	108	16	M	
British Chancellor ..	1954	11197	16808	547	70	14	M	ex Clyde Chancellor 64, ex British Chancellor 61.
British Chivalry	1949	11217	16847	547	70	14	M	ex Clyde Chivalry 63, ex British Chivalry 58.
British Comet ..	1960	22741	35268	683	86	16	ST	
British Commodore	1967	38288	67862	820	108	15½	M	
British Confidence ..	1965	37978	67944	816	108	15½	ST	
British Cormorant ..	1961	11132	16039	525	69	15	M	
British Corporal	1954	10071	14577	517	65	12½	M	ex Clyde Corporal 64, ex British Corporal 60.
British Crusader	1954	11148	15848	547	70	14	M	ex Clyde Crusader 64, ex British Crusader 57.
British Cygnet	1962	11137	15441	525	69	15	M	ex BP Explorer 69, ex BP Endeavour 67, ex British Cygnet 64.
British Diplomat	1963	30815	49320	748	100	16½	ST	
British Dragoon	1963	31144	52928	726	102	16	ST	
British Engineer	1954	21597	33539	665	87	15	ST	
British Ensign	1964	43093	75578	815	113	16	ST	
British Fame ..	1949	10942	16849	547	70	14	M	
British Fern ..	1964	13252	19800	561	74	14½	M	
British Fidelity	1969	15260	24414	559	82	14	M	
British Flag ..	1953	11376	16750	547	70	14	M	
British Freedom	1950	11011	16849	547	70	14	M	
British Grenadier	1963	32303	54788	760	97	16	ST	
British Guardian	1953	11359	16481	547	70	14	M	ex Clyde Guardian 63, ex British Guardian 58.
British Guardsman ..	1963	32038	54611	760	97	16	ST	
British Gunner	1954	10076	14571	517	65	12½	M	ex Clyde Gunner 63, ex British Gunner 61.

BP Tanker: BRITISH LAUREL   [*Fotoship*

BP Tanker: BP ENTERPRISE   [*J. Y. Freeman*

Name	Date	Tons Gross	Tons Dwt	Length (feet)	Breadth (feet)	Speed (knots)	Engines	Former Names
British Hawthorn ..	1964	13119	20551	561	74	$14\frac{1}{2}$	M	
British Hazel ..	1964	12964	20462	561	74	$14\frac{1}{2}$	M	
British Hero ..	1954	11358	16481	547	70	14	M	
British Hussar	1962	32341	53860	760	97	16	ST	
British Ivy ..	1965	13271	19800	561	74	$14\frac{1}{2}$	M	
British Kestrel	1962	11171	15922	525	69	15	M	
British Lancer ..	1963	32331	54544	760	97	16	ST	
British Lantern	1960	22780	36914	683	86	16	ST	To Greece
British Laurel	1965	13512	20826	561	74	$14\frac{1}{2}$	M	
British Liberty	1968	15115	24000	557	81	14	M	
British Light ..	1959	22783	36754	683	86	16	ST	
British Loyalty	1968	15118	23900	557	81	14	M	
British Maple ..	1965	13278	20774	561	74	$14\frac{1}{2}$	M	
British Mariner	1963	43378	74635	815	113	16	ST	
British Merchant	1954	20745	33643	665	86	15	ST	
British Merlin..	1962	10945	16116	526	69	15	M	ex BP Enterprise 68, ex British Merlin 65.
British Oak ..	1953	11307	16562	547	70	14	M	
British Officer	1955	11362	16519	547	70	14	M	
British Osprey	1962	11132	16055	526	69	15	M	
British Patrol ..	1954	11193	16518	547	70	14	M	
British Poplar	1965	13530	20774	561	74	$14\frac{1}{2}$	M	
British Prestige	1962	27045	44878	710	95	$16\frac{1}{2}$	ST	
British Reliance	1950	11026	16867	547	70	14	M	
British Resource	1949	11200	16880	547	70	14	M	
British Sailor ..	1953	20729	33738	665	86	15	ST	To Egypt
British Seafarer	1951	11220	16880	547	70	14	M	
British Security	1969	15095	23900	557	81	14	M	
British Sergeant	1954	10073	13907	517	65	$12\frac{1}{2}$	M	ex Clyde Sergeant 63, ex British Sergeant 60.
British Signal ..	1961	22785	36854	683	86	16	ST	
British Skill ..	1952	18291	29891	643	81	$15\frac{1}{2}$	ST	
British Soldier	1954	20794	33548	665	86	15	ST	
British Sovereign	1954	20781	34049	665	86	15	ST	
British Splendour	1950	11233	16823	547	70	14	M	
British Sportsman ..	1951	11231	16798	548	70	14	M	
British Talent	1952	18289	30132	643	81	$15\frac{1}{2}$	ST	
British Tenacity	1969	15095	23900	557	81	14	M	
British Unity ..	1969	15260	24386	559	82	14	M	
British Venture	1963	23397	38040	678	86	16	M	
British Victory	1955	20980	34118	665	86	15	M	
British Vine ..	1965	13408	19989	559	74	$14\frac{1}{2}$	M	
British Vision ..	1954	11190	16768	547	70	14	M	

British Renown 1974 132,000

British Resolution 1974 132,000

BP Tanker Co. Ltd.

(MANAGERS: ASSOCIATED STEAMSHIPS PTY. LTD., MELBOURNE)

Name	Date	Tons Gross	Tons Dwt	Length (feet)	Breadth (feet)	Speed (knots)	Engines	Former Names
BP Endeavour	1967	13187	19480	561	74	15	M	
BP Enterprise	1969	13185	19890	561	74	15	M	

BP Medway Tanker Co. Ltd.

Name	Date	Tons Gross	Tons Dwt	Length (feet)	Breadth (feet)	Speed (knots)	Engines	Former Names
British Explorer	1970	108000	212160	1070	160	16	ST	
British Inventor	1970	108000	212160	1070	160	16	ST	

BP Thames Tanker Co. Ltd.

British Beech ..	1964	12973	20750	561	74	14½	M	
British Holly ..	1965	13271	20638	561	74	14½	M	
British Willow..	1965	13136	19890	561	74	14½	M	

BP Tyne Tanker Co. Ltd.

British Admiral	1965	61768	111274	918	128	16	ST	
British Commerce ..	1965	37814	67579	816	108	16	M	

Tanker Charter Co. Ltd.

British Architect	1958	22729	37342	683	86	16	ST	
British Aviator	1958	22818	35562	683	86	16	ST	
British Courage	1957	21682	35529	680	86	16	ST	
British Duchess	1958	27279	44824	710	95	16½	ST	
British Energy..	1958	22831	37244	683	86	16	ST	
British Faith ..	1958	20709	33666	665	86	16	ST ToGreece, ren. STELI
British Glory ..	1957	20687	33702	665	86	16	ST	
British Honour	1958	20678	33454	665	86	16	ST	
British Industry	1957	20751	33472	665	86	16	ST	
British Judge ..	1959	27124	44804	710	95	16½	ST	
British Justice..	1957	20750	33769	665	86	16	ST	
British Queen..	1959	32187	53383	760	97	16	ST	
British Statesman ..	1959	27182	44701	710	95	16½	ST	
British Trader..	1957	20687	33636	665	86	16	ST	
British Valour..	1957	22681	35246	680	86	16	ST	
British Vigilance	1957	11349	16672	547	70	14	M	

Clyde Charter Co. Ltd.

British Beacon	1959	22779	36834	683	86	16	ST	
British Curlew	1960	11157	15389	525	69	15	M	
British Destiny	1959	27122	44869	710	95	16	ST	
British Fulmar	1959	11169	15983	525	69	15	M	
British Gannet	1959	11238	15262	525	69	15	M ToFngland
British Gull ..	1960	11156	15939	525	69	15	M	
British Kiwi ..	1960	11178	16183	525	69	15	M	
British Mallard	1960	11174	15866	525	69	15	M	
British Power ..	1959	27586	44799	710	95	16	ST	
British Robin ..	1960	11211	15450	526	69	15	M	
British Star ..	1959	22739	36954	683	86	16	ST	
British Swift ..	1959	11174	15404	525	69	15	M To England
British Trust ..	1959	11211	15913	526	69	15	M To England

BP Tanker: BRITISH GANNET [*F. W. Hawks*

BP-Lowland Tanker Co: BORDER CHIEFTAIN [*Fotoship*

The Lowland Tanker Co. Ltd.

(COMMON BROS. (MANAGEMENT) LTD.)

FUNNEL: *Red with black top divided by red, white and green tartan band with " BP " shield.*

HULL: *Black with red boot-topping.*

Name	Date	Tons Gross	Tons Dwt	Length (feet)	Breadth (feet)	Speed (knots)	Engines	Former Names
Border Castle	1961	13048	20455	569	73	14	M	
Border Chieftain	1962	13017	20502	569	73	14	M	
Border Falcon..	1961	13238	20504	569	73	14	M	
Border Laird ..	1955	11366	16200	547	70	13½	M	
Border Minstrel	1954	11339	16186	547	70	13½	M	
Border Pele ..	1961	13228	19610	569	73	14	M	
Border Reiver..	1955	11356	16182	547	70	13½	M	
Border Shepherd	1960	13339	20582	572	73	14	M	
Border Terrier	1956	11347	16028	547	70	13½	M	

Warwick Tanker Co. Ltd.

(HOULDER BROS. & CO. LTD.)

FUNNEL: *Black with " BP " shield over white Maltese Cross on broad red band.*

HULL: *Black with red boot-topping.*

Name	Date	Tons Gross	Tons Dwt	Length	Breadth	Speed	Engines
Bidford Priory	1960	22748	37148	683	86	16	ST
Brandon Priory	1960	22735	35703	683	86	16	ST

Soc. Maritime des Pétroles B.P.

(FRENCH FLAG)

FUNNEL: *Black with green band bordered by two yellow bands and "BP" shield.*

HULL: *Black with red boot-topping.*

Name	Date	Tons Gross	Tons Dwt	Length	Breadth	Speed	Engines
Amboise ..	1961	30971	49366	748	100	16	ST
Azay le Rideau	1964	31959	51110	746	100	16	ST
Blois	1970	128000	240000	1085	160	15½	ST
Chambord ..	1955	21142	32572	668	86	16	ST
Chaumont ..	1958	20867	32770	668	86	16	ST
Chenonceaux ..	1955	21432	32532	668	86	16	ST
Cheverny ..	1956	21430	32670	668	86	16	ST
Montsoreau ..	1968	67280	124082	900	138	16	ST

TH. BROVIG

FUNNEL: *Yellow with house flag panel.*

HULL: *Grey.*

Name	Date	Tons Gross	Tons Dwt	Length (feet)	Breadth (feet)	Speed (knots)	Engines	Former Names
Balla Brovig ..	1955	13969	20100	580	75	14	M	ex Benguela 66.
Bente Brovig ..	1959	12155	19429	581	72	15	M	ex Olivia 69.
Cecile Brovig ..	1958	13296	20250	560	72	15	M	ex Staberg 69.
Cis Brovig ..	1969	56636	106100	912	128	15½	M	
Dea Brovig	1951	10917	16385	531	68	14	M	
G. C. Brovig ..	1951	10917	16345	531	68	14	M	
Gunda Brovig ..	1962	13089	19720	577	72	15	M	ex Olymp 68.
Gunvor Brovig	1957	12111	18500	565	70	14½	M	ex Beaulieu 64.

Also cargo ships.

BURMAH OIL TRADING LTD.

FUNNEL: *Yellow with black top and blue ' L ' on broad white band.*

HULL: *Grey with red boot-topping.*

El Lobo	1959	12078	16600	547	73	14	M	

Burmah Pearl

Burmah Peridot 1974 72,200

CANADIAN PACIFIC (Bermuda) LTD.

FUNNEL: *Green incorporating a modern design with a triangle, a segment of a circle and part of a square.*

HULL: *Black with red boot-topping.*

Lord Mount Stephen ..	1966	41521	71534	758	118	16	M	
Lord Strathcona	1967	41524	71747	758	118	16	M	
Port Hawkesbury	1970	126000	250000	1109	170	15½	M	
T. S. Shaughnessy	1971	133700	—	—	—	15½	M	
Fort Steele	1974	18.500					M	

F. D. Sinclair 1974 133,700

Fort Kipp

Fort Edmonton

CAYZER, IRVINE & CO. LTD.

Scottish Tanker Co. Ltd.

FUNNEL: *Black with two red bands divided by narrow light blue band.*

HULL: *Black with pink boot-topping.*

Hector Heron	1959	12795	18650	560	70	14	M	

Brovig: CIS BROVIG, the largest and most recent tanker in the line

[WSS collection]

CHANDRIS GROUP

FUNNEL: *Blue, black top, white cross.*
HULL: *Grey.*

Chandris Shipping Co. Ltd.

Name	Date	Tons Gross	Tons Dwt	Length (feet)	Breadth (feet)	Speed (knots)	Engines	Former Names
Evgenia Chandris	1969	103194	205600	1080	144	16	ST	*(Greece)*
Kania Chandris	1973	142,100						*(Lib.)*

(LIBERIA)

CHEVRON SHIPPING COMPANY

Chevron Transport Corporation

FUNNEL: *Black with blue, white and red chevrons on white disc.*
HULL: *Black.*

Chevron Edinburgh 1974 118,200

Name	Date	Tons Gross	Tons Dwt	Length (feet)	Breadth (feet)	Speed (knots)	Engines	Former Names
A. N. Kemp ..	1950	18127	28276	625	84	16	ST	
Atholl McBean	1950	18127	28276	625	84	16	ST	
Chevron Transporter..	1950	18127	28276	625	84	16	ST	ex T. S. Petersen 60.
D. L. Bower ..	1970	96997	212000	1037	160	16	ST	
E. J. McClanahan	1956	12232	17770	558	70	15½	ST	
Elmer R. Peterson ..	1964	29859	51080	753	103	16	ST	
Gage Lund ..	1951	18125	28276	625	84	16	ST	
George L. Parkhurst ..	1960	39965	69225	825	116	17	ST	
H. J. Haynes†	1970	96997	212000	1037	160	16	ST	
Howard G. Vesper ..	1966	33672	63163	784	105	17	ST	
J. E. Gosline ..	1966	33672	66527	784	105	17	ST	
J. T. Higgins ..	1970	96997	212000	1037	160	16	ST	
John A. McCone†	1969	96997	212018	1037	160	16	ST	
K. H. Crandall	1965	30298	50765	755	103	17	ST	
Otto N. Miller	1963	29858	51070	753	103	17	ST	
Paul Pigott ..	1951	18127	28276	625	84	16	ST	
R. G. Follis ..	1965	33672	63090	784	105	17	ST	
Ralph B. Johnson	1965	33672	63090	784	105	17	ST	
Robert Watt Miller ..	1951	18125	28276	625	84	16	ST	
Roy G. Lucks ..	1954	30298	50940	755	103	17	ST	
T. L. Lenzen ..	1960	24992	42277	713	97	17	ST	
T. S. Petersen ..	1962	29856	51110	753	103	17	ST	
William M. Allen	1963	38473	69480	825	117	17	ST	

† Owned by Equitable Life Assurance Society.

(LIBERIA)

Tankers Facilities Corporation

Name		Date	Tons Gross	Tons Dwt	Length	Breadth	Speed	Engines
Asa V. Call	..	1962	38472	69375	825	117	16	ST
George A. Davidson	..	1959	24992	42174	713	97	17	ST

(U.S.A.)

Standard Oil Company of California

FUNNEL: *Black with blue, white and red chevrons on white disc.*

CHEVRON OREGON 1975 17700

Name	Date	Tons Gross	Tons Dwt	Length (feet)	Breadth (feet)	Speed (knots)	Engines	Former Names
Arizona Standard ..	1945	10533	16697	524	68	14½	TE	ex Fort Mims 62.
F. S. Bryant ..	1946	8488	12610	460	65	14	ST	
H. D. Collier ..	1945	10246	16430	524	68	14½	TE	
Hawaii Standard	1945	10543	16284	524	68	14½	TE	ex Rock Landing 62.
Hillyer Brown	1953	10648	17058	524	68	16	ST	
Idaho Standard	1944	10449	16590	524	68	14½	TE	ex Idaho Falls 57.
J. H. MacGaregill	1945	10246	16365	524	68	14½	TE	
J. H. Tuttle ..	1943	11658	17883	547	70	15½	ST	
J. L. Hanna ..	1945	10246	16280	524	68	14½	ST	
Nevada Standard	1943	10626	16284	524	68	14½	TE	ex Clarke's Wharf 62.
Oregon Standard	1944	10449	16568	524	68	14½	TE	ex Fort Clapsop 57.
Utah Standard	1946	8489	12553	460	65	14	ST	ex R. G. Follis 65.
Washington Standard ..	1944	10519	16570	524	68	14½	TE	ex Kettle Creek 57.

CHEVRON HAWAII

CHEVRON MISSISSIPPI

CHEVRON WASHINGTON 1975   GT**(NETHERLANDS)**

Chevron Tankers (Nederland) N.V.

Name	Date	Tons Gross	Tons Dwt	Length (feet)	Breadth (feet)	Speed (knots)	Engines	Former Names
Chevron Arnhem	1958	21394	34307	660	89	16	ST	ex Caltex Arnhem 69.
Chevron Eindhoven ..	1958	22110	32052	660	89	16	ST	ex Caltex Eindhoven 68.
Chevron Leiden	1944	13785	22403	566	78	14	TE	ex Caltex Leiden 68, ex Fort Ridgely 50.
Chevron Rotterdam ..	1956	20992	32325	666	89	16	ST	ex Caltex Rotterdam 68.
Chevron The Hague ..	1945	13894	22352	566	78	14	TE	ex Caltex The Hague 67, ex Boonesborough 50.

(NETHERLANDS)

Maats tot Financiering van Bedrijfspanden N.V.

Name	Date	Tons Gross	Tons Dwt	Length (feet)	Breadth (feet)	Speed (knots)	Engines	Former Names
Chevron Amsterdam	1960	20943	31911	666	89	16	ST	ex Caltex Amsterdam 68.
Chevron Madrid	1961	31617	48211	734	106	17	ST	ex Caltex Madrid 68.
Chevron Naples	1961	20939	31356	666	89	16	ST	ex Caltex Naples 68.
Chevron Nederland ..	1963	31575	48210	735	106	17	ST	ex Caltex Nederland 69.

Chevron Shipping Company: T. S. PETERSEN   [R. J. Weeks

Chevron Shipping Company: ASA V. CALL   [R. J. Weeks

Cities Service Tankers: CITIES SERVICE NORFOLK

[A. Duncan]

(PANAMA)
Overseas Tankship Corporation

Name	Date	Tons Gross	Tons Dwt	Length (feet)	Breadth (feet)	Speed (knots)	Engines	Former Names
Chevron Antwerp ..	1950	16659	24215	595	77	15½	ST	ex Caltex Antwerp 68.
Chevron Brussels	1951	16660	24191	595	77	15½	ST	ex Caltex Brussels 68.
Chevron Liege	1951	16860	24214	595	77	15½	ST	ex Caltex Liege 68.

(PANAMA)
Chevron Shipping Company

Chevron Genoa	1944	13938	22388	566	78	14	TE	ex Caltex Genoa 68, ex Cedar Breaks 52.
Chevron Venice	1945	14153	22646	560	78	14	TE	ex Caltex Venice 68, ex Cabusto 52.

(LIBERIA)
Ocean Tankship Corporation

Chevron Frankfurt	1967	41923	78872	760	122	15¾	ST
Chevron Copenhagen	1974	11820					ST

Chevron Tankship (U.K.) Ltd.

E. Horesby Wasson ..	1970	109550	214200	1070	160	15½	ST
James E. O'Brien	1969	109550	214200	1070	160	15½	ST

(U.S.A.)
CITIES SERVICE TANKERS CORPORATION

FUNNEL: *Green with white ' △ ' within white clover-leaf outline.*
HULL: *Black with red boot-topping.*

Bradford Island	1945	10171	16599	524	68	14½	TE
Cities Service Baltimore ..	1956	19474	32825	661	90	16½	ST
Cities Service Miami ..	1956	19474	32825	661	90	16½	ST
Cities Service Norfolk ..	1956	19443	32825	661	90	16½	ST

(LIBERIA)

Grand Bassa Tankers Inc.

Name	Date	Tons Gross	Tons Dwt	Length (feet)	Breadth (feet)	Speed (knots)	Engines	Former Names
Burl S. Watson	1961	40621	69965	825	117	16	ST	
Cities Service Valley Forge	1954	22595	39255	707	93	17½	ST	ex W. Alton Jones 59.
Cradle of Liberty	1954	22610	39281	707	93	17½	ST	
J. Ed. Warren ..	1963	40621	70030	825	117	16	ST	
Liberty Bell ..	1954	22610	38281	707	93	17½	ST	
Statue of Liberty	1954	22610	39255	707	93	17½	ST	
W. Alton Jones	1959	40621	69965	825	117	16	ST	

ren LAND OF LIBERTY

(GREECE)

COLOCOTRONIS GROUP

FUNNEL: *Yellow, black top with wide red band divided by narrow white band and red 'K'.*

HULL: *Grey or black, red boot-topping.*

Name	Date	Tons Gross	Tons Dwt	Length (feet)	Breadth (feet)	Speed (knots)	Engines	Former Names
Chief Colocotronis	1964	52619	96845	869	122	16	M	ex Berge Chief 70.
Conqueror Colocotronis	1956	20855	32985	659	86	16	M	ex Hoegh Falcon 68.
Defender Colocotronis	1955	8768	13077	489	63	14	M	ex Fina Luxembourg 70, ex Purfina Luxembourg 60, ex Purfina Nederland 56.
Defiant Colocotronis	1964	35412	60040	775	106	15½	M	ex Bruse Jarl 70.
Dynamic Colocotronis	1965	35774	59300	776	106	15	M	ex Bjorgholm 69.
Emmanuel Colocotronis	1957	21185	33250	666	86	16	ST	ex Fina Canada 68.
Epic Colocotronis	1965	37469	63615	738	108	16	M	ex Hoegh Hood 68.
Fearless Colocotronis	1962	31830	54925	734	104	17	M	ex Berge Jarl 69.
Gallant Colocotronis	1961	29333	50080	742	100	17½	ST	ex Hoegh Gallant 69, ex Bergebig 61.
General Colocotronis	1965	47544	85700	817	124	17	ST	ex Barbro 69.
Glorious Colocotronis	1958	19231	30920	657	81	16	M	ex Polycrusader 68, ex Gustaf Brodin 64.
Glorious Colocotronis	1966	45161						ex Clyde Maru

Colocotronis Group: YANGOS COLOCOTRONIS

Name	Date	Tons Gross	Tons Dwt	Length (feet)	Breadth (feet)	Speed (knots)	Engines	Former Names
Heroic Colocotronis	1952	15848	23925	606	77	16	M	ex Texaco North America 68, ex North America 60.
Historic Colocotronis	1965	42824	78085	800	120	16	M	ex Hoegh Lance 69.
Intrepid Colocotronis	1956	17940	22992	621	78	15½	ST	ex Ilse Fritzen 70.
John Colocotronis	1956	21185	31522	666	86	16	ST	ex Fina Italia 68, ex Purfina Italia 60.
Katingo ..	1950	11136	16270	538	69	13	M	ex Polyviking 65, ex Purfina Congo 60, ex Petrocongo 50.
Leader Colocotronis	1959	12821	19825	560	72	15	M	ex Kristina 68.
Majestic Colocotronis	1965	35659	59300	776	106	16	M	ex Fagerfjell 69.
Patriotic Colocotronis	1965	34501	58350	775	105	16	M	ex Tank Countess 69.
Polemic Colocotronis	1954	12859	18120	581	72	14	M	ex Biscaya 69, ex Richard Kaselowsky 67.
Resolute Colocotronis	1958	13227	19670	560	72	15	M	ex Eberhart Essberger 70.
Sir Frederick ..	1954	19053	29675	662	83	16	ST	ex Elisabeth 65.
Valiant Colocotronis	1960	30347	51500	730	102	16	ST	ex Hoegh Galleon 69.
Vassiliki Colocotroni	1951	11045	17224	542	70	13	M	ex Fina Angleterre 66, ex Purfina Angleterre 60.
Victorious Colocotronis	1958	13186	20125	560	72	14	M	ex Arild Maersk 68.
Yangos Colocotronis	1960	41982	75912	838	115	17	ST	ex Hoegh Gannet 68.
Zoe Colocotroni	1953	15899	25716	605	77	14	M	ex Brajara 67.

Ioannis Colocotronis 1975   *ST*

Some ships operate under Liberian flag.

Vassilike Colocotronis 1975   *ST*

COMMON BROS. (MANAGEMENT) LTD.

(KUWAIT)

Kuwait Oil Tanker Co.

FUNNEL: *Red, black top, broad and narrow white bands with oval green device on broad band.*

HULL: *Black with red boot-topping.*

Name		Date	Tons Gross	Tons Dwt	Length (feet)	Breadth (feet)	Speed (knots)	Engines	Former Names
Al Babiah	..	1970	107400	208500	1069	158	16	ST	
Al Funtas	..	1969	107409	208800	1067	158	16	ST	
Al Sabbiyah	..	1965	35751	57160	760	106	16	ST	
Arabiyah	..	1969	107436	208907	1067	158	16	ST	
Kazimah	..	1959	29155	46765	736	100	16	ST	
Warbah ..	..	1964	35760	57132	760	106	16	ST	

COURT LINE LTD.

FUNNEL: *Yellow with black top.*
HULL: *Grey with red boot-topping.*

Halcyon Days ..	1958	12751	19375	560	72	15	M	ex Edith Borthen 63.
Halcyon Wave..	1960	16591	25850	616	79	16	M	ex Naess Clansman 67, ex Snestad 60.

Caribbean Tankers Ltd.

Derwentdale* ..	1964	42343	72550	799	118	16	M	ex Halcyon Breeze 67.

* On charter to Ministry of Defence (Navy Dept.).

CUNARD STEAMSHIP CO. LTD.

(CUNARD BROCKLEBANK LTD.)

FUNNEL: *Yellow, black top and red ' M ' in blue bordered white diamond.*
HULL: *Black with red boot-topping.*

Lucigen ..	..	1962	12800	20203	559	72	15	M	
Luminous	..	1968	14923	24605	557	81	15	M	
Lustrous	..	1968	14923	24507	558	81	15	M	
Luxor ..	..	1960	12700	19944	556	72	15	M	ex Haukefjell 60.

(NORWAY)

A/S THOR DAHL

FUNNEL: *Grey with blue fish (resembling a " C ") on broad white band between two narrow red bands.*
HULL: *Grey with red boot-topping.*

Thorshammer..	1969	120000	230000	1066	158	15½	ST	
Thorsheimer ..	1965	41570	73700	800	121	16	M	
Thorshov ..	1967	54480	101473	890	128	16	M	
Thorshovdi ..	1968	54478	102797	890	128	16	M	
Thorskog ..	1967	54704	101469	890	128	16	M	TO NORWAY, NEW·CALEO
Thorstar ..	1966	41690	72350	800	121	15½	M	

Also cargo ships.

Thor Dahl: THORSTAR   [*F. R. Sherlock*

D' Amico Societa Di Navigazione: MARE ADRIACUM   [*WSS collection*

D'AMICO SOC. DI NAV. S.p.A.
VARIOUS OTHER COMPANY TITLES

FUNNEL: *Yellow with blue star and red top.*
HULL: *Black or grey with red boot-topping.*

Name	Date	Tons Gross	Tons Dwt	Length (feet)	Breadth (feet)	Speed (knots)	Engines	Former Names
Cristina D'Amico	1969	20693	32000	666	86	16	ST	
Elena D'Amico	1954	12967	19420	583	75	15	ST	ex Frisco 67.
Giovannella D'Amico Chemist ..	1959	12983	19315	557	72	15	M	ex Giovannella D'Amico 65.
Linda Giovanna	1940	9985	15963	533	63	13	M	ex Braconda 57.
Mare Adriacum	1954	20451	32153	656	86	17	M	
Marinella D'Amico ..	1959	12982	19367	558	72	16	M	
Mina D'Amico	1954	20489	31688	656	86	16	ST	
Mirella D'Amico	1954	20417	31717	656	86	16	ST	
Sofia D'Amico ..	1958	13065	19900	560	72	15	M	ex Grena 68.

Also other ships.

J. & J. DENHOLM (MANAGEMENT) LTD.
Hopepark Shipping Co. Ltd.

Hopepark ..	1968	87041	167314	1010	146	17	ST	
Nordic Chieftain 1974 85000							M	

H. DITLEV-SIMONSEN & CO.

FUNNEL: *Yellow with swallow-tail house flag and narrow black top.*
HULL: *Grey with red boot-topping.*

Vanja	1966	41247	71200	785	121	17	M	
Varenna† ..	1970	55000	95800	842	128	15½	M	
Velma	1965	41259	71200	785	121	17	M	
Vianna† ..	1970	55000	95800	842	128	15½	M	
Vincita	1957	12645	19250	557	71	15	M	
Vitoria* ..	1967	44523	72250	849	106	16½	M	
Vivi	1957	10375	15600	532	64	15	M	
Vincita	*1974*	*55000*					M	

* Ore/bulk/oil carrier. † Bulk/oil carrier.

O. Ditlev-Simonsen, Jnr.

Vibit	1963	12665	19200	557	71	15	M	

S. Ditlev-Simonsen & Co.

Vibeke	1959	12653	19380	557	71	15	M	

Also other ships.

THOMAS ENTZ TANKER G.m.b.H.

FUNNEL: *Black with white ' E ' within white-bordered red ring.*
HULL: *Grey.*

Name	Date	Tons Gross	Tons Dwt	Length (feet)	Breadth (feet)	Speed (knots)	Engines	Former Names
Elisabeth Entz†	1961	24461	35000	701	90	16	ST	
Helma Entz ..	1958	12430	19810	558	72	15	ST	

† Ore/oil carriers.

JOHN T. ESSBERGER

FUNNEL: *Black with blue ' E ' on white band.*
HULL: *Grey.*

Elsa Essberger..	1968	53160	100000	891	128	16	M	
Helga Essberger	1967	44681	80730	830	124	16	M	
Liselotte Essberger ..	1967	44679	76588	830	124	16	M	
Wilhelmine Essberger ..	1963	36139	57750	775	106	15	ST	ex Aker 67, ex Trolltop 67.

ESSO PETROLEUM CO. LTD.

FUNNEL: *Black with " Esso " in red inside blue ring on broad white band.*
HULL: *Black or grey with red boot-topping.*

Esso Anglia ..	1968	97082	170800	1056	157	16½	ST	
Esso Bernicia ..	1968	96903	199100	1062	155	16½	ST	
Esso Cambria ..	1969	127158	255000	1142	170	16½	ST	
Esso Cardiff ..	1963	31720	50761	743	102	17	ST	
Esso Edinburgh	1963	30981	51332	743	102	17	ST	
Esso Fawley ..	1967	11046	18087	534	72	16	M	
Esso Glasgow ..	1944	10720	16143	524	68	14	TE	ex Wauhatchie 47.
Esso Hampshire	1962	48141	85175	861	113	17	ST	
Esso Hibernia	1970	126500	253000	1140	170	16½	ST	
Esso Lancashire	1962	49397	85002	861	113	17	ST	
Esso Lincoln ..	1962	31720	50769	743	102	17	ST	
Esso London ..	1964	53342	94247	861	125	17	ST	
Esso Mercia ..	1967	87002	166820	1010	146	16½	ST	
Esso Milford Haven ..	1967	11046	18087	534	72	16	M	
Esso Newcastle	1963	31729	51306	743	102	17	ST	
Esso Northumbria	1969	126543	253000	1143	170	16½	ST	
Esso Oxford ..	1953	17539	28175	630	83	16	ST	
Esso Pembrokeshire	1961	49250	84717	861	113	17	ST	
Esso Portsmouth	1959	25715	39889	733	90	16½	ST	
Esso Salisbury..	1957	24008	38094	696	90	16½	ST	
Esso Scotia ..	1969	127158	250300	1141	170	16½	ST	
Esso Ulidia ..	1970	127150	253000	1143	170	16½	ST	
Esso Warwickshire	1962	48049	84688	561	113	17	ST	
Esso Westminster	1954	17568	28232	630	83	16	ST	
Esso York ..	1955	17180	28233	630	83	16	ST	
Esso Yorkshire	1963	52544	94241	861	125	16½	ST	

Also coastal tankers.

Esso Severn   1974   12300

Ditlev-Simonsen: VELMA

[R. J. Weeks

Thomas Entz Tanker: ELISABETH ENTZ

[Malcolm Cranfield

Esso Petroleum Co: ESSO WARWICKSHIRE   [R. J. Weeks

Esso Petroleum Co: ESSO WESTMINSTER   [John G. Callis

(U.S.A.)

Humble Oil & Refining Co.

Name	Date	Tons Gross	Tons Dwt	Length (feet)	Breadth (feet)	Speed (knots)	Engines	Former Names
Esso Baltimore	1960	30682	49517	740	102	17	ST	
Esso Bangor ..	1953	17330	26780	628	83	16	ST	
Esso Baton Rouge	1970	38144	75647	810	125	17	ST	
Esso Boston ..	1960	30680	49557	740	102	17½	ST	
Esso Chester ..	1952	17327	27200	628	83	16	ST	
Esso Dallas	1950	17578	27340	628	83	16	ST	ex Esso Bermuda 62.
Esso Florence ..	1954	17378	27135	628	83	16	ST	
Esso Gettysburg	1957	25186	39029	715	93	16	ST	
Esso Houston ..	1964	35291	67879	800	117	17	ST	
Esso Huntingdon	1953	17548	26729	628	83	16	ST	
Esso Jamestown	1957	23831	39066	715	93	16	ST	
Esso Lexington	1958	25182	39028	715	93	16	ST	
Esso Lima ..	1949	17777	27335	628	83	16	ST	
Esso Miami ..	1950	17291	27320	628	83	16	ST	ex Esso Havana 61.
Esso New Orleans	1965	34833	67847	800	117	17	ST	
Esso New York	1950	17420	27335	628	83	16	ST	
Esso Newark ..	1952	17378	27230	628	83	16	ST	
Esso Philadelphia	1970	38144	75649	810	125	17	ST	
Esso San Francisco ..	1970	38144	75649	810	125	17	ST	
Esso Scranton	1944	10565	16535	524	68	14½	TE	
Esso Washington	1957	23762	39089	715	93	18	ST	

Handwritten annotations in left margin: "Exxon" variants beside several ship names. Also "Exxon Connecticut 1969" under Name heading. Next to Esso Miami: "TO USA, ren. PECOS".

(FRANCE)

Esso Standard Soc. Anon. Francaise

Esso Alsace *(Lib.)*	1960	25451	38872	698	95	17	ST	
Esso Bourgogne	1959	25449	38882	698	95	17	ST	
Esso Lorraine ..	1961	32056	48424	747	103	17	ST	
Esso Parentis ..	1958	25274	37730	697	95	17	ST	
Esso Paris	1969	96226	193900	1066	157	16½	ST	

Handwritten: Esso Languedoc 1973 126200

Also smaller ships.

(BELGIUM)

Esso Marine (Belgium) S.A.

Esso Antwerp ..	1967	42094	76209	809	125	16½	M	
Esso Brussels ..	1960	26843	40800	700	97	17	ST	*To Greece, ren. SPIRO*
Esso Ghent ..	1959	26416	41353	700	97	17	ST	ex Esso Horizon 64, ex Stanvac Horizon 62.
Esso Liege ..	1969	31489	47537	740	102	17	ST	

(NETHERLANDS)

Esso Tankvaart Maats N.V.

Esso Den Haag	1963	53141	89882	862	125	17½	ST	

(NETHERLANDS ANTILLES)
Esso Tankvaart Nederlandse Antillen

Name	Date	Tons Gross	Tons Dwt	Length (feet)	Breadth (feet)	Speed (knots)	Engines	Former Names
Esso LaGvaira *1974 126192*								
Esso Europoort	1970	127150	250000	1141	170	16	ST	
Esso Nederland	1970	127158	249952	1141	170	16	ST	
Esso Saba *1974*		*126,300*						

(WEST GERMANY)
Esso Tankschiff Reederei G.m.b.H.

Esso Bonn 1974

Name	Date	Tons Gross	Tons Dwt	Length (feet)	Breadth (feet)	Speed (knots)	Engines
Esso Bayern ..	1964	52338	90600	870	125	$17\frac{1}{2}$	ST
Esso Berlin ..	1958	24478	36470	693	90	17	ST
Esso Bremen ..	1959	32029	48535	740	102	$17\frac{1}{2}$	ST
Esso Deutschland	1963	54440	90187	856	125	$17\frac{1}{2}$	ST
Esso Essen ..	1960	31014	48535	740	102	$17\frac{1}{2}$	ST
Esso Frankfurt	1955	18060	26942	631	83	15	ST
Esso Hamburg	1955	18040	26620	631	83	15	ST
Esso Koln ..	1961	32056	48274	740	102	17	ST
Esso Munchen	1956	18038	26620	631	83	15	ST
Esso Nurnberg	1960	24501	36370	693	90	17	ST
Esso Stuttgart ..	1959	31017	50420	740	102	17	ST
Esso Hamburg 1974 126000							*ST*

Also smaller tankers.

(DENMARK)
Dansk Esso A/S

FUNNEL: *Yellow with narrow black top and " Esso " sign on broad white band.*

HULL: *Grey with red boot-topping.*

Name	Date	Tons Gross	Tons Dwt	Length	Breadth	Speed	Engines
Esso Aalborg ..	1959	20503	32370	677	84	$15\frac{3}{4}$	M
Esso Aarhus ..	1956	16887	26350	622	77	$15\frac{1}{4}$	M
Esso Danmark ..	1960	20925	34070	677	84	$15\frac{3}{4}$	M
Esso Callunda 1974 13500							*M*

Also smaller ships.

(SWEDEN)
Esso Rederi A/B

Name	Date	Tons Gross	Tons Dwt	Length	Breadth	Speed	Engines
~~**Esso Stockholm**~~	1961	30239	52440	746	102	16	ST *To Pan.reg, TASMN VOYAG*

(SWEDEN)
Standard Petroleum A/B

Name	Date	Tons Gross	Tons Dwt	Length	Breadth	Speed	Engines	Former Names
Esso Gothenburg	1956	17902	26753	625	83	17	ST	ex Esso Nederland 62.

Esso Petroleum Co: ESSO DEN HAAG   [*F. W. Hawks*

Esso Petroleum Co: <u>ESSO DEUTSCHLAND</u>   [*F. R. Sherlock*

Esso Petroleum Co: ESSO SLAGEN

[*Malcolm Cranfield*

Esso Petroleum Co: ESSO PORTOVENERE

[*D. Clegg*

(NORWAY)
A/S Petrolea

Name		Date	Tons Gross	Tons Dwt	Length (feet)	Breadth (feet)	Speed (knots)	Engines	Former Names
Esso Slagen	..	1968	11059	18500	534	72	16	M	

(ITALY)
'' La Columbia '' Soc. Mar. per Azioni

Esso Augusta	..	1969	80000	140000	974	134	16	ST	
Esso Milano	..	1966	39426	67000	800	117	16½	ST	
Esso Napoli	..	1961	31622	47497	741	102	17	ST	
Esso Roma	..	1960	23231	36163	690	90	17	ST	
Esso Torino	..	1966	39270	60740	801	117	16½	ST	
Esso Trieste	..	1959	23275	36273	690	90	17	ST	ex Esso Coventry 63.
Esso Venezia	..	1955	14991	21710	590	77	15	ST	

(ITALY)
''La Prora'' S.p.A. Trasporte

Esso Brega†	..	1968	30700	22000	682	96	15	ST
Esso Liguria†	..	1969	30450	22000	682	96	15	ST
Esso Portovenere†		1969	30700	22000	682	96	15	ST

† Liquefied gas carriers.

Esso Standard Eastern Tankers Ltd.

Esso Macquarie	1953	11301	16645	529	70	13	M	ex Lustrous 64.

(LIBERIA)
Esso Tankers Inc.

Esso Africa	1975							
Esso Bataan	..	1970	13154	21100	558	77	15	M
Esso Brasilia	..	1959	23562	36003	693	90	17	ST	ex Esso Rotterdam 70.
Esso Chittagong		1970	12994	21076	558	77	15	M
Esso Copenhagen		1970	112763	250200	1143	170	15½	ST
Esso Kure	..	1970	13500	21100	558	77	15	M
Esso Skandia	..	1970	112763	249900	1141	170	16	ST
Esso Wilhelmshaven		1970	113750	249900	1141	170	16	ST
Esso Montreal	1974	18800					M
Esso Indonesia	1974	115,000		279			
Esso Kawasaki	1975	139,800					
Esso Bayonne	1974	17,800					M
Esso Honolulu	1974	131,000					ST
Esso Bayway	1974	12,800					
Esso Coral Gables	1974	13,700					

(PANAMA)

Esso Transport Company Inc., Esso Transport & Tanker Co. Inc., Esso Transport & Shg. Co., and Esso Transport & Navigation Co.

Name	Date	Tons Gross	Tons Dwt	Length (feet)	Breadth (feet)	Speed (knots)	Engines	Former Names
Esso Adventure	1960	10124	13822	490	75	14	ST	ex Stanvac Adventure 62.
Esso Aruba ..	1959	29993	47970	740	102	17	ST	
Esso Australia..	1955	16996	26603	630	83	16	ST	ex Stanvac Australia 63.
Esso Austria ..	1962	45445	78776	851	117	17	ST	
Esso Bangkok ..	1968	12994	21056	558	77	15	M	
Esso Barcelona	1964	34542	66943	800	116	17	ST	
Esso Bogota ..	1949	17612	27403	628	83	16	ST	ex Esso Genova 63.
Esso Bombay ..	1968	12994	21113	558	77	15	M	
Esso Brooklyn..	1943	10399	16424	502	68	15	ST	ex Dartmouth 51.
Esso Castellon..	1968	39085	76290	809	125	16½	M	
Esso Colombia	1955	23414	35793	690	90	16	ST	
Esso Cristobal..	1957	29139	49846	773	90	17	ST	ex Esso Cuba 62.
Esso El Salvador	1959	21627	36028	690	90	17	ST	ex Esso Liverpool 64.
Esso Europa ..	1969	113700	249900	1141	170	16½	ST	
Esso Goa ..	1969	12994	20989	561	77	15	M	
Esso Honduras	1960	21627	36021	693	90	17	ST	ex Esso Dublin. 64.
Esso Interamerica	1969	12994	20987	558	77	15	M	
Esso Karachi ..	1969	12000	20989	561	77	15	M	
Esso Kobe ..	1968	12000	21034	558	77	15	M	
Esso Libya ..	1962	48881	89956	861	125	17	ST	
Esso Malacca ..	1970	12994	20980	561	77	15	M	
Esso Malaysia ..	1967	77845	190800	1063	155	16½	ST	
Esso Montevideo	1949	17420	27355	628	83	16	ST	
Esso Nagasaki..	1969	12994	21118	558	77	15	M	
Esso Nicaragua	1958	21927	36117	690	90	17	ST	ex Esso Bristo 64.
Esso Norway ..	1969	84996	190100	1062	155	16	ST	
Esso Orion ..	1954	6836	10219	425	64	12	ST	ex Esso Liguria 69. To Ken-ren· ferrys
Esso Panama ..	1953	29141	51028	773	90	16½	ST	
Esso Penang ..	1969	12994	21106	558	77	15	M	
Esso Philippines	1964	34063	66419	800	116	16	M	
Esso Port Dickson ..	1968	12994	20950	558	77	15	M	
Esso Puerto Rico	1959	25278	32918	690	90	17	ST	
Esso Santos ..	1950	17328	27315	628	83	16	ST	
Esso Spain ..	1962	53507	80534	861	125	17	ST	
Esso Yokohama	1969	12994	21106	558	77	15	M	
Esso Zurich ..	1965	37336	66612	800	116	16	M	

(URUGUAY)

Esso Standard Oil Co. (Uruguay) S.A.

Name	Date	Tons Gross	Tons Dwt	Length (feet)	Breadth (feet)	Speed (knots)	Engines
Esso Uruguay ..	1958	29139	49844	773	90	17	ST

Fearnley & Eger: FERNCASTLE

[R. J. Weeks

Francaise de Transports: SOLOGNE

[D. Clegg

(VENEZUELA)

Creole Petroleum Corporation

Name		Date	Tons Gross	Tons Dwt	Length (feet)	Breadth (feet)	Speed (knots)	Engines	Former Names
Esso Amuay	..	1959	24727	35328	650	91	15	ST	
Esso Caracas	..	1959	24088	35588	696	91	16	ST	
Esso Carapito	..	1959	24727	36000	650	91	15	ST	
Esso Maracaibo		1959	24088	35588	696	91	16	ST	

(VENEZUELA)

Cia. de Petroleo Lago

Esso La Guaira		1954	7435	10905	425	66	12	SR(2)	
Esso Margarita		1953	7435	10905	425	66	12	SR(2)	

(U.S.A.)

Skouras Lines Inc.

Esso Seattle	..	1958	19291	31792	666	84	16	ST	ex Saroula 64.

(NORWAY)

FEARNLEY & EGER

VARIOUS COMPANY TITLES

FUNNEL: *Black with blue Maltese Cross on white panel on red band.*
HULL: *Grey or black with red boot-topping.*

Ferncastle	..	1967	52510	95750	872	128	16	M	
Ferncrest	..	1966	52510	95750	872	128	16	M	
Fernhaven	..	1969	108758	216549	1073	158	16½	ST	
Fernmanor	..	1964	45206	69718	817	119	16	M	
Fernpark	..	1963	35278	57840	774	106	17	M	
Fernstar†	..	1967	55209	98543	836	129	15½	M	
Kristian Birkeland*	..	1968	16532	—	561	80	17	M	

† Ore/oil carrier.   * Liquefied gas carrier.

SOC. FRANCAISE de TRANSPORTS PÉTROLIERS S.A.
(S.F.T.P.)

FUNNEL: *Black.*
HULL: *Grey with red boot-topping.*

Name		Date	Tons Gross	Tons Dwt	Length (feet)	Breadth (feet)	Speed (knots)	Engines	Former Names
Armagnac	..	1961	33621	48549	746	102	16	ST	
Artois	..	1958	13284	20004	561	74	14	M	
Bearn	..	1960	32726	51580	759	100	17	ST	
Bourgogne	..	1966	41328	74390	785	121	16½	M	ex Nyholm 69.
Dauphine	..	1968	59958	117272	902	136	16	M	
Franche Comte		1965	47777	70007	832	114	17	ST	
Lorraine	..	1958	18048	26890	630	81	15	M	
Poitou	..	1954	13295	19845	558	74	15	M	
Saintonge	..	1969	60104	117250	902	136	16	M	
Sologne	..	1955	13322	19788	558	74	15	M	
Touraine	..	1964	36240	55378	774	105	17	ST	

FURNESS WITHY & CO. LTD.

FUNNEL: *Dark red with black top, black base and black band.*
HULL: *Black with red boot-topping.*

Name		Date	Tons Gross	Tons Dwt	Length	Breadth	Speed	Engines	Former Names
Tudor Prince	..	1961	12647	18685	559	72	14½	M	*To Lib., ren STOLT TUDOR*

Prince Line Ltd.

FUNNEL: *As above with Prince of Wales' feathers.*

Name		Date	Tons Gross	Tons Dwt	Length	Breadth	Speed	Engines	Former Names
Stuart Prince	..	1960	12668	18625	559	72	14½	M	*To Lib, ren STOLT STUART*

Also other ships.

GETTY OIL COMPANY

FUNNEL: *Black, light yellow band with "GETTY" in black letters.*
HULL: *Black.*

Name	Date	Tons Gross	Tons Dwt	Length	Breadth	Speed	Engines	Former Names
Delaware Getty	1954	17054	27421	628	83	16	ST	ex Flying A. Delaware 68.
Louisiana Getty	1944	13659	22300	566	77	14	TE	ex Byron D. Benson 68.
New York Getty	1954	17054	27421	628	83	16	ST	ex Flying A. New York 68.
Wilmington Getty	1944	13659	22300	566	77	14	TE	ex William F. Humphrey 68, ex Black Jack 47.

Getty Oil Co: OKLAHOMA GETTY

(LIBERIA)

Hemisphere Transportation Corporation

Name	Date	Tons Gross	Tons Dwt	Length (feet)	Breadth (feet)	Speed (knots)	Engines	Former Names
California Getty	1968	58994	129328	886	140	16	ST	
George F. Getty	1957	33704	53917	786	103	16½	ST	
Minnehoma ..	1957	33768	54094	786	103	16½	ST	
Oklahoma Getty	1957	33791	53966	786	102	16½	ST	
Texas Getty* ..	1965	28263	52769	722	106	16½	ST	
Tidewater ..	1957	33705	53901	776	103	16½	ST	
Washington Getty* ..	1963	28542	52853	722	106	16½	ST	

* Ore/oil carrier.

(LIBERIA)

Gettymar Corporation

Name	Date	Tons Gross	Tons Dwt	Length (feet)	Breadth (feet)	Speed (knots)	Engines	Former Names
J. Paul Getty ..	1960	44698	77936	844	110	16½	ST	
Sarah C. Getty	1963	46649	84263	884	110	16½	ST	

(LIBERIA)

Getty Tankers Ltd.

Name	Date	Tons Gross	Tons Dwt	Length (feet)	Breadth (feet)	Speed (knots)	Engines	Former Names
Veedol	1955	28339	47000	734	101	16½	ST	
Wafra	1956	28339	46997	734	101	16½	ST	

(LIBERIA)

Transoceanic Shipping Corporation

Name	Date	Tons Gross	Tons Dwt	Length (feet)	Breadth (feet)	Speed (knots)	Engines	Former Names
Maryland Getty	1959	28648	46892	737	101	16½	ST	
Massachusetts Getty ..	1958	28682	46856	737	101	16½	ST	
Pennsylvania Getty ..	1958	28674	46866	737	100	16½	ST	
Virginia Getty ..	1959	28648	46909	734	100	16½	ST	

(SWEDEN)

GRANGESBERG-OXELOSUND TRAFIK A/B

FUNNEL: *Black with yellow ' G ' within yellow ring on broad blue band.*
HULL: *Grey with red boot-topping.*

Name	Date	Tons Gross	Tons Dwt	Length (feet)	Breadth (feet)	Speed (knots)	Engines	Former Names
FFM Vassijaure†	1955	15504	—	596	75	14½	M	
Matarengi ..	1960	24193	39200	655	89	15	M	
Torne (OBO)	1974							

Also ore carriers. † Chemical tanker.

GULF OIL CORPORATION

FUNNEL: *Blue grey with " GULF " in orange disc.*

HULL: *Blue grey with red boot-topping.*

Name		Date	Tons Gross	Tons Dwt	Length (feet)	Breadth (feet)	Speed (knots)	Engines	Former Names
Gulflube..	..	1948	8197	12799	472	64	15½	ST	
Gulfservice	..	1952	11369	17728	551	68	15½	ST	
Gulfsupreme	..	1961	19030	30806	645	84	17	ST	

Also smaller ships.

Blackships Inc.

Name		Date	Tons Gross	Tons Dwt	Length	Breadth	Speed	Engines	Former Names
Gulfbear	..	1945	12811	20105	572	75	14½	TE	ex Gulfshore 57, ex Somme 47.
Gulfbeaver	..	1943	12716	19900	572	75	14½	TE	ex Gulfmeadows 57, ex Great Meadows 48.
Gulfcrest	..	1959	18700	30806	645	84	17	ST	
Gulfdeer	..	1944	12842	20104	572	75	14½	TE	ex Gulfland 57, ex Moor's Fields 48.
Gulfjaguar	..	1944	12652	19900	572	75	14½	TE	ex Gulfhaven 58, ex Spring Hill 48.
Gulfking	..	1957	20138	33008	661	90	16½	ST	
Gulfknight	..	1958	20025	33008	661	90	16½	ST	
Gulflion	..	1944	12214	19397	572	75	14½	TE	ex Gulfray 58, ex Bushy Run 47.
Gulfoil ..	..	1960	18776	29239	645	84	17	ST	
Gulfpanther	..	1944	12565	19910	572	75	14½	TE	ex Gulfwell 57, ex Fort William 48.
Gulfpride	..	1959	18700	29239	645	84	17	ST	
Gulfprince	..	1958	20143	33008	661	90	16½	ST	
Gulfqueen	..	1957	20914	33008	661	90	16½	ST	
Gulfsolar	..	1959	18700	29150	645	84	17	ST	
Gulftiger	..	1945	12668	19906	572	75	14½	TE	ex Gulfhorn 58, ex Roxbury Hill 47.

Britama Tankers Ltd.

(GULF OIL MARINE AGENCY)

Name		Date	Tons Gross	Tons Dwt	Length	Breadth	Speed	Engines	Former Names
Gulf Briton	..	1961	26298	40503	715	96	17	ST	
Gulf Dane	..	1961	26652	42969	715	96	17	ST	
Gulf Finn	..	1963	26652	40600	715	96	17	ST	
Gulf Scot	..	1961	26652	40603	715	96	17	ST	

(LIBERIA)
Bantry Transportation Company

Name	Date	Tons Gross	Tons Dwt	Length (feet)	Breadth (feet)	Speed (knots)	Engines	Former Names
Universe Iran	1969	149623	326933	1133	175	15	ST(2)	
Universe Ireland	1968	149609	326585	1133	175	15	ST(2)	
Universe Japan	1969	149623	326562	1133	175	15	ST(2)	
Universe Korea	1969	149623	326676	1133	175	15	ST(2)	
Universe Kuwait	1968	149609	326848	1133	175	15	ST(2)	
Universe Portugal ..	1969	149623	326676	1133	175	15	ST(2)	

(LIBERIA)
Afran Transport Co.

Name	Date	Tons Gross	Tons Dwt	Length (feet)	Breadth (feet)	Speed (knots)	Engines	Former Names
Afran Mercury	*1974*	*14400*					*MT*	
Cabimas ..	1955	21875	31956	665	87	15½	ST	
Ceuta	1959	21012	30670	660	86	15½	ST	
J. Frank Drake	1964	29719	48700	750	102	17	ST	
Lagunillas ..	1955	21147	31934	665	87	15½	ST	
Mona Pass ..	1945	10225	16666	524	68	14	TE	ex Gulf Pass 65, ex Raton Pass 48.
Philippine Sea..	1961	25500	39015	710	93	17	ST	*To Algeria, new· G-ASSI-TOUIL*
Ralph O. Rhoades	1963	29739	48567	750	102	16½	ST	
Ragusa	1959	21012	30670	660	86	15½	ST	
Raudhatain ..	1957	21403	32039	662	87	15½	ST	ex Arabian Gulf 60.
Tasman Sea ..	1961	25500	38937	710	93	17	ST	
William Larimer Mellon ..	1965	29721	48847	753	102	17	ST	

(U.S.A.)
Delships Inc.

Name	Date	Tons Gross	Tons Dwt	Length (feet)	Breadth (feet)	Speed (knots)	Engines	Former Names
Gulfseal ..	1945	12305	19758	572	75	14½	TE	ex Gulfkey 58, ex Kathio 48.
Gulfspray ..	1960	18776	29150	645	84	17	ST	

(LIBERIA)
Argo Tankers Inc.

FUNNEL : *Grey with narrow black top and red band.*
HULL : *Black.*

Name	Date	Tons Gross	Tons Dwt	Length (feet)	Breadth (feet)	Speed (knots)	Engines	Former Names
Arctic Sea ..	1959	25464	39059	710	93	16½	ST	
Bering Sea ..	1959	25462	39328	710	93	16½	ST	

Gulf Oil Corporation: UNIVERSE IRELAND on her maiden voyage to Bantry Bay, Eire

[Gulf Oil (G.B.) Ltd]

Gulf Oil Corporation: Stern view of UNIVERSE IRELAND   [*Gulf Oil (G.B.) Ltd*

Gulf Oil Corporation: GULF SCOTT   [*R. J. Weeks*

Nedgulf Tankers N.V.
(MANAGERS VINKE & Co.)

Name	Date	Tons Gross	Tons Dwt	Length (feet)	Breadth (feet)	Speed (knots)	Engines	Former Names
Gulf Hansa ..	1962	31350	47620	742	102	17	ST	
Gulf Hollander	1962	27139	42600	724	97	17	ST	
Gulf Italian ..	1962	31350	47840	742	102	17	ST	
Gulf Swede ..	1962	27139	42777	724	97	17	ST	

Belgulf Tankers S.A.

Belgulf Enterprise ..	1962	12541	18000	561	71	16	ST	
Belgulf Glory ..	1958	12018	18000	556	71	15½	ST	
Belgulf Progress	1959	12018	18000	556	71	15½	ST	
Belgulf Strength	1962	12544	18000	561	71	16	ST	
Belgulf Union	1962	12539	17757	561	71	16	ST	

HADLEY SHG. CO. LTD.
Warwick & Esplen Ltd.

FUNNEL: *Yellow with black top and black " HSC " in white diamond.*
HULL: *Black with red boot-topping.*

Cerinthus ..	1954	12174	18877	556	69	14½	ST	
Clymene ..	1961	12251	19313	559	69	14½	ST	

HANSEN-TANGENS Red. A/S
Yngv. Hansen-Tangen

FUNNEL: *Yellow with white ' H ' on red band between two red rings.*
HULL: *Black with red boot-topping.*

Adna	1953	11457	16524	549	68	15	M	ex Ferdinando Fassio 62.
Katarina ..	1966	28199	50975	715	97	16	M	
Kristina ..	1965	35823	59050	775	106	16½	M	ex Turcoman 68.
Regina ..	1964	26621	43900	706	95	15½	M	ex Nova 67.
Stolt Sagona ..	1958	11722	17918	550	70	14½	M	ex Sagona 67.
Sunrana ..	1959	13221	19670	560	72	15	M	ex John Augustus Essberger 70.

Gulf Oil Corporation: BELGULF GLORY

[*Malcolm Cranfield*

Hadley Shipping Co: CERINTHUS

[*V. H. Young*

SIGURD HERLOFSON & CO. A/S

FUNNEL: *Yellow with red ' H ' on white diamond on broad blue band.*
HULL: *Grey with red boot-topping.*

Name	Date	Tons Gross	Tons Dwt	Length (feet)	Breadth (feet)	Speed (knots)	Engines	Former Names
Obo Prince* ..	1968	52400	96400	842	128	15	M	
Tank Baroness	1958	16371	25800	616	80	15½	M	
Tank Duchess ..	1956	13229	20100	577	74	13½	M	
Tank Monarch	1954	18324	29000	650	81	14½	M	
Tank Princess ..	1963	22581	36150	665	88	15½	M	
Tank Rex ..	1963	30648	49500	750	102	15½	M(2)	

Also cargo ships.   * Bulk/oil carrier.

LEIF HOEGH & CO. A/S

FUNNEL: *White with blue top and house flag interrupting white band.*
HULL: *Grey with red boot-topping.*

Name	Date	Tons Gross	Tons Dwt	Length (feet)	Breadth (feet)	Speed (knots)	Engines	Former Names
Hoegh Laurel ..	1965	46609	85480	817	124	17	ST	
Hoegh Rainbow*	1970	57450	99600	820	128	16	M	
Hoegh Ranger*	1966	42096	64150	796	106	16	M	
Hoegh Ray* ..	1967	42095	64170	796	106	16	M	
Hoegh Rider* ..	1968	57848	93683	820	128	15½	M	
Hoegh Rover*..	1968	57848	93683	821	128	15½	M	
Hoegh Shield†	1969	6817	—	403	61	17	M	

Also cargo ships.   * Ore/oil carriers.   † Liquefied gas carrier.

HOULDER BROS. & CO. LTD.
Houlder Line Ltd.

FUNNEL: *Black with white Maltese cross on broad red band.*
HULL: *Black with red boot-topping.*

Stolt Grange ..	1958	12391	18890	559	72	15	ST	ex Denby Grange 68.

Also other ships.

South American Saint Line Ltd.

Joya McCance..	1964	26836	42910	699	92	17	ST	ex Beauval 67.

Nile S.S. Co. Ltd.

Name	Date	Tons Gross	Tons Dwt	Length (feet)	Breadth (feet)	Speed (knots)	Engines	Former Names
Clerk-Maxwell*	1966	8298	9035	462	63	15	M	

* Liquefied gas carrier.

Ocean Gas Transport Ltd.

Humboldt*	.. 1968	5200	5115	384	54	15	M	

* Liquefied gas carrier.

Methane Tanker Finance Ltd.

FUNNEL: *Black with three narrow white bands.*

Methane Progress*	.. 1964	21876	28000	621	82	17¼	ST	

* Liquefied gas carrier.

HUNTING & SON LTD.

Hunting (Eden) Tankers Ltd.
Field Tank S.S. Co. Ltd.
Northern Petroleum & Bulk Freighters Co. Ltd.

FUNNEL: *Black with seven-point blue star over narrow red and white bands.*

HULL: *Black with red boot-topping.*

Dewdale†	.. 1965	35642	63588	775	108	15½	M	ex Edenfield 67.
Forthfield	.. 1955	12129	18910	556	69	14½	ST	
Teesfield	.. 1959	12146	18025	556	71	14	M	
Thamesfield	.. 1959	20743	33880	660	85	16½	ST	

Also cargo ships.   † On charter to Min. of Defence (Navy Dept.).

IMPERIAL OIL LTD. (Marine Division)

FUNNEL: *Red with blue band between two white bands.*
HULL: *Light blue with brown boot-topping.*

Name	Date	Tons Gross	Tons Dwt	Length (feet)	Breadth (feet)	Speed (knots)	Engines	Former Names
Imperial Acadia	1966	7068	13700	440	60	15	M	
Imperial Bedford	1969	9500	13980	486	70	15	M	
Imperial Quebec	1957	4680	6355	375	63	13	M	
Imperial Sarnia	1948	4947	6750	409	53	12½	ST	
Imperial St. Clair	1974	9100					M	

Also smaller ships.

Caribbean Oil & Transport Inc.

Imperial St. Lawrence	..	1957	23455	35810	693	91	16½	ST

Western Oil & Trading Company

Imperial Ottawa	1967	59267	110187	907	136	16½	ST

JOHN I. JACOBS & CO. LTD.

FUNNEL: *Yellow with black top.*
HULL: *Black with red boot-topping.*

Hollywood	..	1969	15500	25200	557	81	16	M	
Laurelwood	..	1969	15500	25200	557	81	16	M	
Pearleaf*	..	1960	12353	18500	568	72	15	M	
Texaco Durham†		1959	12354	18025	556	71	14½	M	ex Regent Falcon 70.

* On charter to Min. of Defence (Navy Dept.).
† On charter to Regent Petroleum Tankship Co. Ltd.

Doxford & Sunderland Shipbuilding & Engineering Co. Ltd.

FUNNEL: *Green, with cross of St. Cuthbert, black top.*

North Sands	..	1965	39450	69683	800	110	16	M

Hunting & Son: TEESFIELD [Malcolm Cranfield

John I. Jacobs: NORTH SANDS [J. Mathieson

ANDERS JAHRE

FUNNEL: *Black with white and blue houseflag on broad red band, or yellow with house flag.*

HULL: *Grey with green boot-topping.*

Name		Date	Tons Gross	Tons Dwt	Length (feet)	Breadth (feet)	Speed (knots)	Engines	Former Names
Jabetta ..	..	1959	25300	42555	707	90	16½	ST	
Jagarda ..	..	1962	32455	51612	740	102	17	ST	*To Lib., ren. BURMAH AMBER*
Jagranda	..	1963	50755	89800	868	121	15	ST	
Jakinda ..	..	1958	25271	40290	707	90	16½	ST	
Jalinga ..	..	1970	128000	250000	—	—	15½	ST	
Jarama*	..	1969	57850	95700	867	125	16	M	
Jaranda	..	1967	51831	98333	850	125	15½	M	
Jarelsa ..	..	1964	34056	59031	738	106	17	M	
Jarena ..	..	1968	52324	100480	865	125	16	M	
Jaricha ..	..	1962	32878	52203	740	102	16	ST	
Jarmina*	..	1970	62300	96000	867	125	16	M	
Jarmona	..	1964	34056	59051	738	106	17	M	
Jasankoa	..	1967	91944	164934	984	158	16½	ST	
awachta	..	1963	32763	52555	740	102	17	ST	
Jastella		1974	128000					ST	

Also cargo ships.   * Ore/bulk/oil carrier.

" K " STEAMSHIP CO. LTD.

Kaye Tanker Management Co. Ltd.

FUNNEL: *Black with white " K " in white diamond frame.*

HULL: *Black with red boot-topping.*

Kayeson..	..	1961	28132	47184	712	98	16	ST	*To Royal Mail Lines*

A. F. KLAVENESS & CO. A/S

FUNNEL: *Black with white ' K ' on red band.*

HULL: *Light grey.*

Siljestad†	..	1970	90000	151600	994	140	16	ST
Solstad ..	..	1969	57732	108500	909	128	15½	M *To Norway, ren. FRUEN*
Stiklestad	..	1967	53336	103000	870	128	15½	M

Also cargo ships.   † Bulk/oil carrier.

KNUT KNUTSEN O.A.S.

FUNNEL: *Black with two red bands.*
HULL: *Black with white line and red boot-topping.*

Name	Date	Tons Gross	Tons Dwt	Length (feet)	Breadth (feet)	Speed (knots)	Engines	Former Names
Anna Knudsen..	1966	41442	74300	785	121	15½	M	
~~Hilda Knudsen~~	1956	19178	31830	650	82	15	M(2)	
John Knudsen ..	1967	41441	74300	785	121	15½	M	
~~Tore Knudsen~~	1956	11920	18050	563	70	15	M	*To Cyprus, ren Petrolina I*

Also cargo ships.

J. LAURITZEN

FUNNEL: *Red with white band with white ' J ' above and ' L ' below.*
HULL: *Red.*

Name		Date	Tons Gross	Tons Dwt	Length (feet)	Breadth (feet)	Speed (knots)	Engines
Kinna Dan	..	1966	41108	68900	789	118	16½	M
Selma Dan	..	1964	33847	55750	753	106	16	M
Tanja Dan	..	1964	33746	55850	753	106	16	M

Also cargo ships.

ACHILLE LAURO

FUNNEL: *Blue with white star and black top.*
HULL: *Black.*

Name		Date	Tons Gross	Tons Dwt	Length (feet)	Breadth (feet)	Speed (knots)	Engines
Coraggio	..	1953	17257	26300	628	82	16	M(2)
Tenacia ..	..	1952	17257	26300	628	82	16	M(2)
Volere	..	1951	17048	25964	626	82	16	M(2)

Also passenger and cargo ships.

LIVANOS GROUP

VARIOUS COMPANIES

FUNNEL: *Black with broad white band with blue " L " between two Greek key bands also in blue.*
HULL: *Grey with red boot-topping.*

Name	Date	Tons Gross	Tons Dwt	Length (feet)	Breadth (feet)	Speed (knots)	Engines	Former Names
Athina Livanos	1954	19462	29402	645	84	17	ST	
Atlantic Baron	1953	12696	20080	561	71	15	ST	
Atlantic Baroness ..	1953	12712	20090	561	71	15	ST	
Atlantic Emperor ..	1949	17325	26868	628	83	17	ST	
Atlantic Empress	1964	31716	60906	776	106	17	ST	
Atlantic King ..	1957	25172	39733	695	95	16	ST	
Atlantic Knight	1956	14839	22500	599	77	14½	ST	
Atlantic Lady ..	1955	12985	19980	561	74	15	ST	
Atlantic Lord ..	1953	11322	18080	554	71	14½	M	
Atlantic Marchioness ..	1968	40962	87007	840	127	16	M	
Atlantic Marquess ..	1968	40962	86878	840	127	16	M	
Atlantic Monarch	1968	48936	103800	907	127	16	ST	
Atlantic Prince	1964	39066	76590	814	122	17	ST	
Atlantic Princess	1966	40884	86842	840	127	15½	M	
Atlantic Queen	1957	24813	39872	695	95	17	ST	
Atlantic Union	1958	21144	32570	662	87	16	ST	
Atlantic Universe ..	1960	21138	32467	662	87	16½	ST	
Eugenie Livanos	1954	19406	29402	645	84	17	ST	
G. S. Livanos ..	1958	25988	44214	712	93	17	ST	
George Livanos	1954	18790	29402	645	84	17	ST	
Mary Livanos ..	1960	13592	20145	565	74	15½	ST	
Stavros G. Livanos	1964	44726	80806	814	122	17	ST	

Atlantic Empress 1974
Atlantic Baron 12,690 1974
Atlantic Baroness 1974

Also cargo ships.

LONDON & OVERSEAS FREIGHTERS LTD.

FUNNEL: *Yellow with red star on white over blue band.*

HULL: *Black, boot-topping red with white line.*

Name	Date	Tons Gross	Tons Dwt	Length (feet)	Breadth (feet)	Speed (knots)	Engines	Former Names
Bayleaf† ..	1955	12123	17930	557	71	14½	M	ex London Integrity 59.
Brambleleaf† ..	1954	12123	18706	557	71	14	M	ex London Loyalty 59.
London Confidence ..	1962	21393	33370	665	88	15	M	
London Harmony ..	1959	13022	19214	560	72	14	M	
London Independence	1961	22256	36205	698	88	16½	M(2)	
London Pride ..	1971		— 251500	—	—	16	ST	
London Enterprise 1974 71500							M	

Also cargo ships.   † On charter to Ministry of Defence (Navy Dept.).

London & Overseas Tankers Ltd.

Name	Date	Tons Gross	Tons Dwt	Length (feet)	Breadth (feet)	Speed (knots)	Engines	Former Names
Overseas Ambassador ..	1962	22272	36235	698	88	16¾	M(2)	
Overseas Discoverer ..	1962	22222	36180	698	88	16½	M(2)	

Livanos Group: ATLANTIC PRINCESS   [R. J. Weeks

London & Overseas: OVERSEAS ADVENTURER   [D. Clegg

London & Overseas Bulk Carriers Ltd.

Name	Date	Tons Gross	Tons Dwt	Length (feet)	Breadth (feet)	Speed (knots)	Engines	Former Names
Overseas Adventurer ..	1963	13721	19770	560	72	15¼	M	

MALMROS REDERI A/B

FUNNEL: *White, black top with green* M.

HULL: *Grey.*

Name	Date	Tons Gross	Tons Dwt	Length	Breadth	Speed	Engines	Former Names
Frans Malmros*	1968	60536	108183	870	131	16	ST	
Jacob Malmros*	1968	60555	108109	870	131	16½	ST	
Malmohus ..	1965	52521	93250	857	128	16½	ST	
Paul Endacott†	1964	19077	22090	592	82	16	M	*to Lib., ren, NORFOLK*
† **Malmros Multina**	1974	34000				18	M	*MULTINA*

* Ore/oil carrier.   † Liquefied gas carrier.

MELSOM & MELSOM

FUNNEL: *Yellow with blue ' M ' on white diamond on red band and black top.*

HULL: *Black with white line.*

Name	Date	Tons Gross	Tons Dwt	Length	Breadth	Speed	Engines	Former Names
Polarbris* ..	1970	73526	138000	919	143	16	ST	
Polarsol ..	1960	21592	34050	665	86	17	M	
Polarvik ..	1963	36870	63860	775	109	17	ST	

* Bulk/oil carrier.

P. MEYER

FUNNEL: *Grey with white ' M ' over two red bands.*

HULL: *Light grey with red boot-topping.*

Name	Date	Tons Gross	Tons Dwt	Length	Breadth	Speed	Engines	Former Names
Havbor ..	..	1963	26519	41800	701	96	17	M(2)
Havfrost*	..	1966	8709	11460	464	63	15	M
Havgas*	..	1965	8996	11355	464	63	15	M
Havmoy†	..	1968	42501	72600	800	106	16	M
Havtor†	..	1967	42506	72700	800	106	16	M

Also cargo ships.   † Ore/oil carrier.   * Liquefied gas carrier.

Malmros Rederi: PAUL ENDACOTT   [John G. Callis

Mobil O ilCorporation: MOBIL LIBYA, at Port Stanvac, South Australia   [J. Y. Freeman

MOBIL OIL CORPORATION

FUNNEL: *Black with " MOBIL " in blue with letter ' O ' in red.*

HULL: *Black or dark grey with white bulwark line and red boot-topping. Superstructure—blue/green.*

Name	Date	Tons Gross	Tons Dwt	Length (feet)	Breadth (feet)	Speed (knots)	Engines	Former Names
Colina	1943	10198	17291	524	68	14½	TE	
Eclipse	1954	16242	26010	588	83	17	ST	
Mobil Aero ..	1959	18616	31018	641	84	16	ST	
Mobil Lube ..	1958	18669	31145	645	84	16½	ST	
Mobil Meridian	1961	28218	49298	736	102	17	ST	ex Stanvac Meridian 61.
Mobiloil ..	1959	18616	32730	641	84	16	ST	
Socony-Vacuum	1954	17444	28642	605	84	16½	ST	
Syosset	1945	9932	16526	502	68	14½	ST	

Also smaller vessels.

Mobil Tankers Ltd.

Mobil Acme ..	1960	12755	19740	549	74	15½	ST	
Mobil Endurance	1962	31289	54345	742	104	16½	ST	
Mobil Energy ..	1962	32527	54345	742	104	16½	ST	
Mobil Enterprise	1961	31290	54307	735	104	16½	ST	
Mobil Pegasus..	1969	112657	211660	1069	158	16½	ST	

Mobil Shipping Co. Ltd.

Australian Progress ..	1960	10186	13857	490	75	15	ST	ex Mobil Progress 64, ex Stanvac Progress 62.
Mobil Astral ..	1964	59514	101282	888	128	17	ST	
Mobil Daylight	1964	58034	101058	888	128	17	ST	
Mobil Pinnacle	1970	112650	211660	1070	158	16	ST	
Mobil Transporter†	1957	37781	63835	818	106	14½	ST	ex Mobil Mariner 64, ex Stanvac Mariner 62.
Sylvan Arrow ..	1955	20413	31300	660	86	16½	ST	

† Bulk/oil carrier.

Mobil Tankers Co. (Liberia) Ltd.

Mobil Comet ..	1963	58430	101297	888	128	17	ST	
Mobil Japan ..	1965	43265	86382	835	122	16½	ST	
Mobil Radiant..	1953	17428	27675	635	83	16½	ST	ex Aramis 68.
Mobil Valiant ..	1964	42001	78008	875	104	16	ST	
Mobil Vigilant..	1964	31262	53490	735	104	16	ST	
Mobil Mariner	1974	121,590						
Mobil Marketer	1974	18,000		302				M
Al Haramain	1975							
Mobil Refiner	1974	18,200						

6

Mobil Carrier Ltd.

Name		Date	Tons Gross	Tons Dwt	Length (feet)	Breadth (feet)	Speed (knots)	Engines	Former Names
Mobil Libya	..	1965	48908	84256	835	122	16¾	ST	

(PANAMA)

Mobil Tankers Co. S.A.

Marion ..	..	1960	28814	47025	736	100	16	ST	

(PANAMA)

Iberian Tankers Ltd.

Waneta ..	..	1952	26155	54335	755	104	16	ST	
Wapello	..	1953	30626	53657	763	104	16	ST	
Winamac	..	1939	11981	19254	540	74	14½	ST	ex Mobilube 54.

(FRANCE)

Mobil Oil Francaise
(Dept. Transports Maritimes)

Aramis ..	..	1963	53801	97801	905	127	17	ST	ex Mobil Brilliant 69.
Athos ..	..	1965	48024	84620	835	122	17	ST	
D'Artagnan	..	1959	31298	52195	756	100	17	ST	
D'Artagnan		1974	121500					ST	
Athos		1974	145000						

(WESTERN GERMANY)

Mobil Oil A.G.

Tasso	..	..	1962	30569	53287	742	104	16½	ST	

(PANAMA)

Nocos Tankers Inc.

toGreece, ren 'GALAXY

Mobil Aladdin ..	1954	17888	28651	637	83	16½	ST	ex Porthos 69.
Mobil Exporter*	1959	38012	65000	800	94	16½	ST	ex Wabasha 69.

* Bulk/oil carrier.

(U.S.A.)

Kurz Tankers Inc. etc.

Mobil Fuel	..	1957	18669	31145	645	84	16½	ST	
Mobil Power	..	1957	18669	31145	645	84	16½	ST	
Mobilgas	..	1956	17462	28608	610	84	16½	ST	

A. P. Moller: DAGMAR MAERSK [R. J. Weeks

A. P. Moller: ELISABETH MAERSK [R. J. Weeks

A. P. MOLLER

FUNNEL: *Black with seven-pointed white star on broad pale blue band.*
HULL: *Light blue with red boot-topping.*

Name	Date	Tons Gross	Tons Dwt	Length (feet)	Breadth (feet)	Speed (knots)	Engines	Former Names
A. P. Moller ..	1966	53261	98107	864	128	17	ST	
Anglo Maersk	1963	31941	52720	750	103	16	ST	
Arthur Maersk	1958	13143	20310	560	72	14¾	M	
Caroline Maersk	1960	25057	41780	696	91	15½	ST	
Dagmar Maersk	1969	104681	209400	1067	155	15	ST	
Dirch Maersk ..	1968	103148	205600	1080	144	15	ST	
Dorthe Maersk	1968	103148	205700	1080	144	15	ST	
Eleo Maersk ..	1959	18164	31000	635	81	15½	M	
Eli Maersk ..	1966	52602	97740	872	128	16	M	
Elisabeth Maersk	1968	53227	100700	881	128	17	ST	
Emma Maersk	1964	36831	63730	775	109	17	ST	
Evelyn Maersk	1968	53227	100600	881	128	17	ST	
Gerd Maersk ..	1963	36847	63630	775	109	17	ST	
Gjertrud Maersk	1960	17071	27930	637	74	15	M	
Henning Maersk	1963	22089	36340	686	84	15½	M	
Jakob Maersk ..	1966	48664	88000	859	122	16	ST	
Jane Maersk ..	1966	48697	87000	859	122	16	ST	
Karen Maersk	1964	21613	36340	686	84	15½	M	
Kristine Maersk	1962	26636	42950	708	94	16	ST	
Marie Maersk	1962	21628	34050	686	84	15½	M	
Oluf Maersk ..	1963	21609	35900	686	84	15½	M	ToGreece, ren .AEGIS PRESIDENT
Peter Maersk ..	1964	31979	51400	750	103	16	ST	
Prima Maersk..	1965	33018	53400	771	103	16	ST	
Sine Maersk ..	1965	43921	77450	816	120	16	M	
Sofie Maersk ..	1965	43921	77450	816	120	16	M	
Kristine Maersk	1974	170000						

Also cargo ships.

Grete Maersk 1974 19,900
Katrine Maersk 1974 168,200
Kristine Maersk 1974 168,200

MOSVOLD, TORREY

Mosvold Shipping Co. A/S & Mosvold Bulktransport A/S

FUNNEL: *Black or yellow with interlocking white rings on red band.*
HULL: *Black, red boot-topping.*

Name	Date	Tons Gross	Tons Dwt	Length (feet)	Breadth (feet)	Speed (knots)	Engines	Former Names
Mosduke	1967	45012	81339	800	122	16½	M	
Mosking	1964	36200	67934	780	118	16	ST	
Mosli	1964	34179	58853	734	110	16	M	
Mosprince	1966	44992	81471	800	122	16½	M	
Mosqueen	1964	40893	71417	780	118	16	ST	
Mostank	1957	12591	19682	560	71	14	M	
Mostun Sanko*	1968	42615	65000	783	118	15½	M	

* Ore/oil carrier.

A/S MOSVOLD REDERI

Name	Date	Tons Gross	Tons Dwt	Length (feet)	Breadth (feet)	Speed (knots)	Engines	Former Names
Moster	1965	42204	70867	785	122	17	M	

A. P. Moller: KAREN MAERSK

Mosvold: MOSKING

A/S J. LUDWIG MOWINCKELS REDERI

FUNNEL: *Yellow with black top separated by red, white and blue bands.*
HULL: *Grey with red boot-topping.*

Name			Date	Tons Gross	Tons Dwt	Length (feet)	Breadth (feet)	Speed (knots)	Engines	Former Names
Borga	..	..	1955	13737	20400	591	75	15	M	
Frosta	..	..	1961	22485	36985	665	90	17	ST	
Hada	..	..	1956	11974	18150	556	72	14	M	ToGreece, ren. Christiana
Hitra	..	..	1961	22485	36985	665	90	17	ST	Transoceanic
Molda	..	..	1966	75494	143620	932	142	16	ST	
Strinda	..	..	1957	13734	20350	591	75	15	M	ToGreece, ren. Isabella
Troma	..	..	1966	47527	82340	817	124	16½	ST	

Also cargo ships.

WM. H. MULLER & CO.'S T.M.N.V.

FUNNEL: *Yellow with red and blue diagonal stripes on white panel.*
HULL: *Black with red boot-topping.*

N.V. Nationale Tankvaart Maats

Forest Hill	..	1960	12718	19900	560	72	15	M
Forest Lake	..	1960	12718	19900	560	72	15	M
Forest Town	..	1960	12718	19900	560	72	15	M

N.V. Tanker Handel Maats " Tahama "

Tahama	..	1958	12730	19990	560	72	15	M
Tamara	..	1958	12730	19900	560	72	15	M

NAESS GROUP

VARIOUS COMPANY TITLES

FUNNEL: *Black with blue " N " on white diamond on broad red band.*
HULL: *Grey with green boot-topping.*

Naess, Denholm & Co. Ltd. (Managers)

	Name	Date	Tons Gross	Tons Dwt	Length	Breadth	Speed	Engines	
	Naess Champion	1962	54489	90629	875	123	16	ST	To Lib. ren Burmah Jet
	Naess Endeavour	1960	30731	51088	741	104	17	ST	To Lib. ren Burmah Cameo
ordic	Naess Louisiana†	1964	18589	26503	620	85	16	M	To Lib. ren Burmah Zircon
	Naess Sovereign	1961	54466	95134	875	123	16	ST	
ordic	Naess Texas†	1964	18589	26562	620	85	16	M	

† Liquid sulphur carrier.

Naess Group: NAESS TEXAS

[F. W. Hawks]

(NETHERLANDS)
Nederlandse Norness Scheepv. Maats. N.V.

Name	Date	Tons Gross	Tons Dwt	Length (feet)	Breadth (feet)	Speed (knots)	Engines	Former Names
Carbo Tiger* ..	1958	16139	25920	615	77	14	M	ex Naess Tiger 68. *To L16 -, ren 'STOLT EAGLE*

* Chemical tanker.

(NETHERLANDS)
Nortuna Scheepv. Mij. N.V.

Naess Courier†	1966	26280	41931	708	88	15½	M	

† Bulk/oil carrier.

(NORWAY)
VARIOUS COMPANIES

Naess Crusader	1957	21120	33825	679	87	17	ST	
Nordic Rover	*1963*	*23981*					*M*	*ex Naess Comet*
Nordic Regent	*1963*	*23981*					*M*	*ex Naess Meteor*

(LIBERIA)
VARIOUS COMPANIES

Name	Date	Tons Gross	Tons Dwt	Length (feet)	Breadth (feet)	Speed (knots)	Engines	Former Names
Benjamin Coates	1960	28897	47486	737	100	16	ST	
Carbo Dragon ..	1957	15937	25025	615	77	15	M	ex Naess Dragon 69.
Maria Forsyth ..	1959	28694	48082	740	100	16	ST	ex Naess Challenger 69.
Naess Enterprise	1970	67443	133400	900	138	16	M	
Naess Leader ..	1958	26650	42875	713	97	16½	ST	
Naess Mariner	1957	26650	42828	713	97	16½	ST	
Naess Norseman* ..	1965	37966	71183	820	104	17	M	*To L16., ren. BURMAH ONYX*
Naess Pride ..	1961	40649	66525	848	108	16	ST	
Naess Spirit ..	1960	40468	70380	848	108	16	ST	*To L16., ren. BURMAH CORAL*
Russell H. Green	1965	34837	60427	775	106	16½	M	
Nordic Commander 1975							*ST*	

* Bulk/oil carrier. *NORDIC CONQUEROR 1972 143959*

NAESS PATRIOT 1973 69904
NORDIC CLIPPER 1973 83714
NORDIC CRUSADER 1973 86098

(FRANCE) *ex Naess Viking* *ex Naess Crusader*
CIE. NATIONALE DE NAVIGATION

FUNNEL: *Black with houseflag incorporating the letters " C.N.N. ".*
HULL: *Grey.*

Concorde	..	1967	45229	72900	800	115	17	M
Frimaire	..	1970	84000	140000	947	145	16	M
Nivose ..	..	1965	45033	66000	801	115	17	M
Passy ..	..	1961	20433	32846	678	84	16	M
Ventose	..	1965	45033	66000	801	115	17	M

Niarchos Group: WORLD FAITH

[R. J. Weeks]

CIE. NAVALE DES PÉTROLES

FUNNEL: *Yellow with white and red comet over blue band.*

HULL: *Black with red boot-topping.*

Name		Date	Tons Gross	Tons Dwt	Length (feet)	Breadth (feet)	Speed (knots)	Engines	Former Names
Aldebaran	..	1965	57177	99689	915	123	16½	M	
Altair	..	1959	31174	48346	737	102	15¾	M	
Betelgeuse	..	1968	61766	121432	924	128	16	M	
Batman	..	1957	21547	33089	663	86	15½	M	ro England, ren , Langley
Cassiopee	..	1968	61766	121444	924	128	16	M	
Djemila	..	1953	8354	12655	475	62	12	M	
Emeraude	..	1970	111983	223600	1082	158	16	ST	
Ninive	..	1955	19674	29892	649	84	14½	M	
Polaire	..	1959	31174	48346	737	102	15¾	M	
Rigel	..	1960	31182	47602	737	101	16	M	
Roger Gasquet		1964	53632	91885	866	122	16½	M	
Samarrah	..	1957	18170	29800	633	84	15	M	
Sirius	..	1961	33060	51803	778	102	16	M	
Vega	..	1962	33060	51831	778	102	16	M	
Opale		1975	138200					#ST	

Also smaller ships.

THE NIARCHOS GROUP

FUNNEL: *Black with white " N " interrupting red over white over blue band.*

HULL: *Black, red boot-topping.*

VARIOUS COMPANIES

Constantine	..	1965	34827	60000	775	106	16½	ST	
Eugenie	..	1964	34827	60999	775	106	16½	ST	ex World Inheritor 64.
Eugenie S. Niarchos	..	1970	97000	210000	1037	160	16	ST	
Evgenia Niarchos	..	1956	30158	47818	757	97	17	ST	
Maria Isabella	..	1964	34827	60000	775	106	16½	ST	
Northern Joy	..	1964	38649	76790	814	122	16½	ST	
Philip S. Niarchos	..	1963	50872	90400	834	122	16	ST	
Spyros	..	1964	34593	61028	775	106	16½	ST	
Spyros Niarchos		1956	30709	47783	757	97	17	ST	
World Banner		1958	20546	33273	661	90	16½	ST	
World Beauty	..	1957	27902	46654	736	102	16½	ST	
World Bond	..	1957	20533	33273	661	90	16½	ST	
World Faith	..	1964	47344	86500	870	122	16½	ST	
World Friendship	..	1965	49437	90000	870	122	16½	ST	
World Gallantry		1957	13750	21580	590	74	16	M	
World Grace		1954	27277	47590	740	87	17	ST	
World Grandeur		1955	25317	42462	705	98	17	ST	
World Gratitude		1954	27278	47438	756	87	17	ST	ren. Wamsutta(storage vessel)
World Guardian		1955	27278	47468	756	87	17	ST	storage vessel
World Guidance		1955	27278	44648	740	87	17	ST	
World Ideal	..	1957	26032	42200	713	97	17	ST	

Name	Date	Tons Gross	Tons Dwt	Length (feet)	Breadth (feet)	Speed (knots)	Engines	Former Names
World								
Independence	1957	26032	41799	715	97	17	ST	
World Industry	1957	25490	41005	710	96	17	ST	
World Influence	1957	26031	42120	714	97	16½	ST	
World								
Inheritance ..	1958	25222	40037	695	95	17	ST	
World Inspiration	1957	25489	41000	710	96	17	ST	
World								
Intelligence ..	1957	25357	40058	695	95	17	ST	
World Justice ..	1954	20864	33100	660	88	16	ST	
World Kindness	1968	41477	87340	845	122	17	M	
World Knowledge	1969	41477	87340	845	122	17	M	
World Sea ..	1953	12877	20200	556	72	15	ST	ex Saxonsea 56.
World Sincerity	1955	20165	32900	663	86	16½	ST	
World Spirit ..	1958	25888	41050	700	97	17	ST	
World Unity ..	1952	20667	32895	653	86	16½	ST	

World Monarch 1974 118500

(PANAMA)
VARIOUS COMPANIES

Name	Date	Tons Gross	Tons Dwt	Length (feet)	Breadth (feet)	Speed (knots)	Engines	Former Names
World Merit ..	1950	25305	40970	751	83	16	ST	To Cyprus, ren. MINIM ex Mobil Radiant 66, ex Sovac Radiant 55.
World Miracle	1949	25360	43310	751	83	16	ST	ex Mobil Tide 65, ex Mobil Astral 63, ex Sovac Astral 55.

(GREECE)
VARIOUS COMPANIES

Name	Date	Tons Gross	Tons Dwt	Length (feet)	Breadth (feet)	Speed (knots)	Engines	Former Names
Elena	1967	88866	202000	1034	155	16	ST	
Princess Sophie	1958	43373	71282	859	116	17	ST	
World								
Enterprise ..	1953	21284	33293	663	86	16	ST	
World Hope ..	1961	15979	26026	615	77	15½	M	To Greece, ren. YALTON

(WEST GERMANY)
RUDOLF A. OETKER TANKSCHIFF REEDEREI K.G.
(Rudolf A. Oetker)

FUNNEL: *White with red top.*
HULL: *Grey.*

Name	Date	Tons Gross	Tons Dwt	Length (feet)	Breadth (feet)	Speed (knots)	Engines	Former Names
St. Michaelis ..	1966	44895	76270	822	124	16	M	
St. Nikolai ..	1965	38858	63260	773	110	16	M	
St. Petri ..	1966	44895	76270	822	124	16	M	

Oetker Tankschiff: ST PETRI   [*F. R. Sherlock*

Fred Olsen: BORGEN   [*R. J. Weeks*

Onassis Group: OLYMPIC CHARIOT, pictured in 1963   [*F. W. Hawks*

Onassis Group: OLYMPIC VALLEY   [*D. Clegg*

FRED OLSEN & CO.

(NORWAY)

FUNNEL: *Yellow with white and blue house-flag.*

HULL: *Grey with green boot-topping.*

Name		Date	Tons Gross	Tons Dwt	Length (feet)	Breadth (feet)	Speed (knots)	Engines	Former Names
Bollsta	..	1965	28668	51357	710	102	16½	M	
Borgen	..	1966	46696	87711	810	128	16	M	
Borgila	..	1965	51576	99416	847	128	16	M	
Borgsten	..	1964	49311	91356	870	122	17	M	

Also cargo and short-sea ships.

(NORWAY)

OLSEN & UGELSTAD

FUNNEL: *Black with white "OU" monogram interrupting two white bands.*

HULL: *Black with red boot-topping.   Dark green upperworks.*

Name		Date	Tons Gross	Tons Dwt	Length (feet)	Breadth (feet)	Speed (knots)	Engines	Former Names
Hovdefjell	..	1958	16686	26130	621	74	16	ST	
Lysefjell	..	1960	13075	20700	578	74	14	M	
Vardefjell*	..	1964	36136	57320	775	106	16	M	
Fagerfjell		1974	65000						

Also cargo ships.   * Ore/oil carrier.

(LIBERIA)

THE ONASSIS GROUP

FUNNEL: *Orange with large white disc having blue and white pennant houseflag and five interlocking coloured rings above and below.*

HULL: *Black or white with red boot-topping.*

VARIOUS COMPANY TITLES

Name	Date	Tons Gross	Tons Dwt	Length (feet)	Breadth (feet)	Speed (knots)	Engines	Former Names
Olympic Accord	1969	98726	216500	1056	158	16	ST	
Olympic Action	1970	111500	220000	1056	158	16	ST	
Olympic Adventure	1970	97466	216000	1056	158	16	ST	
Olympic Archer	1970	97500	216000	1056	158	16	ST	
Olympic Armour	1969	109579	216508	1057	158	16	ST	
Olympic Arrow	1970	96627	212000	1059	158	16	ST	
Olympic Athlete	1969	97468	216490	1057	158	16	ST	
Olympic Breeze	1954	13934	21995	597	74	16	ST	
Olympic Brook	1955	13709	21382	591	74	16	ST	
Olympic Challenger	1959	37958	66336	845	108	17	ST	

Name	Date	Tons Gross	Tons Dwt	Length (feet)	Breadth (feet)	Speed (knots)	Engines	Former Names
Olympic Destiny								
Olympic Champion ..	1960	37744	66278	845	108	17	ST	
Olympic Chariot ..	1963	30574	61300	771	106	16	ST	
Olympic Chivalry ..	1964	30581	61300	771	106	16	ST	
Olympic Cloud	1953	14221	21955	597	74	16	ST	
Olympic Dale	1954	18476	29043	650	74	16	ST	
Olympic Eagle	1958	27602	49113	736	103	16	ST	
Olympic Falcon	1958	27602	46787	736	103	16	ST	
Olympic Fame	1965	47403	87970	870	122	16	ST	
Olympic Flame	1950	17791	28385	625	84	16½	ST	
Olympic Freedom	1964	47493	87970	870	122	16	ST	
Olympic Games	1964	32380	61362	771	106	16	ST	
Olympic Garland ..	1965	38607	73986	805	121	16½	M	
Olympic Gate..	1965	32478	61162	771	106	16	ST	
Olympic Glory	1964	38598	69689	805	121	16	M	
Olympic Goal	1965	38607	73992	805	121	16	M	
Olympic Grace	1965	32407	64234	771	106	16	ST	
Olympic Gulf ..	1954	20495	32191	662	87	15	ST	ex Melika 66.
Olympic Ice ..	1954	17999	29201	644	74	16	ST	
Olympic Lake..	1954	17999	29134	644	74	16	ST	
Olympic Laurel	1949	24682	39631	707	84	16½	ST	
Olympic Light	1953	14009	21441	590	74	16	ST	
Olympic Mountain ..	1953	18781	29340	644	74	16	ST	
Olympic Rainbow ..	1954	13934	22017	597	74	16	ST	
Olympic Rider	1960	32008	58000	817	95	17	ST	
Olympic Rock..	1954	17999	29097	644	74	16	ST	
Olympic Runner	1959	32007	59000	817	95	17	ST	
Olympic Sky ..	1955	13934	22012	597	74	16	ST	
Olympic Snow	1954	13665	21337	590	74	16	ST	
Olympic Splendour ..	1954	20595	34333	667	87	16½	ST	
Olympic Star ..	1949	17792	28385	625	84	16½	ST	
Olympic Storm	1954	14047	22034	597	74	16	ST	
Olympic Sun ..	1955	18790	30125	641	84	16½	ST	
Olympic Thunder ..	1950	24741	41562	708	84	16½	ST	
Olympic Torch	1949	24689	39670	705	84	16½	ST	
Olympic Valley	1953	13652	21279	590	74	16	ST	
Olympic Valour	1950	20453	31761	663	87	16	ST	
Olympic Wind	1954	14047	23020	597	74	17	ST	
Tina Onassis ..	1953	28798	49722	776	96	16½	ST	

PACIFIC MARITIME SERVICES LTD.

(Furness Withy & Co. Ltd.)

FUNNEL: *Yellow.*

HULL: *Black with red boot-topping.*

Name	Date	Tons Gross	Tons Dwt	Length (feet)	Breadth (feet)	Speed (knots)	Engines
William Wheelwright	1960	30976	51566	754	98	16	ST

Onassis Group: OLYMPIC GOAL

[F. R. Sherlock

PHILLIPS PETROLEUM COMPANY

FUNNEL: *Black, wide band with "PHILLIPS 66" on shield.*
HULL: *Black.*

Name	Date	Tons Gross	Tons Dwt	Length (feet)	Breadth (feet)	Speed (knots)	Engines	Former Names
⊗ **Phillips California** ..	1954	10473	16191	515	68	15	ST	ex Flying A. California 66.
Phillips Washington ..	1954	10473	16191	515	68	15	ST	ex Flying A. Washington 66.

Philtankers Inc.

Name	Date	Tons Gross	Tons Dwt	Length (feet)	Breadth (feet)	Speed (knots)	Engines	Former Names
Phillips Arkansas† ..	1969	18013	20000	606	84	17	M	
Phillips Kansas*	1963	43521	80303	850	106	16½	ST	ex Delaware Getty 66.
Phillips Louisiana* ..	1964	43520	80261	850	106	16½	ST	ex Louisiana Getty 66.
Phillips Oklahoma ..	1963	51518	94426	835	123	16½	ST	ex California Getty 66.
Phillips Oregon	1964	51542	94576	838	123	16½	ST	ex Oregon Getty 66.
Phillips Texas ..	1961	28805	49635	737	100	16	ST	ex Denmark Getty 66.

* Ore/oil carrier.   † Liquefied gas carrier.

PURFINA-TRANSPORTS

FUNNEL: *Black with Purfina Shield over red over white bands.*
HULL: *Grey, red boot-topping.*

Name	Date	Tons Gross	Tons Dwt	Length (feet)	Breadth (feet)	Speed (knots)	Engines	Former Names
Fina Angola ..	1959	21581	33418	667	87	17	ST	ex Purfina Angola 60.
Fina Belgique ..	1966	48157	73880	820	117	16	M	
Fina France ..	1957	21347	32821	667	87	17	ST	ex Purfina France 60.
Fina Scandinavie	1964	35000	57000	775	106	16	M	

Petrofina S.A.

Name	Date	Tons Gross	Tons Dwt	Length (feet)	Breadth (feet)	Speed (knots)	Engines	Former Names
Fina Allemagne	1958	13120	19506	560	72	15½	M	ex Purfina Allemagne 60.
Fina America ..	1958	21401	33418	667	87	17	ST	
Fina Norvege ..	1965	38704	63834	818	106	16	M	
Reine Fabiola ..	1965	34426	60366	775	106	16	M	

Phillips Petroleum Co: PHILLIPS KANSAS   [R. J. Weeks

E. T. Radcliffe: HAMILTON   [F. W. Hawks

E. Rasmussen: POLYSTAR in New Zealand waters [Malcolm Cranfield

E. Rasmussen: POLYMONARCH [R. J. Weeks

EVAN THOMAS RADCLIFFE & CO. LTD.

Radcliffe Tankers Ltd., & E.T.R. Tankers Ltd.
Anthony Radcliffe S.S. Co. Ltd.

FUNNEL: *Yellow with narrow black top and golden-coloured fleur-de-lys on broad blue band.*

HULL: *Grey with red boot-topping.*

Name		Date	Tons Gross	Tons Dwt	Length (feet)	Breadth (feet)	Speed (knots)	Engines	Former Names
Hamilton	..	1960	13315	19690	560	72	15½	M	
Llangorse	..	1960	22080	35077	665	85	15½	ST	
Llanishen	..	1958	21346	33757	665	85	16	ST	

(NORWAY)

EINAR RASMUSSEN

FUNNEL: *Black with blue ' R ' on white diamond on blue band.*

HULL: *Grey, red boot-topping.*

Name		Date	Tons Gross	Tons Dwt	Length	Breadth	Speed	Engines
Polyana	..	1956	15734	24900	605	77	15	M
Polycastle	..	1963	26622	44650	706	95	16	M
Polyclipper	..	1954	11737	18125	559	70	15¼	M
Polyduke	..	1959	16548	26050	616	79	16¼	M
Polyglory	..	1961	16542	26050	616	79	16¼	M
Polykarp	..	1964	26623	44685	706	95	16	M
Polymonarch	..	1967	49817	95310	847	128	16	M
Polyqueen	..	1964	39249	71715	795	118	16	M
Polysaga*	..	1969	95400	152750	1010	144	16	M
Polystar ..	..	1962	12780	20250	560	72	15½	M

* Ore/oil carrier.

(NORWAY)

HILMAR REKSTEN

FUNNEL: *Black with two blue bands on broad white band.*

HULL: *Grey.*

Name		Date	Tons Gross	Tons Dwt	Length	Breadth	Speed	Engines	Former Names
Arrian ..	..	1953	13489	21106	583	72	15½	ST	ex Andrew Dillon 62.
Aurelian	..	1969	109439	219000	1075	152	16	ST	
Clementine Churchill	..	1966	51615	95830	851	125	16½	ST	
Cyprian	..	1966	35637	65100	775	109	17	ST	
Gratian ..	..	1966	51417	95448	837	124	16½	ST	
Hadrian	..	1959	40835	68238	854	102	16	ST	
Julian ..	..	1966	49231	93150	818	128	16½	ST	
Kong Haakon VII	..	1969	109423	220000	1069	152	16	ST	
Lucian ..	..	1965	35619	65100	775	109	17	ST	
Majorian	..	1951	16116	26400	606	80	13	M	
Octavian	..	1954	26249	45550	722	86	14	M(2)	
Sir Winston Churchill	..	1966	51642	95300	851	125	16½	ST	
Valentinian	..	1965	50758	94100	837	124	16½	ST	
Vespasian	..	1955	12700	20880	557	72	15¾	ST	
Vespasian		1974	140000						
Lucian		1974	19000					LGT	

ROPNER SHG. CO. LTD.

FUNNEL: *Green with red and white check square.*
HULL: *Green with white line and dark green boot-topping.*

Name		Date	Tons Gross	Tons Dwt	Length (feet)	Breadth (feet)	Speed (knots)	Engines	Former Names
Thirlby	..	1958	13105	20070	559	72	14	M	

Also cargo ships.

ROYAL MAIL LINES LTD.

FUNNEL: *Yellow with red insignia.*
HULL: *Yellow.*

Stolt Abadesa	1962	13398	20180	565	72	15½	M	ex Abadesa 69.
ex Kayeson	1961	28132					ST	

(NETHERLANDS)
ROYAL ROTTERDAM LLOYD

Koninklijke Rotterdamsche Lloyd N.V.

FUNNEL: *Black.*
HULL: *Grey, orange boot-topping.*

Doelwijk	..	1963	31051	53180	760	103	16½	ST	

(SWEDEN)
SALENREDERIERNA A/B & REDERI A/B SALENIA

FUNNEL: *Blue with white ' S ' and black top.*
HULL: *Grey, red boot-topping.*

Name		Date	Tons Gross	Tons Dwt	Length	Breadth	Speed	Engines	Former Names
Anco Span	..	1970	15100	23550	557	87	16	M	
Anco Spring	..	1958	13034	19540	558	72	15	M	ex Dodona 64.
Anco Spur	..	1970	15100	23550	557	81	16	M	
Dagmar Salen		1963	35575	60328	800	104	17	ST	
Sea Saga	..	1958	22365	36510	686	86	16½	M(2)	
Sea Sapphire	..	1962	35572	57000	800	104	17	ST	
Sea Scout	..	1957	15729	26025	605	77	15½	M	ex Seven Seas 67.
Sea Song	..	1959	25811	43045	700	96	17	M(2)	
Sea Sovereign		1970	107286	210500	1037	160	16	ST	
Sea Spirit	..	1966	64028	121185	871	134	16½	ST	
Sea Spray	..	1966	64031	121185	871	134	16½	ST	
Sea Swallow	..	1960	25752	38325	698	95	16½	M	ex Vendelso 67.
Seven Seas	..	1967	52170	97550	870	128	17	ST	
Seven Stars	..	1967	52173	97550	870	128	17	ST	
Sven Salen	..	1958	25779	40460	700	96	17	M(2)	
Sea Swift		1974	125300					ST	

Also cargo ships.

Sea Saint   1974   171000   ST

Ropner Shipping Co: THIRLBY [D. Clegg

Salenrederierna: SEA SONG [Malcolm Cranfield

Shell Group: DARINA   [J. Y. Freeman

Shell Group: DORCASIA   [J. Y. Freeman

Lepeta 197
Leonia 197
Lima 197
Limatula 197
Linga 197
Liparus 197

Limnea 197
Limopsis 197
Liria 197

SHELL GROUP

MAIN TANKER FLEETS OWNED OR MANAGED BY COMPANIES OF THE SHELL GROUP

FUNNEL: *Red with yellow sea-shell (scallop) and narrow black top.*

HULL: *Black or grey.*

Lotorium 1975

Shell Tankers (U.K.) Ltd.

Genota 1975 48,600   LGT
Geomitra 1974 48,600   LGT

Pomella 1967 15842   ex Horama

Name		Date	Tons Gross	Tons Dwt	Length (feet)	Breadth (feet)	Speed (knots)	Engines	Former Names
Arianta	..	1959	13148	19310	560	72	14½	ST	
Daphnella	..	1966	39929	66802	800	110	16	M	
Darina	..	1966	39796	66950	800	110	16	ST	
Donacilla	..	1966	40170	70010	800	110	16	M	
Donax	..	1966	42068	74000	800	116	16	M	
Donovania	..	1966	39042	69760	794	110	16	M	
Dorcasia	..	1967	39505	69760	800	110	16	M	
Drupa	..	1966	39796	70383	800	110	16	ST	
Mactra (French flag)	..	1969	104723	208560	1067	155	16	ST	
Mangelia	..	1968	105138	206525	1067	155	16	ST	
Marinula (Curacao flag)	..	1968	98876	195500	1077	144	16	ST	
Marisa (flag)	..	1968	105495	206937	1066	155	16	ST	
Marticia	..	1970	105250	207500	1066	155	16	ST	
Medora	..	1968	105252	207332	1066	155	16	ST	
Megara	..	1968	105245	206750	1066	155	16	ST	
Melania	..	1969	104561	209000	1067	155	16	ST	
Melo	..	1969	105138	206942	1067	155	16	ST	
Meta (Curacao flag)	..	1969	105521	206913	1067	155	16	ST	
Mitra	..	1969	98876	195500	1077	144	16	ST	
Murex	..	1968	104772	208800	1067	155	16	ST	To France - Shell
Mysella	..	1970	104500	208800	1067	155	16	ST	
Mysia	..	1969	105248	207000	1067	155	16	ST	
Mytilus	..	1969	105521	206900	1067	155	16	ST	
Naticina	..	1967	60703	118580	870	138	15	M	
Opalia	..	1963	32122	52768	748	103	16	ST	Cadet training ship
Pallium	..	1959	13007	19570	560	72	14½	ST	
Partula	..	1959	13007	19539	560	72	14½	ST	
Plagiola	..	1954	11007	15100	525	67	14	ST	
Platidia	..	1955	11007	15100	525	67	14	ST	
Serenia	..	1961	42082	67850	818	113	16	ST	
Solen	..	1961	42162	71270	818	113	16	ST	
Velutina	..	1950	18929	29648	643	81	16	ST	
Verena	..	1950	18925	29722	643	81	16	ST	
Voluta	..	1962	24406	38497	665	90	16	ST	
Gastrana		1974	118700					ST	
Lembulus		1974	131400					ST	
Latirus		1974	138500					ST	
Latia		1974	138500					ST	
Lampas		197							
Lancella		197							

(LIBERIA)

Hercules Tankers Corporation

VESSELS ON BAREBOAT CHARTER AND MANAGED BY SHELL TANKERS (U.K.) LTD.

Capiluna	..	1960	28434	47067	736	102	15	ST	
Capisteria	..	1960	28435	47067	736	102	15	ST	
Capulonix	..	1959	28435	47067	736	102	15	ST	

Fulgar 197
Felania 197
Fossarina 197
Fossarus 197
Fusus 197

325

Felipes 197
Ficus 197
Flammulina 197

Fotoship

Shell Group: ASPRELLA

[R. J. Weeks

Shell Group: MUREX

327

Shell Group: ZENATIA

[R. J Weeks

Shell Group: DOSINA

[D. Clegg

Tanker Owners S.A.

VESSELS ON BAREBOAT CHARTER AND MANAGED BY SHELL TANKERS (U.K.) LTD.

Name		Date	Tons Gross	Tons Dwt	Length (feet)	Breadth (feet)	Speed (knots)	Engines	Former Names
Lovellia	..	1959	28435	47183	736	103	15	ST	
Patro	..	1959	28410	47183	736	102	15	ST	
Lotha		*197*							

Shell Bermuda (Overseas) Ltd.

Name		Date	Tons Gross	Tons Dwt	Length (feet)	Breadth (feet)	Speed (knots)	Engines	Former Names
Alinda	..	1959	12301	18317	559	69	14½	ST	ex San Ernesto 64.
Hadra	..	1954	12169	18125	556	69	14½	ST	
Hadriania	..	1954	12160	18175	556	69	14½	ST	
Haminea	..	1955	12191	18104	556	69	14½	ST	
Harpula	..	1955	12258	18082	556	69	14½	ST	
Hastula	..	1956	12180	18215	556	69	14½	ST	ex San Fabian 66.
Hatasia	..	1956	12161	18140	556	69	14½	ST	
Haustellum	..	1954	12122	18180	556	69	14½	ST	
Haustrum	..	1954	12090	18125	556	69	14½	ST	
Heldia	..	1955	12149	18947	556	70	14½	ST	
Helisoma	..	1956	12149	18220	556	70	14½	ST	
Hemicardium		1953	12215	18847	556	69	14½	ST	ex San Fernando 65.
Hemifuses	..	1954	12182	18746	556	69	14½	ST	
Hemiglypta	..	1955	12180	18153	556	69	14½	ST	
Hemimactra	..	1956	12278	18992	556	69	14½	ST	ex San Fortunato 64.
Hemiplecta	..	1955	12192	18116	556	69	14½	ST	
Hemitrochus	..	1959	12265	18904	560	69	14½	ST	ex San Emiliano 65.
Hima	..	1957	12257	18163	556	69	14½	ST	*TO Greece, ren: PETROLA WI*
Hindsia	..	1955	12212	18115	556	69	14½	ST	
Hinea	..	1956	12211	18115	556	69	14½	ST	
Hinnites	..	1956	12186	18165	556	69	14½	ST	
Holospira	..	1956	12180	18217	556	69	14½	ST	ex San Felipe 65.
Horomya	..	1956	12183	18250	556	69	14½	ST	
Humilaria	..	1958	11955	18075	556	71	15	ST	ex San Edmundo 64.
Hyala	..	1954	12164	17915	556	69	14½	ST	
Hydatina	..	1956	12161	18070	556	69	14½	ST	
Hygromia	..	1956	12161	18011	556	69	14½	ST	
Hyria	..	1954	12132	17916	556	69	14½	ST	
Valvata	..	1960	21180	33749	661	87	16	ST	ex San Conrado 65.
Verconella	..	1958	20894	32252	660	85	16	ST	ex San Gerardo 64.
Vermetus	..	1959	21179	33749	661	87	16	ST	ex San Calisto 65.
Vertagus	..	1959	20893	32252	660	85	16	ST	ex San Gaspar 64.
Vexilla	..	1955	20776	32287	660	84	16½	ST	
Vibex	..	1955	20798	32095	660	84	16½	ST	
Vitta	..	1957	20889	33630	660	84	16½	ST	ex San Gregorio 65.
Volvatella	..	1956	20801	32308	660	84	16½	ST	

Tanker Finance Ltd.

Name		Date	Tons Gross	Tons Dwt	Length (feet)	Breadth (feet)	Speed (knots)	Engines	Former Names
Acavus ..	..	1958	12326	18285	559	69	14½	ST	
Achatina	..	1958	12326	18285	559	69	14½	ST	
Aluco ..	..	1959	13148	19340	560	72	14½	ST	
Amastra	..	1958	12273	18037	559	69	14½	ST	
Amoria ..	..	1960	12324	18062	559	69	14½	M	
Anadara	..	1959	12280	18500	559	69	14½	ST	
Asprella	..	1959	12321	18225	560	69	14½	ST	
Aulica ..	..	1960	12321	18255	560	69	14½	ST	
Axina ..	..	1958	12283	18230	559	69	14½	ST	
Halia ..	..	1958	12183	19172	556	69	14½	ST	
Haminella	..	1957	12189	18193	556	69	14½	ST	
Hanetia	..	1957	12189	18253	556	69	14½	ST	
Hemisinus	..	1957	12207	18149	556	69	14½	ST	
Varicella	..	1958	21843	33423	665	85	15½	ST	
Venassa	..	1959	21391	32695	665	87	16	ST	
Vitrina ..	..	1957	20802	32078	660	84	16	ST	
Zaphon ..	..	1957	39470	69689	842	105	16½	ST	
Zenatia ..	..	1957	39160	66350	842	105	16½	ST	

Conch Methane Tankers Ltd.

(MANAGERS—SHELL TANKERS (U.K.) LTD.)

FUNNEL: *Black, with three narrow white bands.*

Name		Date	Tons Gross	Tons Dwt	Length (feet)	Breadth (feet)	Speed (knots)	Engines
Methane Princess*	..	1964	21876	24219	621	82	17¼	ST

* Liquefied gas carrier.

Shell International Marine Ltd.

(MANAGERS—ASSOCIATED STEAMSHIPS PTY. LTD.)

Name		Date	Tons Gross	Tons Dwt	Length (feet)	Breadth (feet)	Speed (knots)	Engines
Cellana ..	..	1968	16005	24772	561	80	14½	M
Susus		1975	19300					M
Lepton		1975	140000					ST
Felania		1974	19300					M

(FRANCE)

Soc. Maritime Shell

Name		Date	Tons Gross	Tons Dwt	Length (feet)	Breadth (feet)	Speed (knots)	Engines
Dolabella	..	1966	41506	71803	800	115	16	ST
Isanda ..	..	1955	33820	62206	787	102	15	ST
Isara ..	..	1958	33753	62206	787	102	16	ST
Isidora ..	..	1955	33705	59000	787	103	16	ST
Isocardia	..	1955	33711	60000	787	103	16	ST
Isomeria	..	1956	33765	60000	787	102	16	ST
Magdala	..	1968	105296	208445	1065	155	16	ST
Miralda	..	1969	105295	212000	1065	155	16	ST
Myrtea ..	..	1969	105396	210967	1065	155	16	ST
Sitala ..	..	1961	49410	73148	849	117	16½	ST
Sivella ..	..	1963	49320	81566	849	117	16½	ST
Vola ..	..	1956	20518	34427	660	84	16	ST
Volvula ..	..	1956	20732	32150	660	84	16	ST
Lucina		1974	138500					ST

Also smaller ships.

Murex	1968	104772				
Gastrana	1974	48700	330			ST LNG
Batillus	1976					
Bellamya	1976					

Shell Tankers N.V.

Name		Date	Tons Gross	Tons Dwt	Length (feet)	Breadth (feet)	Speed (knots)	Engines	Former Names
Camitia	..	1955	9094	12985	501	62	12½	M	
Cinulia	..	1955	9094	12985	501	62	12½	M	
Crania	..	1955	9094	12985	501	62	12½	M	
Kabylia	..	1955	12097	18172	556	69	14½	ST	
Kalydon	..	1955	12017	18224	556	69	14½	ST	
Kara	..	1955	12146	18218	556	69	14½	ST	
Katelysia	..	1954	12143	18170	556	69	14½	ST	
Kenia	..	1955	12101	18225	556	69	14½	ST	
Kermia	..	1955	12139	18155	556	69	14½	ST	
Koratia	..	1954	12154	18050	556	69	14½	TE	
Korenia	..	1955	12152	18101	556	69	14½	TE	
Korovina	..	1954	12121	18069	556	69	14½	ST	
Kosicia	..	1957	12146	18240	556	69	14½	ST	
Kossmatella	..	1953	12144	17892	556	69	14½	TE	ex Helix 62.
Krebsia	..	1954	12107	18184	556	69	14½	ST	
Kryptos	..	1955	12098	18169	556	69	14½	ST	
Kylix	..	1955	12119	18140	556	69	14½	ST	
Vasum	..	1955	21062	33855	660	84	16¼	ST	
Vivipara	..	1957	20634	32265	660	84	16	ST	

Somerset Shipping Co.

VESSELS ON BAREBOAT CHARTER AND MANAGED BY SHELL TANKERS N.V.

Philidora	..	1959	30165	50125	735	102	15	ST
Philine	..	1959	30165	50125	735	102	15	ST
Philippia	..	1959	30165	50125	735	102	15	ST

N.V. Curacaosche Scheepvaart Maats

Dallia	..	1967	39482	70050	800	110	16	M
Daphne	..	1966	39482	69900	800	110	16	M
Diadema	..	1966	38132	69295	800	110	16	M
Diloma	..	1966	38260	69220	800	110	16	M
Dione	..	1967	39135	70870	800	110	16	M
Dosina	..	1966	38818	69250	800	110	16	M
Macoma	..	1967	104303	206679	1067	155	16	ST
Metula	..	1968	104379	206719	1067	155	16	ST
Neverita	..	1968	57906	109710	869	131	14½	M
Niso	..	1966	63292	119378	870	138	14½	M

SHELL GROUP (continued)

(NETHERLANDS)
Maats. tot. Financiering van Bedrijfspanden N.V.

Name		Date	Tons Gross	Tons Dwt	Length (feet)	Breadth (feet)	Speed (knots)	Engines	Former Names
Abida	..	1958	12226	18090	559	69	14½	M	
Acila	..	1958	12221	18040	559	69	14½	M	
Acmaea	..	1959	12222	18090	559	69	14½	M	
Acteon	..	1961	12226	18090	559	69	14½	M	
Arca	..	1959	12222	18348	559	69	14½	ST	
Atys	..	1960	12239	18350	559	69	14½	ST	
Kelletia	..	1957	12146	18240	556	69	14½	ST	
Khasiella	..	1956	12119	18255	556	69	14½	ST	
Kopionella	..	1955	12146	18181	556	69	14½	ST	
Ondina	..	1961	31030	52450	750	103	16	ST	
Onoba	..	1962	31540	49940	748	103	16	ST	
Sepia	..	1961	42410	68125	818	113	16	ST	
Viana	..	1960	22347	35160	665	85	15½	ST	
Vitrea	..	1962	21873	33589	665	85	15½	ST	
Zafra	..	1960	26144	39530	700	94	16½	ST	
Zaria	..	1960	26144	39530	700	94	16½	ST	

Deutsche Shell Tanker G.m.b.H.

Caperata	..	1950	18233	28280	625	84	16	ST	
Caprella	..	1950	18257	28280	625	84	16	ST	
Caprinus	..	1950	18256	28280	625	84	16	ST	
Capsa	..	1950	18258	28280	625	84	16	ST	
Capulus	..	1950	18256	28280	625	84	16	ST	
Diala	..	1966	39426	65499	800	110	16	ST	
Myrina	..	1967	95836	191250	1050	155	16	ST	
Nacella	..	1968	59868	115000	869	138	14½	M	
Narica	..	1967	59868	115250	869	138	14½	M	
Oliva	..	1963	33056	48800	740	102	16	ST	
Lagena		1974	133000						

(VENEZUELA)
Cia Shell de Venezuela Ltd.

Shell Aramare		1960	23523	34124	665	85	16	ST	
Shell Caricuao		1954	11224	15252	520	67	12½	SR(2)	ex Gaza 60.
Shell Charaima		1954	11224	15681	520	67	12½	SR(2)	ex Glebula 60.
Shell Mara	..	1958	29313	43400	722	98	16	ST	ex Isselia 66.
Shell Murachi*		1950	7012	7002	424	63	12	SR(2)	ex Gyrotoma 60.
Shell Naiguata		1960	23533	33958	665	85	16	ST	

Also smaller ships.   * Liquefied gas/oil carrier.

(ARGENTINA)
Estrella Maritima S.A. de Nav. y Comercio

Cazador	..	1949	6441	9301	445	55	12	M	
Estrella Argentina	..	1960	22083	33214	665	85	15½	ST	ex Videna 69.
Harvella	..	1956	12224	18168	556	69	14½	ST	
Kalinga	..	1953	12185	18012	556	69	14½	ST	ex Hemidonax 55.
Kelita	..	1953	12202	18009	556	69	14½	ST	ex Harpa 55. To Argent
Pecten	..	1955	10711	16050	525	68	13½	M	ex San Patricio Fabian 65.

Also smaller ships.

Shell Group: ONDINA

SINCLAIR REFINING CO. INC.

FUNNEL: *Green with black top and white panel with emblem and ' SINCLAIR ' in red.*

HULL: *Black with red boot-topping.*

Name	Date	Tons Gross	Tons Dwt	Length (feet)	Breadth (feet)	Speed (knots)	Engines	Former Names
P. C. Spencer ..	1953	16153	25214	605	78	16	ST	
Sheldon Clark ..	1942	10883	16807	529	72	14½	ST	
Sinclair Texas	1963	27469	47772	736	102	17	ST	

Marlin Tanker Corporation

Sinclair Venezuela ..	1963	31886	52150	760	102	16½	M(2)	

I. M. SKAUGEN & CO.

FUNNEL: *Yellow, black top with white diamond, blue and red border and black ' S '.*

HULL: *White.*

Skaugum ..	1965	42377	77370	801	118	16½	M	
Stolt Skaukar ..	1959	16721	26110	621	74	16	ST	ex Skaukar 64.

Also cargo ships.

CHRISTEN SMITH SHIPPING CO.

Belships Co. Ltd. Skibs A/S

FUNNEL: *Blue with blue " CS " and anchor monogram on white disc.*

HULL: *Grey or dark blue with red boot-topping.*

Belmaj	1964	28986	50210	724	101	16	M	
Belobo	1974	43,000					M	

Also cargo ships.

Sorensen & Son: ACINA

[F. R. Sherlock

S. H. SMITH SORENSEN

FUNNEL: *Yellow with white star on blue band between two red bands.*
HULL: *Grey.*

Name	Date	Tons Gross	Tons Dwt	Length (feet)	Breadth (feet)	Speed (knots)	Engines	Former Names
Ø. B. Sorensen	1956	17875	28240	631	79	14	M To S'pore, ren CHERRY DUK
Stolt Orator ..	1953	8985	13550	514	63	13½	M	ex Orator 65.

C. H. SORENSEN & SONS

FUNNEL: *Yellow with white ' S ' on broad blue band between narrow red and white bands.*
HULL: *Grey with red boot-topping.*

Name	Date	Tons Gross	Tons Dwt	Length (feet)	Breadth (feet)	Speed (knots)	Engines
Acina	1965	28877	50920	726	101	16	M

Also cargo ships.

HARALD STANGE & CO. A/S

FUNNEL: *Yellow with blue and white house flag.*
HULL: *Black.*

Name	Date	Tons Gross	Tons Dwt	Length (feet)	Breadth (feet)	Speed (knots)	Engines
Harald Stange	1959	12788	19470	560	72	15	M

HELMER STAUBO & CO.

FUNNEL: *Yellow with black diamond on broad white band between narrow red bands.*
HULL: *Light grey with red boot-topping.*

Name	Date	Tons Gross	Tons Dwt	Length (feet)	Breadth (feet)	Speed (knots)	Engines
Stavik	1968	52022	98800	888	128	16	M

STEVINSON HARDY (TANKERS) LTD.

FUNNEL: *Blue with yellow " S " and black top.*
HULL: *Black with red boot-topping.*

Name	Date	Tons Gross	Tons Dwt	Length (feet)	Breadth (feet)	Speed (knots)	Engines
Edward Stevinson ..	1961	31317	51615	754	98	15½	ST

STOCKHOLMS RED. A/B. SVEA

FUNNEL: *Black with black " S " on broad white band or blue " S " on yellow band.*

HULL: *Grey with red boot-topping.*

Name		Date	Tons Gross	Tons Dwt	Length (feet)	Breadth (feet)	Speed (knots)	Engines	Former Names
Capella*	..	1967	10775	10595	494	71	16 Toitaly, ren, LUIGI CASALE	M	ex Franklin 67, ex Capella 67, ex Benjamin Franklin 67.
Emanuel Hogberg	..	1964	34872	61100	774	105	17	M	
Scanthiod	..	1959	12311	19660	560	70	15	M	

* Liquefied gas carrier.

SUOMEN TANKKILAIVA O/Y

FUNNEL: *Black with white ' W ' on light blue band between two white bands.*

HULL: *Grey.*

Name		Date	Tons Gross	Tons Dwt	Length	Breadth	Speed	Engines	Former Names
Pensa	..	1954	11115	17000	533	68	14	M	
Presto	..	1959	12869	20905	560	72	$14\frac{1}{2}$	M	
Pronto	..	1960	12874	20872	560	72	$14\frac{1}{2}$	M	
Winha	..	1969	18224	25500	619	72	15	M	
Wipunen	..	1955	12423	20480	567	75	$14\frac{1}{2}$	M	
Wirma	..	1952	12412	19050	557	71	$14\frac{1}{2}$	M	ex Brumaire 66.

TANKERS LTD.

(*Formerly* ATHEL LINE LTD.)

FUNNEL: *Red with black top and " ATHEL " in blue on white diamond.*

HULL: *Black or grey with red boot-topping.*

Name		Date	Tons Gross	Tons Dwt	Length	Breadth	Speed	Engines	Former Names
Anco Duchess	..	1968	11102	17630	525	69	16	M	ex Athelduchess 69.
Anco Duke	..	1968	11102	17680	525	69	16	M	ex Athelduke 69.
Anco Knight	..	1968	10819	17610	525	68	16	M	ex Athelknight 69.
Anco Queen	..	1960	13040	19770	560	72	14	M	ex Athelqueen 66.
Athelchief	..	1958	12041	18700	560	70	14	ST	ex Astropalitis 58.
Athelcrest	..	1957	7548	10290	459	61	14	M	
Athelcrown	..	1949	11149	15646	544	67	12	M	
Athelking	..	1964	35398	62060	775	106	15	M	
Athellaird	..	1949	10924	15626	544	67	12	M	
Athelmonarch		1950	10937	16285	544	67	12	M	
Athelregent	..	1965	35395	62090	775	106	15	M	
Athelstane	..	1955	7517	10350	459	61	13	M	
Athelviscount		1961	12778	19326	559	73	$14\frac{1}{2}$	ST	

Suomen Tankkilaiva: WIRMA negotiating the Kiel Canal

[Malcolm Cranfield]

TEXACO INC.

FUNNEL: *Black with "TEXACO" in black on white disc on broad green band.*

HULL: *Black with red boot-topping or white with green boot-topping.*

Name	Date	Tons Gross	Tons Dwt	Length (feet)	Breadth (feet)	Speed (knots)	Engines	Former Names
Texaco California	1954	12789	20112	565	75	18	ST	ex California 60.
Texaco Connecticut	1953	12789	20143	565	75	18	ST	ex Connecticut 59.
Texaco Florida	1956	12802	20068	565	75	18	ST	ex Florida 60.
Texaco Georgia	1963	16514	25186	605	78	17½	ST	
Texaco Illinois	1944	14324	23592	575	79	14½	TE	ex Illinois 60, ex San Pasqual 47.
Texaco Kansas	1943	14153	23685	575	79	14½	TE	ex Greenpoint 60, ex Crown Point 55.
Texaco Louisiana	1944	10499	16632	524	68	14½	TE	ex Louisiana 60, ex Kernstown 48.
Texaco Maryland	1963	16514	26550	605	78	17½	ST	
Texaco Massachusetts	1963	16515	25728	605	78	17½	ST	
Texaco Minnesota	1943	15622	25930	624	74	14½	TE	ex Minnesota 60, ex Churubusco 50.
Texaco Mississippi	1944	15688	26573	624	74	14½	TE	ex Mississippi 59, ex South Mountain 50.
Texaco Montana	1965	16584	25785	605	78	17½	ST	
~~Texaco Nebraska~~	1943	14251	24672	575	79	14½	TE	ex Hunters Point 61, ex Conoco Denver 56, ex Fort Washington 48.
Texaco New Jersey	1944	12261	20836	572	75	14½	TE	ex New Jersey 61, ex Lake Erie 47.
Texaco New York	1953	12789	20836	565	75	18	ST	ex New York 60.
Texaco North Carolina	1944	10535	16391	524	68	14½	TE	ex North Carolina 60, ex Briar Creek 48.
Texaco North Dakota	1953	12789	19434	565	75	18	ST	ex North Dakota 60.
Texaco Oklahoma	1958	20084	35072	661	90	17	ST	ex Atlantis 60.
Texaco Rhode Island	1964	16584	25413	605	78	17½	ST	
Texaco Wisconsin	1959	20538	33141	661	90	17	ST	ex King's Point 61.
~~Texaco Wyoming~~	1943	14242	23628	575	79	14½	TE	ex Wyoming 60, ex Buena Vista 50.

Texaco Inc: TEXACO VIRGINIA

[Malcolm Cranfield]

Texaco Overseas Tankship Ltd.

Name	Date	Tons Gross	Tons Dwt	Length (feet)	Breadth (feet)	Speed (knots)	Engines	Former Names
Texaco Bahrain	1953	11804	17500	544	70	15	ST	ex Caltex Bahrain 68.
Texaco Bombay	1945	13892	23334	566	78	14	TE	ex Caltex Bombay 68, ex Castle's Woods 51.
Texaco Brisbane	1961	31118	46490	733	104	17	ST	ex Caltex Brisbane 68.
Texaco Brussels	1968	14948	24624	591	78	16	ST	
Texaco Edinburgh ..	1956	12492	18255	559	71	15	ST	ex Caltex Edinburgh 68.
Texaco Europe	1970	104616	205800	1067	155	15	ST	
Texaco Frankfurt	1969	104616	205800	1067	155	15	ST	
Texaco Ghent	1968	14967	24624	592	78	17	ST	
Texaco Greenwich ..	1962	35720	54850	762	109	15	ST	ex Caltex Greenwich 68.
Texaco Hamburg	1969	104616	206100	1067	155	15	ST	
Texaco Kenya	1952	8523	12340	491	62	13	M	ex Caltex Kenya 68.
Texaco Melbourne ..	1945	13899	23313	566	77	14	TE	ex Caltex Melbourne 67, ex Victory Loan 51.
Texaco North America ..	1970	104616	205800	1067	155	17	ST	
Texaco Rome ..	1945	13892	23313	566	77	14	TE	ex Caltex Rome 68, ex Sideling Hill 53.
Texaco Rotterdam ..	1968	14948	23682	593	78	17	ST	
Texaco Saigon ..	1945	13892	22368	566	77	14	TE	ex Caltex Saigon 68, ex Chicaca 52.
Texaco Southampton	1963	35841	54829	762	109	16	ST	ex Caltex Southampton 68.
Texaco Wellington ..	1944	13887	22367	561	77	14	TE	ex Caltex Wellington 67, ex Paulus Hook 52.

Tankship Finance (U.K.) Ltd.

Name	Date	Tons Gross	Tons Dwt	Length (feet)	Breadth (feet)	Speed (knots)	Engines	Former Names
Texaco Cardiff	1958	21877	33350	667	85	16	ST	ex Caltex Cardiff 68.
Texaco Newcastle ..	1958	12478	18130	559	71	15	ST	ex Caltex Newcastle 68.
Texaco Plymouth	1960	31109	46502	733	104	16	ST	ex Caltex Plymouth 68.
Texaco Rochester ..	1959	21877	33351	667	85	16	ST	ex Caltex Bristol 68.

Regent Petroleum Tankship Co. Ltd.

Name	Date	Tons Gross	Tons Dwt	Length (feet)	Breadth (feet)	Speed (knots)	Engines	Former Names
Texaco Durham†	1959	12354	18025	556	71	14½	M	ex Regent Falcon 70.
Texaco Gloucester ..	1959	12834	18764	571	72	15	M	ex Regent Eagle 69.
Texaco Liverpool	1962	30770	49329	746	98	16	ST	ex Regent Liverpool 69.
Texaco Pembroke ..	1965	36454	65340	790	106	17	ST	ex Regent Pembroke 68.
Texaco Westminster	1968	54908	100927	838	128	16	ST	ex Regent Westminster 68.

† Owned by John I. Jacobs & Co. Ltd.

(PANAMA)

Texaco Panama Inc.

Name	Date	Tons Gross	Tons Dwt	Length (feet)	Breadth (feet)	Speed (knots)	Engines	Former Names
Texaco Africa	1974	127000						
Texaco Alaska	1960	24077	41382	700	97	17	ST	
Texaco Bristol	1944	14412	23426	575	79	14½	TE	ex Texaco Alabama 62, ex Alabama 60, ex Hubbardton 48.
Texaco Caribbean ..	1965	13604	20545	575	78	16½	ST	
Texaco Colombia ..	1964	45823	89956	858	125	16½	ST	
Texaco Idaho ..	1959	23420	43149	701	102	16	ST	ex Idaho 60.
Texaco Iowa ..	1959	24035	41282	700	97	16	ST	ex Iowa 59.
Texaco Kentucky ..	1949	17892	29744	625	84	16	ST	ex Kentucky 60.
Texaco London	1944	14396	24498	575	79	14½	TE	ex Glen Cove 61, ex Esso Utica 57.
Texaco Maracaibo ..	1965	47630	91028	858	125	16½	ST	
Texaco New Mexico	1958	18750	29482	630	84	16	ST	ex New Mexico 60.
Texaco Ohio ..	1949	17892	28081	625	84	16	ST	ex Ohio 61.
Texaco Pennsylvania	1949	17872	28081	625	84	16	ST	ex Pennsylvania 60.
Texaco Puerto Rico*	1966	3554	5050	340	52	15	M(2)	
Texaco Texas ..	1949	17892	29744	625	84	16	ST	ex Texas 60.
Texaco Utah ..	1959	26252	47300	736	99	17	ST	ex Utah 60.
Texaco Venezuela ..	1964	32758	61464	778	106	16½	ST	
Texaco Virginia	1958	25525	43146	701	102	16½	ST	ex Texaco Santiago 63, ex Santiago 62.
Texaco Japan	1975							
Texaco Italia	1974							

* Liquefied gas carrier.

Texaco Inc: TEXACO ROTTERDAM   [R. J. Weeks

Texaco Inc: TEXACO BELGIUM   [John G. Callis

Texaco-Regent Petroleum Tankship Co: TEXACO GLOUCESTER   [*D. Clegg*

Trident Tankers: OTTAWA   [*R. J. Weeks*

General Tankers S.A.

Name	Date	Tons Gross	Tons Dwt	Length (feet)	Breadth (feet)	Speed (knots)	Engines	Former Names
Texaco Arizona	1956	18428	29353	625	84	16	ST	ex Arizona 59.
Texaco Arkansas ..	1956	12665	18075	579	72	18	M	ex Arkansas 61.
Texaco Missouri	1957	18750	27883	630	84	16	ST	ex Missouri 60.
Texaco Vermont ..	1955	18428	27710	625	84	16	ST	ex Vermont 60.

(LIBERIA)

Ocean Tankers Company

Texaco Australia	1967	41187	78170	760	122	15½	ST	
Texaco Italia	1974	120000					S T	

(PANAMA)

Chartered Tankers S.A.

Brighton ..	1959	26543	48542	736	102	16	ST	
Texaco Anacortes ..	1961	26252	47193	736	100	16½	ST	
Texaco Hawaii	1960	26252	47216	736	100	16½	ST	
Texaco Maine	1959	26544	46442	736	102	16½	ST	ex Maine 60.
Texaco Oregon	1960	26252	47250	736	99	17	ST	
Trinidad ..	1958	26530	48734	736	102	16	ST	

(NORWAY)

Texaco Norway A/S.

Texaco Belgium	1965	13121	20500	541	78	16½	ST	
Texaco Bogota	1960	13623	22100	561	72	14½	M	
Texaco Brasil ..	1952	10546	15625	533	64	15	M	ex Brasil 60.
Texaco Britannia ..	1954	12915	18007	579	72	15	M	ex Britannia 60.
Texaco Norge ..	1962	13223	21200	579	74	15	M	
Texaco Nueva Granada ..	1955	12901	18001	579	72	15	M	ex Nueva Granada 60.
Texaco Oslo ..	1960	12884	19713	574	72	15	M	
Texaco Skandinavia	1962	13222	21200	579	74	15	M	
Texaco South America ..	1954	12915	18900	579	72	15	M	ex South America 59.

CIE. DE TRANSPORTS MARITIMES PÉTROLIERS

FUNNEL: *Black with red ' TMP ' on blue-bordered white panel.*

HULL: *Grey or white.*

Name	Date	Tons Gross	Tons Dwt	Length (feet)	Breadth (feet)	Speed (knots)	Engines	Former Names
Champs Elysees	1960	32740	52085	759	100	16	ST	ex Centaure 62.
Fructidor ..	1968	48058	75850	833	117	16½	M	
Germinal ..	1964	35694	54498	800	104	16	M	
Messidor ..	1969	49400	80000	833	117	16½	M	
Monceau ..	1959	18557	29586	657	81	16	M	
Pierre Poulain ..	1967	48058	75850	833	117	16½	M	
Alsace	1974	118000					ST	
Post Energie	1974	155000					M	

TRIDENT TANKERS LTD.

FUNNEL: *Black, with black trident emblem superimposed on a white diamond.*

HULL: *Black with buff superstructure, red boot-topping.*

		Date	Tons Gross	Tons Dwt	Length	Breadth	Speed	Engines	
Erne ..	..	1962	14244	20090	560	72	15	ST	
Malwa ..	..	1961	23900	37278	691	90	16½	ST	
Megna ..	..	1961	24549	39316	691	90	16½	ST	ex Foyle 65.
Opawa ..	..	1965	38996	62840	776	106	17	M	to Greece. ren. Anangel Friendsh
Orama ..	..	1964	39051	63000	775	106	17	M	
Orissa ..	..	1965	39035	63075	780	106	17	M	
Ottawa ..	..	1964	51756	93072	851	125	17	ST	
Quiloa ..	..	1960	12779	19026	560	72	14½	ST	
Talamba ..	..	1964	34709	53800	765	106	15½	ST	

P. & O. Steam Navigation Co. Ltd.

		Date	Tons Gross	Tons Dwt	Length	Breadth	Speed	Engines	
Ardlui ..	..	1970	119728	215000	1042	158	16	ST	
Ardshiel ..	..	1969	119678	214100	1064	158	16	ST	
Ardtaraig ..	..	1969	119666	214128	1064	158	16	ST	
Ardvar ..	..	1970	119700	215000	1042	158	16	ST	
Eridge* ..	..	1966	42825	72692	823	104	16	M	
Garonne ..	..	1959	24097	37383	690	90	16	ST	
Grafton* ..	..	1967	43330	73829	823	104	16	M	
Heythrop* ..	..	1967	43330	73800	824	104	16	M	

* Bulk/oil carriers.

British India Steam Navigation Co. Ltd.

		Date	Tons Gross	Tons Dwt	Length	Breadth	Speed	Engines
Ellenga ..	..	1960	23913	37420	691	90	16	ST

Trident Tankers: MALOJA   *[Malcolm Cranfield*

Trident Tankers: ERNE   *[D. Clegg*

Turnbull, Scott Management: STONEGATE   [D. Clegg

Universe Tankships Inc: UNIVERSE DEFIANCE   [Malcolm Cranfield

Moss Hutchison Line Ltd.

Name		Date	Tons Gross	Tons Dwt	Length (feet)	Breadth (feet)	Speed (knots)	Engines	Former Names
Busiris ..	..	1961	24268	37558	691	90	16½	ST	

Charter Shipping Co. Ltd.

Maloja ..	..	1959	12763	19948	559	72	14½	ST	
Mantua ..	..	1960	12899	19943	559	72	14½	ST	

(NORWAY)

TSCHUDI & EITZEN

FUNNEL: *Black with blue and white shield on red band.*

HULL: *Grey.*

Siboen* ..	..	1968	44332	78400	849	106	15½	M
Siboto* ..	..	1968	44326	76500	849	106	15½	M
Sibotre*	..	1969	44327	76500	849	106	15½	M

* Bulk/oil carrier.

TURNBULL, SCOTT MANAGEMENT LTD.

FUNNEL: *Black with white " TS " in red-bordered white shield.*

HULL: *Black with red boot-topping.*

Eastgate	..	1957	11907	18924	556	69	15	ST	To lib., ren. GREAT FAREASTERN
Flowergate*	..	1969	58589	106700	830	131	15	M	
Stonegate	..	1961	12001	18774	559	69	14½	M	

* Ore/oil carrier on charter to Grangesberg-Oxelosund Trafik A/B.

(NORWAY)

S. UGELSTAD

FUNNEL: *Black with blue ' U ' on white panel.*

HULL: *Black.*

Honnør	..	1958	13812	20500	577	74	15½	ST	To lib., ren. OCEAN CHEMIST
Samuel Ugelstad		1956	21178	32010	662	87	15½	ST	

UNIVERSE TANKSHIPS INC.

FUNNEL: *Black.*
HULL: *Black, red boot-topping.*

Name	Date	Tons Gross	Tons Dwt	Length (feet)	Breadth (feet)	Speed (knots)	Engines	Former Names
Energy Progress	*1974*	*135000*						
Commonwealth	1957	26035	43847	712	97	15	ST	ex Petrolene 64.
Frisia	1957	51321	87446	855	125	16	ST	ex Universe Challenger 60.
George Champion ..	1958	51320	87416	855	125	16	ST	
Harold H. Helm	1958	51320	87469	855	125	16	ST	
Petroqueen ..	1953	21577	39628	673	92	16	ST	
Petro Sea ..	1956	26035	48200	712	97	15	ST	
Phoenix ..	1953	26085	49062	722	97	16	ST	
Ulysses† ..	1963	38748	57829	794	106	16½	ST	
Universe Admiral	1957	51320	92049	855	125	15½	ST	
Universe Apollo	1959	72132	122876	950	135	15½	ST	
Universe Commander	1957	51398	92346	855	126	15	ST	
Universe Daphne	1960	72266	115360	950	135	15½	ST	
Universe Defender† ..	1962	35748	57644	794	106	16½	ST	
Universe Defiance ..	1958	51320	92049	855	125	15	ST	
Universe Leader	1956	51400	92373	855	125	15	ST	
Universal Explorer	*1974*	*119,000*						

† Ore/oil carriers.   Also ore carriers.

Universe Guardian *1975*
Universe Ranger *1975* *119,000*   *ST*
Universe Mariner *1974* *123,000*

PHS. VAN OMMEREN (LONDON) LTD.

FUNNEL: *Black with white " V " within a white ring.*
HULL: *Black with red boot-topping.*

Name	Date	Tons Gross	Tons Dwt	Length	Breadth	Speed	Engines	
Avedrecht ..	1963	31214	51304	747	103	15	ST	
Barendrecht ..	1960	21130	32179	665	88	15	M	
Mijdrecht ..	1955	13115	20350	575	74	15½	ST	

Also cargo ships.

H. WAAGE

FUNNEL: *Black with white band.*
HULL: *Grey or black, red boot-topping.*

Name	Date	Tons Gross	Tons Dwt	Length	Breadth	Speed	Engines	
Rinda	*1974*	*117300*						
Rinda*	1967	45003	72100	849	106	16	M	
Runa*	1967	45003	72100	849	106	16	M	
Ruth	1967	52371	100350	848	126	16	M	
Symra	1967	52930	100350	849	128	16½	M	
Runa	*1974*	*113,500*					*ST*	

* Bulk/oil carriers.

Westfal-Larsen: KAUPANGER   [Malcolm Cranfield[

Wilh. Wilhelmsen: TEMPLAR   [R. J. Weeks

OLOF WALLENIUS

FUNNEL: *Yellow with narrow black top and yellow " OW " on green band.*
HULL: *Grey.*

Name	Date	Tons Gross	Tons Dwt	Length (feet)	Breadth (feet)	Speed (knots)	Engines	Former Names
Soya-Atlantic†	1954	15975	23450	596	75	15	ST	
Soya-Baltic† ..	1964	37792	63320	788	108	17	ST	

Also cargo ships.   † Ore/oil carriers.

WESTFAL-LARSEN & CO. A/S

FUNNEL: *Yellow with narrow black top and two narrow black bands.*
HULL: *Grey with green boot-topping.*

Name	Date	Tons Gross	Tons Dwt	Length (feet)	Breadth (feet)	Speed (knots)	Engines
~~Finnanger~~ Austanger	~~1975~~ 1964	12872 ~~22,300~~	~~19980~~ 19980	560	72	15	M
Grenanger ..	1964	12872	19980	560	72	15	M
Hallanger ..	1960	20416	34430	659	86	16½	M
Haukanger ..	1958	13133	20100	560	72	15	M
Kaupanger ..	1960	12862	19950	558	72	15	M
Orkanger ..	1970	12800	—	—	—	15	M
Samnanger ..	1963	33924	56300	775	106	16½	M
~~Varanger~~	1974	22300					M

Also cargo ships.

Torvanger

ROLF WIGANDS REDERI

FUNNEL: *Yellow with two blue bands and blue diamond.*
HULL: *Grey.*

Name	Date	Tons Gross	Tons Dwt	Length (feet)	Breadth (feet)	Speed (knots)	Engines
Borwi	1965	44472	81740	800	122	16	M
Harwi	1964	34966	58555	774	106	16	M
Jonwi	1964	35844	61565	775	106	16	M

WILH. WILHELMSEN

FUNNEL: *Black with two light blue bands close together.*
HULL: *Black with white line and red boot-topping, or all black.*

Name	Date	Tons Gross	Tons Dwt	Length (feet)	Breadth (feet)	Speed (knots)	Engines
Tamano ..	1968	46988	88072	810	128	16½	M
Tarim* ..	1970	81000	150000	961	220	16	M
Taurus ..	1966	51295	93520	840	128	16	M
Teheran* ..	1968	56709	89200	858	128	16	M
Templar ..	1967	46252	82200	804	122	16½	M
Tiberius ..	1966	43264	77100	802	122	16½	M
Titus ..	1959	16417	25700	616	79	16	M
Toluma ..	1959	16417	25700	616	79	16	M
Toscana ..	1961	22725	38450	683	87	16	M
Troms ..	1961	21099	34140	665	86	16	M
Tuareg ..	1965	43572	77100	802	122	16½	M

Also cargo ships.   * Bulk/oil carrier.

CLASSIFIED NAMES

(Tanker Section)

Names beginning					Company
ALVA X——	..	..	..	..	*Alva*
ATHEL—— ..	..	..	..	..	*Tankers Ltd.*
ATLANTIC X——	..	..	..	..	*Livanos*
BEAU—— ..	..	..	..	..	*Biornstad*
BEL—— ..	..	..	..	..	*Christen Smith*
BELGULF X——	..	..	..	..	*Belgulf Tankers*
BERGE—— ..	..	..	..	..	*Bergesen d.y. & Co.*
BO—— ..	..	..	..	..	*Fred Olsen*
BORDER X——	..	..	..	..	*Lowland Tankers*
BRITISH X——	..	..	..	..	*BP Tanker Co.*
BULK—— ..	..	..	..	..	*Universe Tankships*
CHEVRON X——	..	..	..	..	*Chevron Shg Co.*
ESSO X——	..	..	..	..	*Esso Petroieum Co.*
FERN—— ..	..	..	..	..	*Fearnley & Eger*
FINA X——	..	..	..	..	*Purfina-Transports*
FOREST X——	..	..	..	..	*Muller*
GULF—— ..	..	..	..	..	*Gulf Oil*
HAV——	..	..	..	..	*Meyer*
HOEGH X——	..	..	..	..	*Hoegh*
IMPERIAL X——	..	..	..	..	*Imperial Oil*
JA—— ..	..	..	..	..	*Jahre*
KOLL—— ..	..	..	..	..	*Berg*
LLAN—— ..	..	..	..	..	*Radcliffe*
LU—— ..	..	..	..	..	*Cunard*
MOBIL X——	..	..	..	..	*Mobil*
MOS—— ..	..	..	..	..	*Mosvold*
NAESS X——	..	..	..	..	*Naess Group*
OLYMPIC X——	..	..	..	..	*Onassis*
OVERSEAS X——	..	..	..	..	*London & Overseas*
PHILLIPS X——	..	..	..	..	*Phillips*
POLAR—— ..	..	..	..	..	*Melsom*
POLY—— ..	..	..	..	..	*Rasmussen*
SEA X—— ..	..	..	..	..	*Salenrederierna*
SEVEN X——	..	..	..	..	*Salenrederierna*
SI—— ..	..	..	..	..	*Tschudi & Eitzen*
SOYA X——	..	..	..	..	*Wallenius*
STA—— ..	..	..	..	..	*Staubo*
T—— ..	..	..	..	..	*Wilhelmsen*
TANK X——	..	..	..	..	*Herlofson*
TEXACO X——	..	..	..	..	*Texaco*
THORS——	..	..	..	..	*Dahl*
TIDE—— ..	..	..	..	..	*Ministry of Defence*
UNIVERSE X——	..	..	..	..	*Universe Tankship or Gulf (Bantry)*
V——	..	..	..	..	*Ditlev-Simonsen*
WAVE X—— ..	..	..	..	..	*Ministry of Defence*
WI—— ..	..	..	..	..	*Suomen Tank*
WORLD X——	..	..	..	..	*Niarchos*

Names ending					Company
——ANGER ..	..	..	..	..	*Westfal-Larsen*
—— BROVIG ..	..	..	..	..	*Brovig*
—— COLOCOTRONIS	..	..	..	..	*Colocotronis Group*
——DALE ..	..	..	..	..	*Ministry of Defence*
—— D'AMICO ..	..	..	..	..	*D'Amico*

Names ending					Company
—— DAN	..	..	..	..	*Lauritzen*
—— DRECHT	..	..	..	..	*Van Ommeren*
—— ENTZ	..	..	..	..	*Entz*
—— ESSBERGER	..	..	..	..	*Essberger*
——FIELD	..	..	..	..	*Hunting*
——FJELL	..	..	..	..	*Olsen & Ugelstad*
——FONN	..	..	..	..	*Sigval Bergesen*
—— GETTY	..	..	..	..	*Getty*
——IAN	..	..	..	..	*Reksten*
—— KNUDSEN	..	..	..	..	*Knutsen*
——LEAF	..	..	..	..	*Ministry of Defence*
—— MAERSK	..	..	..	..	*Moller*
—— PRIORY	..	..	..	..	*Warwick*
—— RANGER	..	..	..	..	*Ministry of Defence*
——STAD	..	..	..	..	*A. F. Klaveness*
—— STANGE	..	..	..	..	*Stange*
—— STANDARD	..	..	..	..	*Chevron (Standard Oil)*
——WI	..	..	..	..	*Wigand*
——WOOD	..	..	..	..	*Jacobs*

Themes			Company
FRENCH PROVINCES	..	..	*Soc. Francaise T.P.*
LATIN NAMES OF SHELLS	..	..	*Shell Tankers*
CONSTELLATIONS (French)	..	..	*Navale*

INDEX

355

INDEX (continued)